For my husband

Diversion Books
A Division of Diversion Publishing Corp.
443 Park Avenue South, Suite 1008
New York, New York 10016
www.DiversionBooks.com

Copyright © 1995 by Tracy Thompson
All rights reserved, including the right to reproduce this book or portions
thereof in any form whatsoever.

"Journey to the Interior," copyright © 1961 by Beatrice Roethke, Administratrix
of the Estate of Theodore Roethke. From *The Collected Poems of Theodore
Roethke*, by Theodore Roethke. Used by permission of Doubleday, a division
of Bantam Doubleday Dell Publishing Group, Inc.

For more information, email info@diversionbooks.com

First Diversion Books edition October 2014.
Print ISBN: 978-1-62681-520-9
eBook ISBN: 978-1-62681-434-9

THE
BEAST

A Journey Through Depression

TRACY THOMPSON

DIVERSIONBOOKS

In the long journey out of the self,
There are many detours, washed-out interrupted raw places
Where the shale slides dangerously
And the back wheels hang almost over the edge
At the sudden veering, the moment of turning.

—*Journey to the Interior*
THEODORE ROETHKE

Foreword

When *The Beast* was originally published 20 years ago, one of the blurbs referred to me as a "survivor." It's a word that I didn't like then and like even less now. Survivors are people who hang around waiting for the Coast Guard. I survived my encounters with the Beast the way Diana Nyad survived swimming from Cuba to Florida: one stroke, one breath at a time. It was *work*. And even at that, I can only take about half the credit; nobody survives severe depression without the love of family and friends. Nobody survives without a certain element of luck—things like whether you live in an area rich in health care resources (as I do) or in some small town where the nearest shrink is 50 miles away and booked for the next three months, things like how much trial and error it takes to find the combination of drugs that may help, things like whether you are also battling a drug or alcohol problem.

Today, most of the struggles I described in these pages are over. The Beast and I have declared an armed truce. It mostly leaves me alone, but the price of health is eternal vigilance: medications, exercise, a spiritual practice, and a supportive network of family and friends. Life is good, but I don't kid myself: it could always come back. It *has* come back.

For any woman whose history of depression begins in adolescence, as mine did, postpartum depression is almost a one hundred percent probability. Yet when I became pregnant with our first child a year after *The Beast* was published, I convinced myself that pregnancy hormones would simply rewire my brain. (Magical thinking is tough to eradicate.) This was in the mid-1990s, when the "just say no to drugs" mantra was still ascendant and pregnant women got icy stares if they so much as took a sip of wine. So I did what seemed like the responsible thing to do and went off my meds. *Huge* mistake. For the first few weeks of my daughter's life I was consumed with a kind of anxiety so intense that my brain seemed to emit a low-level hum, the way power lines crackle in damp weather. "Sleep when your baby sleeps," the books cheerfully advised, but nobody said what to do if you were gripped by the irrational conviction that your eight-pound nine-ounce infant, rosy with health, was about to die at any moment. Weeks of sleep deprivation devolved into auditory hallucinations; the stress played havoc with my milk production; the inability to breastfeed threw me into a spiral of shame, self-recrimination and despair.

In retrospect, my cavalier confidence about the effects childbirth was apt to have on a person with my vulnerabilities was like the misplaced hubris of those Confederate soldiers of 1860, who swore they could whip the Yankees with cornstalks— until they learned, as one admitted later, "The Yankees didn't fight with cornstalks." The Beast does not fight with cornstalks. Underestimating the power of what I was dealing with meant that my initiation into motherhood was six months of hell, followed by another six months or so of slow recovery. And in what may or may not have been a coincidence, our daughter acted exactly like a baby who had been swimming in stress hormones for nine months: she was colicky and hard to settle, and at four months gave a convincing demonstration of a kind of intense separation anxiety most babies don't develop until much later, if at all. We joked that putting her down to sleep was like defusing a live hand grenade. Four years later, I prepared for the birth of our second daughter with every defensive weapon I could think of: medication throughout pregnancy, a shrink on call, a doula for the first few weeks, a friend network and a husband vigilantly on guard for the reappearance of the hollow-eyed zombie wife. *That* baby blew kisses at us on her way to bed—we have pictures to prove it—and settled down to sleep without a murmur. Feel free to draw your own conclusions.

The Beast made its next major onslaught in 2005-6, around the time of my mother's death. She had been in failing health for a decade, and her passing was the kind of major life transition that most of us experience eventually. But this grief was like a quiet tsunami: a dark, steadily rising force that began at least a year before her death and just kept coming, obliterating the landscape of my life.

I can't describe it any better than that, because many of my memories of that time are gone. ECT—electroconvulsive therapy—wiped them out. We were told, my husband and I, that ECT affected memory; the well-known doctor I talked to at Baltimore's Sheppard Pratt Hospital blandly assured us that most patients experienced some memory loss, but that "almost everybody" found that these were temporary. It was only later that I realized what a ridiculously optimistic assessment that was. It's impossible to report losing something you don't know you're missing—and evidence of ECT-induced memory loss, at least for me, arrived piecemeal, over a period of months and years. In fact, I'll never have a full accounting of everything I've lost, simply because nobody besides me is in a position to know it's gone, and I can only find out by accident. I do know that I have no memory of the Christmas of 2006. I have no memory of a friend I met at a writer's conference who called me later to nail down the dates for a visit. When I had to ask, "Who are you?" she was humiliated; I was horrified. That friendship did not survive. Another decades-long friendship was grievously injured when I asked about my friend's mother; it was only when I heard her gasp that I had a fleeting, sickening memory fragment of speaking at her mother's funeral. To this day, it's not unheard of for one of my daughters or my husband to say, "Remember when we went to that state park in—" or to refer to some event or person, and I draw a complete blank. This is not the kind of forgetting where, in the deepest recesses of your mind, you at least know that you *used* to know something; this is total annihilation, a tiny little foretaste of death.

And yet ECT worked. The improvement was dramatic, and took only a few weeks. Faced with the same choices, I would do it again, though maybe I will never have to. In October 2008, the Food and Drug Administration approved the use of a method known as repetitive transcranial magnetic stimulation (rTMS), which uses powerful magnets instead of electrical pulses to stimulate nerve growth in areas of the brain associated with mood regulation and memory. Supposedly, this carries with it far fewer memory-related side effects. Supposedly. Still, if there ever is a next time, I know there are new treatments, and that research continues. I take some comfort in that.

During that bad time after my mother's death, I remember saying to my shrink, "I never cease to be amazed at the power of this illness to lay me low." If I were to wake up tomorrow once more in the throes of suicidal depression, I'd be amazed all over again. Depression is like that: hard to describe to others who have never felt it, hard to remember clearly once you've gotten through it, hard to recognize in its initial approach. Living with it is like going through life followed by one of those bad guys you see in movies, somebody who wants to put you in a headlock and hold a chloroform-soaked handkerchief over your nose. It's like alcoholism and addiction in the sense that you learn to watch your back; you learn to enlist help in getting others to help you watch it.

In fact, alcoholism and addiction often go hand in hand with depression; it's only human, when confronted with painful feelings, to stuff them down and try to medicate them out of existence. I know there's a distinct possibility that a drug addict lurks inside me, just waiting to come out. I've never qualified as an alcoholic, but I've certainly abused alcohol in the past and might be doing it today if it weren't for the fact that somewhere in the past 20 years my body just decided to rebel. These days, even a glass of wine is likely to make me feel mildly ill. Most antidepressants carry warnings that advise against taking such drugs while using alcohol; my shrink says that I got away with doing that for a long time because I was young and my liver could compensate. Evidently, those days are past. Between my uncooperative liver and federal laws against over-prescribing narcotics, I find myself firmly steered in the direction of sobriety and the hard, messy work of dealing with crap as it arises.

I don't always succeed. I try to keep an eye out for ominous signs: a long period of stress in which I want to cry but can't, for example. Compulsive eating. Hypersensitivity to noise, general irritability. Sleep disturbances of any kind, whether it's sleeping too much or too little. (*Nobody* messes with my bedtime.) At other times, when I seem to be blundering along unaware of rising stress levels, or determined to ignore them, or over-reacting to things generally, my husband will tell me to take some time off, schedule a massage, go have lunch with somebody, go to the gym. This invariably pisses me off, reflecting as it does his complete failure to grasp the seriousness of the situation, whatever the situation may be. But I've learned to listen; sometimes, I can even tell myself before he has to. And sometimes powerful emotions just require a messy and painful emotional purge—a couple of hours of sobbing on the floor of my closet or raging at some unkind stroke of fate, some time spent in bed with the covers pulled over my head. I treat my mental health the same way I treat my physical health—they are really one and the same—and if the inside of my head looks like a war zone, I put myself on the casualty list. It is better to risk the judgment of people who may think of me as some kind of head case for going to bed when there is nothing outwardly wrong with me than to soldier on pretending to be as "normal" as them, and actually become a head case.

Finally, there were also moments of what I can only describe as divine grace, when I was preserved from the effects of my own folly or weakness. Believe it or not, I think of Thomas as an example of that. Earlier readers of this book have taken me to task for sugarcoating that situation, for failing to acknowledge the full effects of his abuse, both emotional and physical. They're right. I did sugarcoat some things. Some of that was unconscious; some of it was for a reason. Had I been more accurate in portraying that relationship, I think it would have shifted the focus from my struggle with depression to the story of one more "man victimizes woman" love affair. It would have become a story about how domestic violence and emotional abuse cause depression—not, as was more accurate, the story of how depression makes a woman more vulnerable to such relationships in the first place.

So where does grace come in? I think I needed a kind of battering ram to break through my iron determination to seem "normal"—and that's what Thomas was. A nicer person, a gentler person, a person less supremely convinced that he was the smartest person in the room, wouldn't have stripped me of all my defenses. A case in point: he humiliated me by telling me again and again what a toxic influence I was on his kids (which, to the extent that it was true, was more an indictment of him than me)—but up to then, it had never occurred to me that depression really does inflict enormous collateral damage on family members. It's hard to overstate the importance of that realization. He was an arrogant prick and first-class control freak, but he was also smart. And at a crucial moment, he insisted that I belonged in an in-patient psychiatric unit, which was my first step toward recognizing what I was dealing with and learning how to cope with it. It was a crossroads in my life, the moment when I stopped trying to escape and turned to face the fact that I was not, and never would be, "normal." Good things came from that awful mess, in ways that were the opposite of what I wanted and that I had no way to understand at the time, and they came through the actions of a person who had zero intention of doing me any favors. If that's not grace, I don't know what is.

One thing I wrote 20 years ago jumps out at me now:

"It seemed to me the basic definition of any mental illness, this persistent, painful inability to simply *be* with someone else." And I wrote that I sometimes still dreamed about that sick sense of disconnectedness, despair and anxiety. I still do; I probably always will. But then I wake up, and the objects around me arrange themselves into the life I have today, with a husband snoring beside me and a dog at the foot of the bed and two daughters in their rooms down the hall—though, by the time you are reading this, one of them will be sleeping in her college dorm—and all of this (with the exception of the dog, though I'm extremely fond of him, too) is more precious to me than anything on earth. On days when one of the kids has done something—or failed to do something, such as clean out the cat litter box—and I want to drop-kick the offender off a cliff, I remember those days 25 years ago when the only way I could move my legs down the sidewalk to get to work was by repeating an inner mantra: "I *will* have a family someday." Today, I do. If the only thing I ever accomplished on this earth was to love those three people and be loved by them, I would count myself happy. But what actually happened was that life gave me that, and so much—*so* much—more.

Prologue

My body aches intermittently, in waves, as if I had malaria. I eat with no appetite, simply because the taste of food is one of my dwindling number of pleasures. I am tired, so tired. Last night I lay like a pile of old clothes, and when David came to bed I did not stir. Sex is a foreign notion. At work today I am forgetful; I have trouble forming sentences, I lose track of them halfway through, and my words keep getting tangled. I look at my list of things to do today, and keep on looking at it; nothing seems to be happening. Things seem sad to me. This morning I thought of the woman who used to live in my old house, who told me she went to Sears to buy fake lace curtains. It seemed a forlorn act—having to save your pennies, not being able to afford genuine lace. (Why? a voice in my head asks. The curtains she bought looked perfectly nice.) I feel as if my brain were a lump of protoplasm with tiny circuits embedded in it, and some of the wires keep shorting out. There are tiny little electrical fires up there, leaving crispy sections of neurons smoking and ruined.

At least that's how it seems. Sitting in the subway station, waiting for the train, I realize I am not thinking straight, so I do what I've done before in this situation: I get out a pen and paper and start writing down what I call my "dysfunctional thoughts." Just between the car and the subway station escalator, I accumulate these: "Everybody but me is in shape. I am fat." Then: "My career is going nowhere. I'm never going to get a promotion at work. They think I'm second-rate." And: "My relationship with David is not working. I'm getting irritable and withdrawn, finding fault. More proof that I can't handle intimacy."

Writing these down doesn't help immediately, as I knew it wouldn't, but I file them away for future reference. I take it on faith that I am thinking in distorted ways at the moment. But I'm never really sure of that when it would most help to know. I don't even know when this current siege began—a week ago? A month ago? The onset is so gradual, and these things are hard to tell. All I know is, the Beast is back.

It is called depression, and my experiences with it have shaped my life—altered my personality, affected my most intimate relationships, changed the course of my career—in ways I will probably never be fully aware of. These days, however, the Beast has been cornered—which is to say that he escapes from time to time, but I have some control over him. I have an array of new antidepressant drugs at my disposal—far more powerful than traditional antidepressants, faster-acting and with fewer side effects—and a psychiatrist with whom I have developed trust and a good working relationship. After many years of pretending the Beast did not exist, I now have deep respect for my adversary.

I call him "Beast" because it suits him—though I imagine "him" not as a creature but as a force, something that has slipped outside the bounds of natural existence, a psychic freight train of roaring despair. For most of my life, the Beast has been my implacable and unpredictable enemy, disappearing for months or years, then returning in strength. He appeared in the most benign of guises, hiding in plain view behind a word I thought I understood, but didn't. I was using the word "depression" as early as fourteen in my diary, but I did so in the nonmedical sense of the word—the ordinary, transient despair of being a teenager. Yet, even in grammar school, there were long stretches—weeks, maybe months, it is impossible now to say—when every morning I counted the hours that had to pass before I could crawl into bed again, times when I escaped to the shower and turned on the water full blast to disguise the sound of my weeping, unhappy over something I could not name. I suspected something was wrong with me, that this flat and colorless world I lived in was different from the one most other people lived in, and I wanted desperately to be "normal." At the same time, I had no real assurance this was not normal.

"Everybody gets lonely sometimes," my mother told me, when I tried to tell her what it was like. How could she help me? I had no words to describe this thing. And she suffered from depression too.

And so, very early, I began to try to understand.

I trace the beginnings of that endeavor back to a winter afternoon when I was fourteen, sitting in my bedroom in a suburb of Atlanta. In my lap was a blank green stenographer's pad; in my hand was a pen. I know the precise date, because it's recorded there in my careful schoolgirl penmanship: December 29, 1969. I was beginning a private journal and, I wrote, I had two reasons for trying this experiment. One was to practice my writing. The other purpose was "to put down the cause of my depressions and to see if I can help myself that way ... It sounds horrible, and it is, but a couple of times I have thought how nice it would be to kill myself!!!"

As time went by, depression became more than just a personal struggle, but also a subject on which I could practice my writer's craft, even in those long years when I did not know what I was describing. It seemed natural to become a journalist—an occupation hospitable to persons with mood disorders. Having a mood disorder is not synonymous with having artistic talent, but it is true that people in the so-called creative professions— writers, actors, artists, musicians—have a higher than normal incidence of such illnesses, and there are also a disproportionate number of alcoholics in these fields whose drinking may be an attempt to medicate the anxiety of depression. I didn't know this when I was twenty-one, the year I became a newspaper reporter. I just knew I loved newspapers. Mostly, I loved the people who wrote for them: the hard-bitten colleagues who chortled over the dead stripper whose will directed the undertaker to put a whip and a jar of peanut butter in her coffin ("What for?" I asked, and they guffawed), but who turned to mush over a story about a child lost in the woods. I wanted, of course, to write brilliant fiction—but real life kept intervening. It was so much more interesting. I watched and noted, and what I saw and felt went into my journal. It was an adolescent undertaking, still; every incident was invested with high drama in those pages, and hardly a day went by when I did not note my psychic temperature. It would be years before I developed an interest in brain biology, before I would be able to see the story I was researching as bigger than myself. But those scraps of raw material would prove useful later, when I searched them for patterns. I was, as they say in the newspaper trade, "saving string."

In 1992, two years after I began to get effective drug therapy for my depression, the personal and the professional merged in an article I wrote about my experience for the *Washington Post*. Several colleagues warned me against writing about such a personal subject. They said that revealing I had suffered a mental illness would harm my career, and for a while I held back, afraid they were right. But the more I thought about it, the more I wondered. Suppose they *were* right? Did silence, in the long run, help me? I also felt the inequity of my situation. My colleagues had written first-person accounts of their heart attacks or their gallbladder surgery, if they had learned something of interest, and their stories were considered valuable contributions to public understanding. Depression was surely as common as heart disease or gallbladder surgery; I knew half a dozen people who had endured serious episodes of it, and just as many who had dealt with it in a family member. They did not talk about it freely, however. Some of my colleagues at the *Post* knew that I had been hospitalized for depression, but they tended to bring the subject up in stairwells, or at private lunches. Over and over, I was struck by the way in which each person categorized his or her experience as unique. *It wasn't really "depression," it was stress.* Or, *I never spread it around, but my father was hospitalized for six months; we thought he'd never get better.* Or, *Nobody in my family has ever seen a psychiatrist, I'm the oddball.* After a while, it seemed logical to suppose that there were a great many people who had some experience with this illness.

There were. By nine a.m. on the Tuesday morning my article appeared, my direct line at the office had recorded a little over forty voice mail messages, not counting calls coming in to other parts of the paper. The pace of calls continued all week.

Really good for talk

mental vs. physical

Relates

For many readers, it was the first news that their pain was, in fact, a medical problem and not a character weakness, that a great many "high achievers" suffered the debilitating effects of depressive episodes and in the intervals still managed to pursue demanding careers—and that help was available. Like me, they had suspected that something was fundamentally wrong with how they felt. But they had gotten stuck at the last conceptual hurdle—which was to say, out loud, "I have a mental illness." Many expressed immense relief; it was as if a familiar word—"depression"—had suddenly become three-dimensional, revealing the adversary behind its ordinary facade. One caller comes vividly to mind. "I'm Peggy," she said. The call was logged early Tuesday morning; she must have just read the paper. She was weeping. "I read your story. I think you may have just saved my life."

After four days of this, overwhelmed with the reaction I had unleashed in myself and others, I went home and, for a little while, pulled the bedcovers over my head.

I emerged, eventually, with the idea of writing about this illness in a new way—not as a memoir of insanity, but as the chronicle of a time I have lived through. To me, it's an era which began on that winter afternoon in 1969 in Atlanta, in a time and place in which people talked vaguely about "nervous breakdowns" and "female trouble," and which continues to the present, when many laymen can converse with some sophistication about disorders of neurotransmitters in the brain. My task would be to subject myself to the same scrutiny I applied when I wrote about other people, to write about an intensely personal subject in the most objective way I could. I would try to apply the tools of journalism—the ability to note significant details and ask the right questions, the dogged pursuit of a pattern of meaning in a jumble of facts—to the art of personal history. I would try to pass through the mirror of self and describe what I saw from the other side.

This is an interesting concept. The brain is the only organ that tries to make sense of its pain. It is as if the bone were trying to understand the break, as if the blood vessel could comprehend its rupture. But this is also its greatest impediment to understanding. The mind clings fiercely to any alternative to chaos, even if that alternative is self-destruction; the tunnel vision of suicide, when death seems the only solution to an intolerable existence, is the brain's categorical rejection of the preposterous notion that anything about its perception of events might be amiss. But the reverse ought also to be true: the healthy mind might be able to understand its own malfunction.

The array of symptoms we call depression is a territory ventured into many times over the centuries, each time by explorers fascinated by different elements of its topography. It seems to us a twentieth-century phenomenon, but in fact, it is an old and well-documented illness. Greek physicians in the time of Hippocrates described a mental condition involving prolonged and inexplicable feelings of fear and anxiety, which they ascribed to an excess of "black bile." The Greek term for that— *melaina chole*—is the root of the English word "melancholy." In the fourteenth century, it was known as "melancholia," which reflected the sadness that is another dominant feature; in the nineteenth century, it had become "neurasthenia," with its hysterical connotations of swooning fits and vague physical malaise. The word "depression," used in a clinical sense, did not come into common usage until this century, and already it has passed back into the domain of the layman. Today, as we struggle to put all the pieces of the picture into a single frame, the most common medical term is "affective disorder." That, and other modern locutions such as "neurobiological disorder," may be more clinically precise, but they lack the music of some words from earlier centuries. So far, nothing has quite worked; we still lack a distinctive and accurate name for this ancient shadow on the brain.

Depression meets with a particularly ambivalent reception in modern America. Our frontier ethic of self-sufficiency has evolved into a modern taste for self-absorption and the inverted quest for status found in victimhood. When it comes to depression, Americans tend either to remain stoic and blind to the most flagrant symptoms, or to adopt the role of wounded children whose problems are entirely the fault of forces beyond their control—a bad upbringing, societal ills, or rotten genes. Sometimes it seems as if the most widely heard spokesmen on this issue are divided into two camps: those who believe depression isn't truly an illness at all, and those whose lives have been one long tragic experience with nothing but depression.

Despite our recent preoccupation with psychopharmacology, depression is a complex illness of both internal and external origins, the interaction of nature and nurture. That makes it all *Both* the harder to define—and our inability to do so may explain why *Controversy* even the most generous medical insurance plans limit coverage for this illness. Yet according to a recent estimate in the *Journal of Clinical Psychiatry*, depression accounts for a $43.7-billion-per-year burden on the American economy, measured in medical costs, lost productivity, and the lost economic contributions of wage earners who die young from depression-related suicide. For American business, depression is the ne'er-do-well relative suspected of skimming money from the cash register; employers ignore or condescend to him, hoping that one day he will just go away. But he won't.

These days, any good bookstore has shelves of books about mood disorders, many of them medically sophisticated, some of the level of pop psychology, and much in between. In cyberspace, people swap questions about medication and coping hints via files with names like "Depression Chatline." Judging from the number of entries, interest in this subject ranks up there with that old standby, "relationships." The pharmacist in my neighborhood in Washington, D.C., jokes about how he should order Prozac by the truckload, since everybody in the neighborhood is taking it.

But, he adds, not everybody wants to personally own up to that.

His words point out the aspect people don't talk about: even in this avalanche of information, the stigma remains. I know of one highly regarded reporter for the *New York Times* who pays his own psychiatric bills, fearful that submitting them to the company health insurance plan will stymie his career. He may be right; in any event, the *Times'* mental health coverage is not generous, so he's not missing out on much. A young White House aide, recruited straight from college because of his obvious intelligence and potential, tells me over lunch how he sneaks out of the office to see his psychiatrist, how he worries that the side effects of his medication will become evident to his co-workers. As my illness has done so many times in the past, his is producing such anxiety that to simply complete a thought is an excruciating task, and writing a complete paragraph can take an entire morning. It is a debilitating state to be in, all the more so in Washington, a city with no time for the slow-witted. Depression robs the mind of its normal power to concentrate and analyze. From the outside, looking at apparently healthy people hiding their depression, the deficits are subtle and easily missed. But to the sufferer, they are as devastating as if a knitting needle had sliced 20 IQ points from his frontal lobe while he slept. This is what the White House aide tells me over lunch, though he doesn't need to. He is in such pain it is palpable, so brittle I think he might shatter before my eyes. He is very sick, and so very ashamed.

I understand his shame; I've felt it myself. Sometimes I still do. To those who have never experienced depression, this must be an infuriating illness—easy to fake, quite possible to conceal, hard to distinguish at times from whining and simple malingering. That frustration no doubt explains some of the treatments for depression, which over the centuries have included emetics, purges, cold showers, or prescriptions for "mother's little helper" pills, all dispensed with a kind of weary tolerance. I sometimes wonder how much this all too human reaction of frustration has to do with the advice of a few doctors who in recent years have opposed the use of psychoactive drugs altogether—and whether any of them would ever think of telling a diabetic patient to try harder to get well.

The stigma of depression is sometimes unwittingly perpetrated by those of us who write about it, who subscribe to the notion that having a mood disorder makes one "special." Many first-person accounts of depression contain a hopelessly compromised message: it is wrong, those writers say, to attach a stigma to an illness which is a medical problem like any other … except that it *is* different, since only artists suffer. This is an elitist view. Grocery store clerks and bus drivers also suffer, but lack the leisure to write about it. And it is a view which ignores some unattractive truths, including the fact that depression tends to foster an array of personality traits which can remain as its permanent legacy: manipulative behavior, passivity, unremitting self-absorption.

I do not believe depression is the special province of any particular group; I don't see it as a "feminist" issue. I am distrustful of data which show that the incidence of depression is much higher among women than among men, because I do not think our culture has ever permitted men to express psychic pain the same ways that women do. Nor can we know with any degree of certainty how the statistics in our century stand in comparison to, say, the incidence of depression in late-nineteenth-century France. Statistics on depression are like statistics about crime; all we know is the reported incidence. They give us broad landmarks, not precise information.

It is one of the ironies of the history of this illness that new drug treatments for it—drugs with names like Prozac, Paxil and Zoloft—emerged in this country about the same time the antidrug crusade reached its zenith. The antidrug slogans are everywhere, emblazoned on shopping bags and on the sides of tractor trailer trucks. "Drugs are a dead end." "Just say no to drugs." "Drugs kill." Hardly any school in the country does not have a sign proudly announcing that it is a "drug-free zone." Added to this is the belief among many non-M.D. psychotherapists that drugs are an illicit shortcut, that the only way to truly solve problems is through years of painful self-analysis. "I'm a little scared of Prozac," one prominent Washington psychotherapist told me at a party once. "I prefer to treat the whole person"—as if, I thought, she somehow understood the brain to be completely unrelated to, say, the colon or the pancreas.

But she's right, in a way. Ray Fuller, one of the Eli Lilly scientists who developed Prozac, put it this way when I interviewed him for a *Washington Post* story several years ago: "If the brain were simple enough for us to understand, we would be too simple to understand it." Altering brain chemistry alters behavior, he said—but the hidden reverse is also true: altering behavior alters brain chemistry. This makes sense to me. And in accepting this, I find no diminishment of the mystery of human consciousness. If anything, the mystery deepens.

Mental illness is a kind of exile into a foreign territory of the mind, although this foreign territory is right next door. It is a room—imagine it as plain white, featureless, empty—which most people may not enter, and from which others may never leave. Those of us who have seen it from the inside may or may not be able to send back bulletins, and until now those bulletins have been understandable to others only in the music of poetry, in music itself, or in the simplest of prose.

"It's cold in here," we may say. "I hurt. I am miserable."

And those on the other side may hear. They may even partly understand. But the message has never come through in clear, everyday language, told with coherence, sophistication, and detail.

Until now, that is. Now that medicine has come up with effective ways to treat depression, those of us who suffer from it have become co-investigators into this new science of the brain; for the first time, sizable numbers of us can return from that featureless white room to add our voices to the debate about psychotropic drugs and their place in society. It's a discussion which, so far, has mostly excluded us, though it shouldn't; no one outranks the patient as an authority on what is happening inside his own head. We are also under an increasing obligation to confront our illness, seek the proper treatment, and to the extent we can, begin the work of changing the behaviors fostered by depression. This is not blaming the victim; it is—to use a trendy phrase—empowering the victim. To fail at this, to surrender to the devouring self-pity this illness can engender, violates an unwritten law of society, which needs all the talents and energies of every member. To remain a victim of depression when I have been given the tools to be healthy, or at least healthier, means that I am withholding a part of me from people who might need whatever I have to give.

Looking back at those carefully rounded letters in the green stenographer's pad, I marvel at how little that fourteen-year-old knew, and how prescient those words were in describing the struggle she faced. And I'm glad she made it.

Chapter One

[handwritten: very poetic, pretty writing]

It is deep in the night; morning is a mirage. And the thing I have dreaded has happened: the beast is outside my window. It is a mechanical beast, and it screams—steel against steel, a heavy thundering of weight. There is the oppressive sense of something huge and black. It is confined for now, but it threatens to bolt loose, breaking all natural laws; if I move, it might notice me. I lie motionless, trying not to breathe. The beast slows, grumbling, then shudders, slides, and finally comes to a raucous, banging stop outside my window. Somehow the silence is worse than the cacophony which preceded it. It is a silence of something about to happen, broken at intervals by another metallic groan as the beast moves, muttering in its sleep. The fear is a bubble which rises from the pit of my stomach to my lips. Then there is a shadow in the doorway: my mother. *[handwritten: 14 y.o.]*

"It's a freight train, Tace," she says tiredly. "Go back to sleep." In a minute, I hear her voice across the hallway, in my parents' bedroom. "I swear, I think she can hear those trains the minute they leave the station in Chattanooga."

I am sitting on my mother's lap. She is kneeling or sitting cross-legged on a bare hardwood floor. I feel warm and happy. There is sunlight coming through the window in front of me, and a breeze moves the sheer curtains. I am laughing.

It is summer, and I am in the backyard, a shelter under a cool canopy of oak trees. My mother's chaise lounge rests on bare dirt, next to the duck pen. She is sitting with the mother of one of my playmates, and they are sipping iced tea from tall frosted metal glasses, and I should be comfortable. But I'm not. I feel a familiar, gnawing fear. What's wrong? Something's wrong. I keep waiting for it to happen. "It's so nice to sit back here when it's raining, the trees are so close you don't get wet at all," my mother is saying. Somehow that casual remark is branded in my brain as if she had said, "The Russians are bombing us," or, "I am dying." Those were the things I expected to hear.

Happy & Fearful

Most of my early memories are like sunlight through a tree, dappled with dread. "My hill-and-dale girl," my mother called me. At night, after everybody was asleep, I would kneel at the cedar chest in my bedroom, making a shrine by spreading the white sheer curtains around me. There I would bargain with God for relief from this awful sense of guilt and impending disaster. If I could be good enough, my father would not lose his job, my mother would not die of cancer, our house would not burn down. I would go to bed holding a cross made of plastic that absorbed light and glowed for a while in the dark, hoping to drift to sleep while the emblem of my Savior watched over me, a magical purplish glow. But the glow often faded before sleep came. On some nights, I drifted in and out of an anxious doze, snapped into consciousness by the crowing of my grandmother's rooster across the cornfield from my bedroom. It might be dawn; it might be three a.m. The sound, like the call of a mockingbird, years later, seemed an accusation aimed at me for sins I could not name.

Verily, I say unto thee, that this night, before the cock crows, thou shalt deny me thrice.

Anxiety was in the air, like a virus.

My mother was afraid. "I had a terrible dream last night," she said one day. The four of us were in the car, at the top of a hill deep in the countryside south of Atlanta. We had been "visiting," dropping by relatives' houses on a Sunday afternoon, an old Southern custom. Now it was late. Ahead of us, the sun had burned to a dull orange and was sinking behind a knotted bramble of bare tree branches, throwing shadows across monochrome fields marked with the stubble of last summer's corn. My mother was always having terrible dreams, prophecies of disaster or interminable slow-motion nightmares in which she could not escape the thing that was pursuing her. It was the legacy of her past: a childhood of poverty, the early loss of both parents, years of deprivation and abuse from relatives. From all of that she had salvaged her Southern fundamentalist faith. Jesus was her refuge, the one Being who had never deserted her or made her feel unworthy; she loved her Savior with the fervor of an abandoned child. But even kindly Jesus warned us of doomsday, and that was what she was talking about now. My sister and I leaned over the front seat; she sat beside my father as he drove, and looked into the sunset.

"The sun was blood-red, like it was the end of the world," she said.

"What happened in the dream, Mama?" Her words gave me a chill. "Were we in it?"

"Yes," she said, shortly. Then she shuddered. "I don't want to talk about it." No matter how I pressed her, she would not say more.I leaned back into the car seat. How horrible it must have been, that she couldn't tell us. The dream was an omen; I believed in omens. We expected the end of the world, the Second Coming of Christ. It could happen at any moment. *For no man knows the day or the hour. I will come on thee as a thief, and thou shalt not know what hour I will come upon thee. The sun shall be darkened, and the moon shall not give her light, and the stars of heaven shall fall, and the powers that are in heaven shall be shaken.* But I knew what her dream was about: it was about me, being left behind. I was not going to heaven.

I could not remember a time when I did not know that. The faith that steeled my mother for life, which my father accepted and which seemed to come so naturally for my older sister, did not come naturally to me.

From the beginning, my confusion centered on this thing

called the Second Coming. It was supposed to be the moment of ultimate rapture for all Christians, when believers were to be caught up in the air and taken directly to heaven. We heard the Bible verses in church. *I tell you, in that night there shall be two men in one bed; the one shall be taken and the other shall be left ... Two men shall be in the field; the one shall be taken, and the other left.* It was a moment all Christians supposedly longed for. But every description sounded terrible, disorienting, and strange to me. I just didn't get it. And the fact that this alternate view made no sense, that I awaited the Second Coming with horror and dread, was proof of my difference from others. And different, to a child, was a curse. Different meant defective.

"I can't feel at home in this world anymore," we sang in church. But the world *was* my home. I was in love with the tangible; in my mind, even the letters of the alphabet possessed shape, color, texture, weight.

This was Georgia, twenty miles south of Atlanta. The time was the early sixties.

One night when I was seven, President Kennedy was on television. I said, "What is it?" The adults stared at the television and did not answer. Afterwards, we had a family conference around the round oak kitchen table about what to do if a nuclear bomb fell on Atlanta. Do not get on the bus, my mother ordered; I will come get you, no matter what. At church, pale men in dark horn-rimmed glasses bent over me and asked me to suppose that godless Russians had threatened to shoot me if I did not renounce Jesus Christ. What would I do? I would renounce Jesus and go home, I thought; maybe then they would leave me alone. But I didn't say that. Telling the pale men that I was ready to knuckle under to the godless Russians was not what they wanted to hear.

The imminence of nuclear war, centered around someplace called Cuba, got tangled up in my mind with the Second Coming. I couldn't decide which scared me more: the godless Russians or Jesus in the sky, coming to judge the quick and the dead. Somehow I always thought both events would take place directly over the marquee of the Roosevelt Drive-In Theater, visible from our back doorstep.

My mother remembers one Fourth of July in either 1962 or 1963. She and my father had stepped out into the driveway around midnight to watch the annual fireworks show put on by the drive-in. My sister and I were asleep, they thought, in the back bedroom. At some point, between whistles and pops, she became aware of screaming from the back of the house. It was the two of us, awakened by the noise. We thought it was the end of the world.

I have no memory of this event. I knew only that annihilation loomed. It could happen while I was asleep, while I was pulling up my socks, while I was fighting with my sister; I could wake up from a nap and discover myself doomed to eternal hell while the rest of my family had gone to heaven in the Great Rapture or the giant mushroom cloud, whichever came first.

One day in fourth grade, I left my seat in the classroom and went down the hall to the girls' room. I walked close to the wall, trying not to take up space. Inside the rest room, I crouched behind a toilet, my arms wrapped around my knees. I did not cry; I was just wordlessly sad. Unable to figure out why, equipped with only a child's logic, I eventually decided I was sad because President Kennedy was dead.

Even then, this rationale did not seem satisfactory.

There were clear signs on at least one side of my family—my father's—that a vulnerability to mood disorders was woven into the family genes.

At some point in the 1930s, one story went, my father's mother simply went to bed and stayed there for a decade. No one knew exactly why, though there was some vague mention of "female troubles." In retrospect, it seems she simply gave up on life. By the time I formed my first memories of my father's mother, she was a bent woman, frailer and more elderly than her years, who sat on the sofa and seemed to absorb all the light and levity in the room. Her need for human contact—any kind—

was insatiable, but her usual way of asking for it was to request personal favors. "Would you trim my toenails?" she would ask. "Would you wash my hair?"

Years later, as an adult, I learned of another child—a girl born before my father, whose existence my grandmother rarely spoke of.Her name was Helen Faye. She had died at the age of three in a household accident. While my grandmother's back was turned, Helen Faye managed to climb up on a stool near the stove, where she upset a pot of boiling water. She died several days later. My father was sent to live with his aunt in Gadsden, Alabama, while his older brother stayed at home to help care for their mother.

My father's father was a roguishly handsome man who was one of Birmingham's first motorcycle policemen. No one in the family ever heard my grandmother call him anything but "Boy"—not in the demeaning sense also known then in the South, as addressed to black men, but as a simple word of endearment, an unusual gesture in a woman so reticent. At some point after Helen Faye's death, he left. In some versions of the story, he simply departed—went out for a pack of cigarettes, as the saying goes, and never came back; in other versions, they had fought over his decision to go look for work in Mobile. His brother found him, years later, working on the docks in San Francisco. When I was an infant, my mother says, there came news that he had remarried. My grandmother was living with my parents then—she spent most of her life, after her bedridden period, shuttling from one son's house to the other—and my mother was awakened in the night by the sound of racking sobs. By then, he had been gone for several years. My grandmother still wore her wedding ring.

So death and abandonment took up residence in our house, trapped under a blanket of suffocating silence, and for comfort there was a kindly Jesus who might come at any moment to judge the quick and the dead.

Of my mother's family I know even less. She has a picture, taken about 1929, of two little girls standing against the side of a house. It appears to be morning. Both have bobbed hair and are carrying Easter baskets. The older one, about seven, looks directly into the camera. The younger one, who is about three, is looking off to one side—distracted for the moment by a butterfly, perhaps, or the appearance of the family cat. Looming across the foreground of that picture are two large shadows, a man and a woman, evidently the adults who are taking the picture. The three-year-old is my mother. The shadows are her only visible reminder of her parents.

She never knew her father. He left not long after that, for reasons never explained, the way men left families in the Depression to seek work elsewhere or simply to rid themselves of the burdens of a wife and children. My mother was told that he had died. She has only vague memories of her mother—a serious, deeply religious woman with auburn hair, who worked in the Nabisco factory in downtown Atlanta, making biscuit boxes. She died of influenza when my mother was four, the winter after that Easter snapshot was made. My aunt—the seven-year-old in that picture—was told that as their mother was dying, she made her own sister promise to take care of her two little girls.

The promise was casually made and just as casually broken; poverty had made my mother's family bitter and mean-spirited. Two children, to them, simply meant a bigger grocery bill. Neither my mother nor her sister has ever spoken of their relatives with anything approaching affection. The only uncle who was financially stable, an accountant with Coca-Cola, did petition to adopt them. But the courts refused to give him custody, citing his alcoholism. For a time, my mother and her sister shuttled between the homes of various relatives, treated like the unwanted children they were. My mother remembers a family argument that ended with the two of them being pushed out of a car and left by the side of a deserted road in the country. How long they were there she does not remember; it seemed like a week, though it was probably not more than an hour. She remembers standing there with her sister in the tall grass, watching the car drive away. She was six years old; her sister was ten.

The two of them wound up as full-time residents of the

Southern Christian Children's Home in downtown Atlanta. During one particularly lean period, money was so scarce that the children got a piece of bread with some pasty peanut butter for dinner at night. My mother learned to eat the bread and save the peanut butter, rolling it into a ball to eat in bed at night before she went to sleep.

My aunt left the children's home at sixteen to make an unwise marriage. My mother was luckier: she was adopted at the age of eight. Not surprisingly, she lavished her unqualified adoration on the man who came to her rescue. He was a rawboned Georgia farmer named John Derrick, whose wife, Cora, could not have children. I called him Pa-Pa. By the time I was four or five, he was retired from Southern Railway, the job he had taken to pay the bills. But at heart he was still a farmer, and up to the year before he died, he was still reflexively putting seeds in the soil. One of my earliest memories is of sitting on his lap while he fished a knife out of a front pocket of his worn overalls to peel an apple for me.

My memories of those years are primitive and sensory.

The dirt road out front is red clay, gluey and slick when wet. I dig it out from under my nails, find it between my toes. I walk behind my grandfather, Pa-Pa, as he plows the upper cornfield with his white mule, Becky. It is early spring, and the crumbling clots of dirt are cold, as if the plow is opening up the winter earth to the steady spring sun. The dirt smells dark, a musky scent of manure and rain.

Later, in another spring, I remember lying on the earth outside the barn, across a dirt lane from where Pa-Pa plowed. He died on a spring day like this, a day like an old lady's idea of heaven: a little too hot, a little too perfumed, a little too floral. I smell honeysuckle. Running under that scent, like the harsh one-note plaint of a diggery doo, is a faint animal stench from the barn. The sun is hot on my back. I lie facedown in the grass, my face pressed to the earth, and while I sleep it seems I can feel the earth move, almost imperceptibly, toward late afternoon.

·   ·   ·

So much sadness—and yet by the time my parents had met and married, life seemed bright, the worst hardships behind them. Pictures of my mother from that period show a beautiful woman with awkward, round-shouldered posture, a pose she adopted because she thought her height was unfeminine. She was slim, with red hair, green eyes, and a gardenia-pale complexion. My father was skinny in those years, with black curly hair and an intense gaze that my sister would later inherit. He came home from World War II, they met while working at Delta Airlines, and they married a year later, following their version of a script that millions of returning veterans and their brides were also following. Pa-Pa carved out eight acres of his woods and cornfields next door to his own house, and my father ordered some house blueprints out of a magazine. He and Pa-Pa built most of the house from scratch, contracting out the skilled labor but mixing cement and hoisting two-by-fours themselves. My mother plastered the walls. The result was a split-level ranch house with a pine-paneled den and a two-sided living room fireplace I still recall with affection. My sister was conceived in that house in the winter of 1953. I was born two years later.

In those years, my father was getting his law degree at night while working by day in the cargo department at Delta. I was lulled to sleep at night by the sound of my mother's Royal manual typewriter in the kitchen, as she typed his school papers. The two of them were well matched. After his motherless childhood, my father soaked up my mother's unqualified love the way thirsty ground accepts water; with my father, my mother felt truly wanted at last. They honeymooned in California, stopping in Los Angeles to visit her sister, by then on her second husband. In a picture from that trip, my mother lounges against a low-slung late-1940s car, wearing slacks and looking radiant and sexy. Yet there is something—a tension in her pose, an unease in her expression—that suggests the camera had captured something from her without her permission. She was shy. But my father had a politician's social gift for being with people; with him, she knew the giddy, vicarious pleasure of popularity. He played on the office softball team and won trophies, pitching left-handed; he played on the office golf team and won trophies, playing right-handed. He played in the church bowling league and brought home so many trophies that my mother stacked them in closets. He joked constantly, even in church; it was years before I realized how much he hid behind that mask of jollity. What made it effective was the fact that he was truly funny. "Did you hear what Tommy said?" people would say to each other at parties, repeating some one-liner. I was his shill, a risible child who instantly rose to his bait; nothing pleased him more than making me laugh. "After the service tonight, there will be a short elders' meeting," the minister intoned from the pulpit, and my father stage-whispered, "What about the *tall* elders?"—knowing that I was defenseless, that there was no way I could repress this rising hilarity.

He was impulsive. Once, he came home from work tearing in the driveway, brakes grinding, horn beeping, yelling at us to get in the car. We screamed up the road to the freeway overpass that was being built near our house, where my father pointed west toward a peculiarly brilliant red sunset. He had wanted us to see it.

After he got his law degree, he moved into management at Delta, and we qualified for free airline passes. But he never planned trips; we just took them. One day, he came home from work and announced, "We're going to Australia," and that weekend we did. It was the first of several similar adventures, which over the years took us to places like Ireland, New Zealand, Hawaii—anyplace my parents had always hankered to explore and wanted us to see. My mother found this no less thrilling than my sister and I did. "Who would have thought," she would say frequently, "that an orphan from the Southern Christian Children's Home would wind up in—" In their best moments, those trips were hilarious, *ad hoc* enterprises. Once, trying to escape from a large and peculiarly uninhabited airport in Auckland, we found ourselves in a rental car, stopped at the end of a road which had put us directly onto a runway. "Now what?" my mother asked, and always the eager wiseacre, I stuck my head between her and my father in the front seat. "What you do now," I said, "is locate the wind sock and take off into the wind."

Sometimes rage would consume him, for no particular reason—a lawn mower that wouldn't start, the mayonnaise jar left open on the kitchen counter. At those times, he frightened me; his fury could clear the room. There was something exaggerated in the way he threw a tool down or slammed a door, a fierceness that seemed to come from nowhere. In him I sensed a deep, unfathomable anger—perhaps because, even then, I sensed that I had it too. Then it would be over. He wandered through the house singing nonsense lyrics to popular tunes. "Toreador / Don't spit on the floor / Use the cuspidor/ That's what it's for," he bellowed; or, "LEP-rosy / Night and day you TOR-ture me / Sometimes I wonder / Why I fall asunder …"

For my mother, his ebullience was a tonic. She was happy. I watched her from the kitchen doorway as she stood at the sink, wearing a green striped seersucker dress, her red hair pulled off her face. Her hands moved in and out of the soapsuds; her face was calm and serious. I thought no one in the world was more beautiful. "Love lifted me," she sang in her clear, true soprano, or, "He hideth my soul in the cleft of a rock / That shadows a dry, thirsty land / He hideth my soul in the depths of his love / And covers me there with his hand."

On the last day of school before the Christmas holidays, December 18, 1968, my bus stopped at its usual spot, across the railroad tracks, within sight of my house. It was a clear and chilly afternoon. "Be sweet," my friend Necie said to me as I filed off behind my sister. The last thing I remember is a glint of sunlight on metal out of the corner of my eye.

The car had come over a slight rise, traveling so fast that I never saw it. It missed my sister by inches. I took the blow in the lower right side of my back and went up over the hood like a rag doll. It was a week before I woke up, on Christmas Eve. On the television set beside my bed, the Apollo 8 astronauts were about to make man's first journey around the dark side of the moon. I caught glimpses of it, in intervals between morphine-induced sleep, through my right eye, the only part of me that wasn't encased in gauze.

The impact had shattered the bones of my lower back and pelvis, and I had deep lacerations on the outside of my left thigh, where I apparently skidded along the road. Lesser lacerations marked me from head to toes; there was even a speck of gravel embedded in my wrist. The internal damage was also significant: intestinal hemorrhages and a bruised spleen. But the worst injury, to me, was to my face: something metal on the car had left a ragged tear of skin that opened just below the hairline above my left eye and exposed the whole left side of my skull, miraculously missing the eye. It took six hours of surgery to put me back into human form, most of that spent by the plastic surgeon working on my face.

The accident coincided with a major growth spurt of puberty. After three weeks, I left the hospital in a wheelchair; in three months, I was walking without a limp. But there was a slashing red scar that covered a quarter of my face, starting just above my left eye, turning the outer edge of my eye up into a distorted squint.

I never knew exactly how the accident happened. I was aware that it was a time of racial tension. Martin Luther King had been assassinated the previous April, and there were dark mutterings among some people at church that the driver, a nineteen-year-old black man, had run me down on purpose, because I was white. Late in the spring, there was a criminal trial. In court, the driver said his brakes had failed. In the courthouse corridor, our families regarded each other with hostility. My family waited for some token of remorse; his family waited to see what form of injustice the court system would inflict.

After lunch, I was called to the witness stand. The questions from the prosecutor were perfunctory. Then he asked me to step down from the witness box and walk in front of the jury. He guided me down the row of jurors slowly. Some of them leaned forward to get a good look at the red scars on my face; I remember an older man who looked at me and flinched. The scars, I realized much later, had nothing to do with proving the defendant had committed a crime. But they were an eloquent, unspoken message from the prosecutor to the twelve white people in the jury box: here was a young white girl who had been robbed of one of a woman's most valuable assets, and a black man had done it.

The defense attorney had no questions. The jury took half an hour to convict. I heard later that the judge gave him three years.

The whole thing was unbearable, so in my mind I sealed it away. Don't worry, people told me; the scars are bad right now, but plastic surgery will fix that. And so I waited. The summer after the accident, I had the first of a series of plastic surgeries—a day or two in the hospital, followed by several weeks spent with a bandaged face, hiding inside the house, looking as if I had been in a bar fight. Each time, I waited for the bandages to be removed, to see the face I had had before; each time, I was disappointed. In fact, the only thing that could heal the scars was the passage of time. To a fourteen-year-old, this was an alien concept. "You're a pretty girl," my mother kept trying to reassure me, but all I had to do was look in the mirror to see that this was untrue. And so I adopted the only tactic left to me: I tried to ignore it.

It worked, some of the time. Once, as I was waiting at a bus stop, a stranger inquired rudely, "What happened to your face?" I looked straight ahead, unable to think of a reply. "Don't worry, darlin'," said my emergency room doctor, a rakish man who was on his third or fourth wife, a former Playboy bunny. "You're gonna be an interestin'-lookin' woman." This wasn't helpful. I wasn't stupid; I knew "interesting" was just one step up from "ugly," and ranked far behind "beautiful" or even "pretty"—and he was proof of how much men valued beauty in women. My plastic surgeon was a man of medical renown who radiated an emotional chill, he observed my face impassively, the way an artist considers his options. In his silence, I heard an eloquent commentary on the impossibility of my dreams.

Finally, despite her moral qualms about allowing me to

wear makeup so young, my mother took me to a Merle Norman studio. There a lady slathered my face with heavy masque foundation, dusted that with powder, dusted the powder with rouge, then took a makeup pencil and drew a new eyebrow over my left eye. Then she sold us a bagful of Merle Norman products. "You look beautiful," she said when she was done, which was untrue; I looked embalmed. But from that moment, I never left the house without my makeup. It maddened me, that I had to wear makeup, that I was scarred and pasty-faced. My sister, then sixteen, had put on another inch in height over the past year, and her face had lost its childish roundness; with her dark hair and large brown eyes, she was developing a dusky prettiness that was enhanced by the startled-doe look she turned on people when they spoke her name. It did not occur to me then that she was suffering too, that she reacted to the attention our parents lavished on me by withdrawing farther into her books and her fantasy life. As far as I can remember, there was very little discussion of the fact that she had nearly gotten killed too. I only knew that I was jealous.

Journal entry, Saturday, MAY 15, 1971:

> Nonny got her hair cut today, so now I am definitely the plainer sister in the family. I always knew I was … She's got all it takes to be really pretty, and she's learning how to take advantage of it. As for me, I look as good as I'm ever going to look.

I had waited for adolescence like any other young girl, as if it would be a Disney dream and something magical would happen. Now, although I longed to hear my father say I was pretty, I knew it would never happen. I didn't even ask. When I came home from the hospital, he had picked me up in his arms and carried me into the house, but I felt no comfort in his touch, only embarrassment. I never knew what he thought about the accident; he never told me. We talked about it only once, years later, in a conversation that was stilted and unnatural. My mother talked about it frequently. To her, my survival was a miracle; she offered her fervent thanks that God had spared her daughter.

Listening to her prayers, it seemed ungrateful of me to complain about the means by which God had accomplished this.

Once again, pale men in dark glasses bent over me at church, this time to murmur their thanks that the good Lord had allowed me to survive, and like a good daughter I echoed their piety. Inside, my rage retreated to a dark corner of my mind. It would be years before I realized I was angry.

By my senior year in high school, I had fallen in with a crowd the rest of the school referred to sardonically as "creamers," as in "cream of the crop," the top of our class in an ordinary Georgia public high school. Being a creamer was the same thing as being called a geek or a nerd, but that was okay with me; at last, I had found a group to belong to. In geek tradition, we stuck together. We even went to the prom en masse, since none of us could work up the nerve to ask anyone else for a date. By graduation, I had garnered a number of academic honors, I played tennis, I had even acquired a boyfriend. I read constantly. My reading list was heavily male, British, and nineteenth-century, though an occasional American got thrown in: Dickens— *Great Expectations* was my favorite book—the Brontë sisters, Thackeray, Hemingway, F. Scott Fitzgerald, James Thurber, Mark Twain. My life was full of the normal teenagethings— sleep-over parties, clubs, working on the school yearbook staff.

But signs of chronic depression were emerging. Even before the accident, I had begun to make frequent trips to the doctor, always complaining of a variety of ailments. Some were real; others had no clear physical cause. I seemed to suffer constantly from stomachaches, headaches, a mysterious cough, strange lumps in my lymph glands—a litany of ailments baffling to my doctors and worrisome to my mother, whose experiences had taught her that there is no such thing as bad news, only catastrophe. Each ailment convinced her I was suffering from a fatal disease. The family doctor referred me to an internist, who referred me to a neurologist, who gave me an EEG. It was normal. My urine was tested for diabetes; my blood was tested for leukemia. Those tests were normal too. Finally, in bafflement, the internist gave up and wrote a prescription for Valium. I was thrilled. Not only was I getting some attention, which I craved, but the Valium meant that I was also—finally—going to get a good night's sleep.

> MAY 1973: It's going on one a.m., but I'm writing until I get sleepy. Last night I had a recurrence of all my old symptoms—insomnia, dozing off only to find myself awakened with a start ten minutes later by my own beating heart, unable to catch my breath ... Tonight I took a dose of cough medicine with codeine, plus ten milligrams of Valium, and I hope I can sleep.... This started about a year and a half ago, when we were going to move, and I have had problems with it off and on since then.

I was seventeen.

The anxiety was like poison ivy. It took nothing to set off that mental itch—a chance remark, remembering an event from the day before—but once it started I found it impossible to stop the cycle. My thoughts twisted in a circle, my pulse hammered, I couldn't concentrate. The only thing I wanted was to make *sense* of this feeling—and the explanation, or apparent explanation, was obvious: I was worried about boys.

But I was a Christian, and Christian girls were supposed to have their minds on higher things. We were supposed to be happy. "Doubt," one Sunday school teacher told us solemnly, "is of the Devil." I was filled with doubt, I was wormy with it. When the principal of our public high school brought a beauty queen to a football pep rally to offer her own personal Christian testimony, I sat in the bleachers with my friend Jim as, one by one, all the people around us went down to rededicate their lives to Christ. I wasn't making a statement; I just hated the emotional coercion.

I also hated my face. There were times when I silently mouthed obscenities at myself in the bathroom mirror, sick at the sight of the red keloid scar which marred my forehead.

But I admitted that to no one; for years, whenever anyone brought up the subject of the accident, I would leave the room, too furious to speak. With nowhere else to direct that anger, I focused it on the most readily available target—myself. The urge to do this, to catalog my inferiorities, was one of the earliest impulses behind the creation of my journal; enclosed in that first volume, I found scraps of paper predating the beginning of my journal in December 1969, but which I had folded and kept with the journal. On one such paper, dated October 23, 1969, I had written:

> Basically I am a very cold and withdrawn person … Most [people] think I am honest, dependable, and trustworthy, a fine young Christian girl, I have to state that this is, I'm afraid, mostly hypocritical … I have tried to be a good Christian, but because of the above-stated tendency for being hypocritical, and also an alarming tendency towards deceit and conceit, I have found it extremely hard … I am much worse than the drunks on the streets or the prostitutes in the barrooms, as they do not pretend to be better than they are. I cannot say the same for myself. P.S. When I read this I will probably start feeling sorry for myself.

At other times, those journal entries show that at some level I understood that my physical ailments and my mental state were linked.

> APRIL 14, 1970: I feel fine in the middle of the day; at night I start feeling depressed, and in the morning I trace the hours on the clock till bedtime. I am really not worth all this self pity, because I have anything that anybody could ever ask for. Well, I must not lie to myself: I have been thinking sometime ~bout attempting suicide because that would put r hospital … I know why I am having fainting spells, and general less than normal health; of all these dark thoughts I keep thinking

But these were episodes. For long periods in between, life was normal, with its regular ups and downs. Sometimes I found it hard to believe I was the same person. In one journal entry from June 1972, I recalled my incredulity when, walking home from the horse barn one day, I had realized how sad I had been only a few weeks earlier. "You mean, you really wanted to die?" I asked myself. "You must have been out of your mind!"

It was like flying low in an airplane, in and out of thunderheads. The normal work of adolescence—acquiring knowledge, achieving emotional maturity, discovering sex, preparing for college and independence—took a back seat to navigating the daily storm front. I was angry, so angry. My father's black rages now seemed trivial, compared to the fury I felt but could not express. It seemed uncontrollable, and for that reason I frightened myself, sought to push it to the back of my mind. And for a long while, I succeeded. When the emotional storms had abated, I felt energized, optimistic, full of myself—the adolescent version of the laughing, risible child I had been. There was a song from my senior year in high school that became linked in my mind to those times: "I can see clearly now, the pain is gone / I can see all obstacles in my way ..."

In black moments, my turmoil spilled out in nervous, melodramatic pronouncements; I was dying for someone to discover what I tried so hard to hide. When the Valium prescription ran out, I replaced it with over-the-counter sleeping pills, which I took by the fistful. Once, riding in a carload of friends on our way to a football game, I announced: "Last night, I had to take ten Sominex to get to sleep." My friend Jim spoke up from the back seat. "I don't think you should take so many pills, Tracy," he said—and I treasured that remark for years, as if it had been a profession of love: he had *noticed*.

At home, the rule of silence prevailed. Once my mother found a drawerful of empty Sominex bottles in my bureau and threw them out; I did not discover until years later that she had sobbed for a day, afraid that I was becoming a drug addict. I did not tell anyone that despite the Sominex I still awoke at four with my heart pounding so loud I could hear it in my ears. I did not tell anyone that when, in the winter of my senior year, I found out that Jim had gone out for a date with one of my best friends, I had gone home and taken half a bottle of aspirin.

I wanted to die, or have my misery noticed, but neither of those things happened.

Chapter Two

I stood at night at the edge of the ocean. It was black, as was the sky; looking out, I could not see where the ocean ended and the sky began. No stars or moon interrupted that blackness. It was unnaturally calm. The boat was just past where the breakers would have begun, if there had been any, and it was lit like a festival. Light streamed from every porthole; twinkling ropes of light fell from the mast. I had to reach it.

Then the scene changed. I was on a small raft, chasing the pleasure ship, setting out to sea on a current that was fast and strong and silent. I was a speck in that vastness. My chest was tight with panic. Though I was taking big, shuddering gulps of air, I was dizzy for oxygen. The boat was pulling away. I had just enough time to intercept it, moving on that swift current, if I could plot the right course. But I had no charts, no way to steer. Then the raft pitched forward. Somehow I knew that the ocean floor had taken a steep downward slope. Far beneath the glassy surface, the ocean floor was falling away. The current was getting faster. The waters were going to suck me down into some huge waterfall that somehow existed below the surface, a silent, downward rush of current. Horrified, I waited for that to come.

I woke up. It was 4:08 A.M.

The Beast came for his first extended visit in the spring of my junior year in college, 1976, his arrival announced by the onset of a peculiar sleep disturbance. I kept a digital clock beside my bed in my dorm room at Emory University. It was an old-fashioned one—no liquid crystal display, but numbers that flipped with each changing minute. That spring, for weeks, every time the "7" in 4:07 A.M. flipped to the "8," I would wake, intensely alert, my consciousness zapping off the walls.

It was the old fear from childhood, returned with a vengeance. I was afraid that something was about to happen, but now my fears were becoming more specific. The trouble was, facts had no boundaries; they unfolded like paper accordions in my head, offering vistas of a catastrophic future. My parents were getting old; that meant someday they would get sick and die. I had made a C on my English paper; that meant I was stupid and would not get a decent job after college. I didn't have a date for Saturday, night; that meant I would be alone forever.

There was a mockingbird who lived in a tree outside my window, which faced a busy street. The mockingbird sang all night, but in the predawn hours he got shriller and more insistent. The cascade of bird noises and the growing rush of traffic outside told me that another day, another crushing load of loneliness and dreary chores, was upon me.

Sometimes the dread sharpened into panic. The usual focus for that was my boyfriend, Sam. We were former high school classmates who had both ended up at Emory, a well-regarded Southern university on a leafy suburban campus in Atlanta's well-to-do northeast. Sam was a stern-faced young man, with a prominent jaw and a nervous habit of reaching up with his right hand to smooth the part in his hair. His father was a lawyer whose practice consisted mainly of divorce cases, contract disputes, young toughs in trouble, and furtive men working on their second or third DUI conviction. He was a nice man, but absentminded and aloof. Sam's life centered around his two sisters. They were vivacious, pretty, and, in my view, hopelessly man-crazy, vying with each other to see who could find the tiniest bikini. I wasn't fond of them, but I tried not to show it. Sam's mother, who lived in Florida with her second husband, was as flirtatious as her daughters. I liked her even less. Sam was the dutiful son, by far the most responsible member of a flighty family. That was one of the things that bound us together; Sam had a lot of experience in rescuing the needy. As for me, I thought of his solicitude as my due, more or less; for all the other people on his caretaking list, I felt only faint disdain. To the women in Sam's family, I was a dreary bookworm Sam inexplicably found attractive. As they looked at me, I could read their thoughts: *Maybe he'll grow out of it.*

Sam also marked the beginning of my first tentative experiments with sex—though, odd as it sounds, those experiments took years to unfold. In the beginning, ours was a chaste relationship. This was the early seventies, and though I went braless to class, scandalizing my mother, the Sexual Revolution of the 1960s had left large pockets of the Bible Belt virtually untouched. In Bible Belt culture, sex was an earth-shattering notion. Within marriage, it was supposedly a mystical union; outside of marriage, it was the first step on a oneway road to moral ruin and depravation. Nobody ever actually told me that sex could simply be fun; I found that out later, on my own. I think now that part of the reason I disliked Sam's sisters so much was that they seemed light-years ahead of me on this subject, and at some level, this simply pissed me off. What pissed me off even more was that they were so provocative, even around their brother, that Sam had long ago developed the habit of keeping a tight lid on his sexual impulses—a state of affairs which put a monkey wrench into my own faltering attempts at seduction.

In other ways, Sam and I found considerable pleasure in each other's company. My family was fond of him, we shared many high school friends, we had similar intellectual interests. Altogether, the relationship would last for the next five years. I assumed at somepoint we would talk about marriage, but at the moment, that seemed premature. Sam wanted to go to medical school, which was likely to mean leaving Atlanta, and his long-term plans involved setting up his own practice in a rural area. I wasn't sure how that was going to fit with my intended literary career.

But just how serious I was about that, I did not want to admit to myself. Seriousness of purpose in career matters did not reconcile with the image of Woman as Wife that I had grown up with. I was attached to that image, exemplified by my mother; it seemed to offer a kind of love and security impossible to find any other way. Yet I suspected, with a sinking feeling that was starting to get familiar, that this was one more area in which there was something wrong with me. What other people found relatively easy, even sometimes hard to avoid—namely, finding a mate during one's college years—was not going to be easy for me. My first intimation of this came the night Sam and I sat out on the lawn outside the Emory medical school, talking vaguely about the futures we imagined, and he remarked, "Of course, my career would have to come before my wife's." *Have to* come first? No negotiation at all? I pressed him for some elaboration, but he found it impossible. How could you elaborate on a point so obvious? *Oh, God*, I thought, and dismay settled over me like an old, clammy blanket. *Oh, God*. I said nothing.

But that spring, as I fell farther into the abyss of serious depression, my hesitations were swept aside by my frantic need for security. I began to feel a compulsion to nail things down between us, to carve into stone the idea that we would marry— if not next year, then the year after, on a date certain. I began to obsess that he was secretly in love with another girl; I panicked if I did not know his whereabouts. On weekends, he would hole up in the library to study; he was having trouble with organic chemistry, and needed to do well in that course to have a shot at medical school. I roamed the stacks, looking for him, and when I found him I would try to drag him away from his books, to spend time with me. I lived from one date to another; I had few other friends. My thoughts raced in a circle, centering always around the same question: Would Sam marry me? Marriage was the glass slipper, the charm that would break this evil spell.

I spent an increasing amount of time alone. If I was with people, I felt as if I were surrounded by strangers on a bus. The world seemed to be telescoping away; I saw everything through the wrong end of a pair of binoculars, watching tiny, animated people at the other end engage in activities I could not fathom. I spent hours walking around campus at all times of day, encased in a loneliness as palpable as armor, armed with an unreasoning hostility. If anyone spoke to me, I glared at them.

At the same time, my senses seemed to be sharpened. I experienced my surroundings—the wet smell of hot pavement after a spring rain, the sound of mourning doves at dawn—with vivid and intense sorrow, as if I were seeing it for the first and last time. Sometimes I felt this to be true, as if I were literally dying.

With a desperation born of the sense that I was losing my mind, I threw myself into schoolwork. Academic failure—which I defined as anything less than a 4.0 average—would have destroyed my tenuous grip on my self-esteem. But it was hard: the sound of my schoolmates' conversation and laughter in the dorm seemed as earsplitting as shattering china. I had little part in these conversations; I was by then a mostly silent presence on the hall, not a part of the dorm's social life. Glaring, aggrieved at this imposition, I would retreat to the library across the street. But even that was too noisy. I was distracted by the sound of someone's breathing close by, the gentle rustle of turning pages, the muffled conversations in the lobby, the sound of doors opening and closing. In a growing fury of frustration, I would sit hunched over my book, reading one paragraph over and over, hell-bent on understanding what the words meant and trying to make them stick in my brain. Today I recall that I was reading the *Confessions of Saint Augustine*, but I remember virtually nothing of what it said. Good*damm*it, I would mutter as another person walked by my table and broke my train of thought. And I would go back to the top of the page and start over. But I didn't really blame other people. I blamed myself. I am so *stupid*, I would say despairingly, over and over. And that was a true catastrophe: the only good thing about myself that I knew with any certainty was that I was intelligent. Once I lost that, what use would I be to anybody?

In the pages of my journal from that year-long episode, the symptoms of a mood disorder were clear:

> My face is wet. My hands are icy—I notice these things one at a time, gradually, like an infant. I am cold. Inside, I am a battlefield—Waterloo after Napoleon, Vicksburg after the siege … Always a war; always fighting one emotion after another.

> I am so restless—no, "restless" is too weak a word to

describe the way I feel; I feel angry in a dozen ways, all bursting out at once, yet all directed inward. I can't sit still a moment, physically or mentally, and my lack of concentration puts me on edge … Where do I get this unreasonable sense of panic?

I can't enjoy anything.

It's as if I'm trading punches with someone through a curtain, and the first time I knew he was there was when he knocked me breathless … The worst thing is not knowing what hit you; after that, it's not knowing what you are afraid of.

There is a deep, gnawing sadness at the core of everything, everything, and on afternoons like this I feel it most. I am empty inside. There is something in the future which is coming … I am afraid that it will suck out my core and I will be completely empty and anguished.

At night I go for walks and think of how much I would like to be drunk. Completely smashed. Out of myself … I would like to forget I ever existed.

I have to find ways to get myself through it, people I love who will help me … I have to because the alternative is simply existing, crawling in a corner to die. Or going over the edge into madness.

My dreams were extraordinary and vivid.

Last night I was walking along Old National Highway, picking up litter … Suddenly I felt a pain and held up my hand. A very neat hole opened up in my palm, just below my third and fourth fingers. Inside it was bloody and pulsating. I was about to give birth through my hand. I thought, "How incredible! I never knew it could be done like this" … Then the pain increased, and I began to pull out wads of cotton from inside my hand, and then a handful of pills, like emptying out an aspirin bottle (only the pills were yellow). I was in great pain, but I knew these were things I had to do myself since no one else would help me. At last the fetus came out, bloody and glistening blue in its sac. I woke up.

Last night I dreamed that the world was full of birds—big, black birds with ugly, shiny bodies that would not fly. They covered the ground like vermin, they crawled up on windowsills and hung over ledges. They covered every flat surface, barely moving, making little sluggish noises to each other. I was supposed to go over to Gwen's. Sam was there, with other people. There was going to be a party. I did not want to go out, but I did, wading through the birds, making myself open the door to her apartment, even though birds hung all over it.

I dreamed of being angry last night. There was a man in my dream, an ugly little dwarf with puke-colored hair, who had debased me in some way, taken advantage of me. It didn't occur to me until after it happened that I should get mad. Then I did. I got so furious that I went back and found the little man and I walked up to him and kicked him. I said, "You have something that belongs to me. Now go get it!" He was walking away from me, trying to ignore me, but I followed him through crowded rooms, shouting, "Get it, you punk! Punk!" I pushed him and scratched his arm with my fingernails. He gave me back whatever it was I had lost. But after I walked away, I saw a rifle pointed at me sticking out of some bushes and I was afraid. I was afraid of retaliation by the little man's friends.

I dreamed of confessing to someone, anyone, that I was getting preoccupied with thoughts of suicide. My dreams were as detailed and specific as real life; in one, I was visiting a psychiatrist—a dark, skinny guy with lots of hair who resembled one of my French professors—and we were discussing a *Cosmopolitan* magazine article about women who kill themselves. "What does that have to do with you?" the "psychiatrist" asked, and in the dream I burst into tears. "How come I can't stop thinking about it?" I sobbed.

In real life, though, confession was unthinkable. There was the social stigma of being labeled hysterical, neurotic, out of control. In white Southern culture, women held their emotions in check. Intensity of feeling could get you labeled crazy, like the pathetic Blanche DuBois—even though the constant effort to suppress emotion gave many Southern women that shrill, slightly hysterical tone which was the basis of the ditsy Southern belle caricature.

My own mother lived not so much by that code, however, as by the one she had learned in a childhood of deprivation and abandonment: Trust no one. She kept her problems to herself—and, over the years, I came to the conclusion that her despondent periods were fundamentally different from my father's mercurial personality. Like me, he was forever navigating the peaks and valleys of a steep and uncharted emotional life—though, being a man of the World War II generation, he would never have willingly displayed this; I deduced it many years later, inferring it from his dense silences, the periods of snappish irritability that came and went for no reason. My mother's periods of depression were, I think, not so much the product of a genetic predisposition as of the psychic trauma of a tumultuous childhood. Her wariness about leaning on any other person turned her focus ever more inward, and that in turn fueled her religious fervor. From my father, I took whatever genetic predisposition I had toward depression; from my mother, I learned ways of behaving when those periods came along. Over the years, I had learned to read the signals of those times when she sank into despair about some problem she would not name: the set face, the silences, the stony look in her eyes, the slightly defensive inward curve of her shoulders. Then there were her constant nightmares, the way she always jumped out of her skin at sudden loud noises, the chronic headache that lasted, it seemed, throughout most of my childhood. To me, all those signals were easy to read, but if I pressed her about what was wrong, she would say, "Nothing." If I pressed harder, she would say, "It's nobody's business but my own, Trace"—in a tone which allowed no further discussion. No mere human was allowed to examine the burden she carried, except possibly my father; she took her problems to the Lord in prayer, and she advised me to do the same. Her reaction was a familiar part of Southern Bible Belt culture, in which a crisis of the mind was, by definition, a crisis of the soul. The cure, therefore, was spiritual.

I was a born-again Christian, having walked down the church aisle at the age of eleven to make my public confession and to be immersed in the baptistry at the front of the church, a huge tank of chlorinated water concealed behind a velvet curtain; the tank was kept filled and ready to go twenty-four hours a day, the theory being that once someone decided to give his life to Jesus, baptism should follow immediately, to avert the possibility that the Second Coming might happen before the deal was, so to speak, sealed. In that time, and in that family, it was not possible to be anything but a born-again Christian—though I showed an early and distressing lack of enthusiasm on the subject of being saved. The reason was not philosophical but emotional and, to some extent, social. I was so convinced of my sinfulness, and so certain that I would never be anything but a sinner, that a public confession of my failings seemed agonizing and pointless. I also had an adolescent horror of getting my hair wet in front of five hundred strangers, because it dried frizzy. Yet I was rapidly approaching what church theology called "the age of reason"— an indefinable point, located somewhere around the age of twelve, but earlier in the case of a kid who was bright, when the child began to take on adult responsibilities for his own moral choices. Every Sunday, my mother waited for me to march down the aisle toward the waiting preacher at the front of the church; every Sunday, I felt her sorrowful gaze boring a hole in the back of my head as I stubbornly remained in my seat. The tension was awful. Eventually, she signed me up for a Saturday morning class at church, designed to reinforce the lessons we had been taught for years on the Steps of Salvation. At the end of this remedial course, I went forward and gave my life to Jesus. My mother was overjoyed. I felt relieved.

Encompassed in that act was the assurance that from now on, God would help me through all problems and crises; if not, it meant I had not really been "saved" after all. Now I began to suspect that this was, in fact, true—that somehow God had not found meacceptable, or that my commitment had been intrinsically faulty. I prayed. But I was getting the distinct sense that I was only talking to myself.

The thing that was going wrong in my brain was a biochemical event imprinted on an existing, unique personality. I cannot tease apart, even now, where personality ended and illness began; they were woven too tightly together. But some of the underlying pattern of personality—the part of me that would have existed independently, with or without any illness— is traceable.

The main thread was my role in my family.

Visitors to my family's house in those days were struck by the degree to which I played the starring role, by how much the father I adored also doted on me. My sister, two years older, was intense and solitary, paralyzingly shy, more at home with animals than people. As children, we had been companions, living out our fantasies of digging to China in the backyard or making rock soup. But as we grew older, the differences in our personalities became increasingly evident. She lived inside her head, where the boundary between real life and fiction was often blurred. A scary car-chase scene in some television drama or film footage of combat in Vietnam terrified her equally; she would watch, curled up on the sofa, her face screwed up with horror, and once she abruptly fled the living room in tears during a Huntley-Brinkley segment on starving children in Biafra. I didn't know what to make of her.

She was untidy where I was neat, a daydreamer in the classroom where I was a teacher's pet. I found her an easy mark for my witticisms. Once I stopped in front of her bedroom, noting the unmade bed, the pile of dirty clothes in a corner. I had been nagging her all day about doing her chores. "What are you saving those for?" I asked, pointing to the dirty clothes. "The Smithsonian?" She lunged at me over the bed, and I fled in serious panic. I had seen her hands, and they were itching for my neck.

My sister was my father's helper, his trusted companion. They worked agreeably together for hours, fixing the lawn mower or mending the pasture fence. My relationship with him was more volatile—but when I wasn't making him mad, I could make him laugh. "He spoiled you to death," my high school friend Jim said to me, years later. "It showed in many, many ways." One Friday afternoon, as I arrived home from the Emory campus across town for a weekend's visit, he met me in the hallway. "Curly, the whole house lights up when you're here," he said. Naturally, I thought; it lit up for me when he was around, too. Weren't we just alike?

That spring, Sam started to get worried about me. He and I had been out one Saturday night when he told me that he wanted to beg off on our plan to spend the next day together; his older sister, who lived about fifty miles away, had organized a last-minute family reunion, and some relatives would be there he hadn't seen in a while. The change in my weekend plans sent me catapulting into hysteria; it was proof that Sam did not love me. I sobbed for hours. He did not give in to me, and his awkward attempts at comfort only added to my desolation. A few days later, he told me how exaggerated my reaction had seemed to him, and how scared he had been by my hysteria.

"I think you should see a doctor," he said.

The last thing I wanted to do was to admit I needed help. That was synonymous with weakness; intellectually superior people did not need "counseling" for "emotional problems." On the other hand, if Sam was worried about me, that was at least a form of attention. And the idea of rescue was darkly appealing.

Torn between neediness and shame, I ducked out of the

dorm one day, went to a telephone booth down the street, and called my internist. No, I told his receptionist through clenched teeth, I could not tell her what the problem was; I needed to *talk to the doctor*. No, I did not mind holding.

After a long wait, he came on the line. "What's the matter, Tracy?" he said.

I don't remember what I told him, but the nature of my distress must have been apparent, even over the phone. "I want you to come in and see me," he said. "Come in this Thursday, at the end of the day. That way, we'll have time to talk."

He was a kind man, a general practitioner in his fifties, with daughters my age, and he was sure that he could help me. He began by prescribing Triavil, a drug which contains an antidepressant and an antipsychotic. (Later, I discovered that he had prescribed a dose too small to have any effect.) On that first Thursday afternoon, I sat in his office, looking at the floor and avoiding eye contact, managing just barely to keep from bursting into tears. At the end of the visit, he suggested that I come in again the next week.

The visits became weekly events. We would sit in his paneled office for forty-five minutes or an hour, usually on Thursday afternoons, while Nita, his receptionist, busied herself outside clearing away the paperwork debris of the day. It was my first experience in admitting the existence of the Beast, this strange despair that had inexplicably decided to stalk me. That was a huge relief, and the attention from him was enormously cheering. But its effects were temporary. After a while, Nita's cheery voice would come through the door: "Good night!" And then it would be time to leave, to catch the crosstown bus back to campus.

It was a dreary time. And yet I managed that spring to get a summer job as an intern at the *Atlanta Journal*. It was a measure of my need to excel that I assembled a file of my clippings from the student newspaper and sold myself as a job candidate when it was all I could do to read a full paragraph. When the letter came in late April notifying me that the internship was mine, I went to the calendar on the back of my dorm door and counted the weeks until June: six. I had that long to escape this mental cloud, to become a normal person.

It was my coming of age, a summer of downtown strippers and hard-boiled newsmen, of sex and drugs and crime, the summer I learned to drink. The paper's "White House correspondent" was a reporter who could be found at almost any time of day at a local bar called the White House. After work, we repaired there to drink concoctions called B-52s. People with hardy livers drank a doubled-up version—B-104s. I have no idea what was in them, other than vodka. My tongue went numb after two sips; they would have made a great dental anesthetic. I sampled them gingerly, until my head felt light. It was my first experience of the liberating effects of alcohol, though it would be years before I actually worked up the nerve to get drunk.

My mother sensed that what she had always feared most was happening: her little girl was slipping away. It wasn't just that working on Sundays meant that I had to miss church; what worried her was my obvious relief at having an excuse. My interest in the tattered remains of Atlanta's hippie culture, in the goings-on in downtown flophouses and strip joints, appalled her. That world of poverty and degradation was the world she had managed to escape, and my fascination with it must have seemed to her a kind of perverse degeneracy—a sign, perhaps, that I was slipping back into the poor-white-trash world of her haunted childhood. She worried about my moral improvement, picking up books I'd left around the house, riffling through their pages in search of whatever it was I found so compelling there. I mocked her for thinking there were dirty parts in *Anna Karenina*, seethed with oppressed superiority when she complained that a television production of *Long Day's Journey into Night* was "all doom and gloom" and that I never wanted to watch anything "uplifting." The battle between us escalated until she was reduced to complaining about my "attitude"—a perfectly accurate description of what was going on, but an accusation she found impossible to elaborate on or substantiate. I had moved beyond her reach.

My job required me to be at work by seven a.m., and the

commute was at least half an hour, even without one of Atlanta's notable traffic jams. If I was going to eat breakfast and put on my makeup (there was, of course, no thought of going without makeup), I had to be up at five-thirty. But by this time, depression had taken over my brain, and sleep was its first casualty. I was insomniac, irritable, raging at the slightest noise in the night, a caldron of anger during the day. After years of suppressing rage, I now felt like a volcano in continuous eruption. Any minor inconvenience could set me off—misplacing a blouse, getting lost somewhere, missing a phone call from Sam, finding myself stalled in a traffic jam. I felt I was going out of control. My fear of doing so was at war with my overwhelming need to express this constant, nameless fury in some physical way. I threw things; I beat helplessly on the floor with my hairbrush; I scratched and tore at my own skin. The provocations were always so minor that I had usually forgotten them by the next day; sometimes I would look at a bruise on my arm and think: What was that for?

Somehow, I kept some shred of control. My tantrums took place mostly behind closed doors. I only broke things that belonged to me; I only scratched myself in places that would not be obvious later. It seemed to me that if I stifled these outbursts completely, I would go crazy, I would literally lose my mind. And yet, after each one, I felt acutely ashamed. If people could only see me, I thought, they would know I was nuts already.

The year 1976 was a presidential election year. At work, during the day, I monitored local elections in the counties south of Atlanta, the labyrinthian political intrigues between candidates for justice of the peace—a judicial office every Georgia county had at least one of, and whose officeholders my editor referred to collectively as "corn-pone Buddhas." All during that summer, I wrote in my journal.

> It's not pity I feel toward myself … but a sense of contemptuous leniency. "Well, she really is sick," I seem to think of myself. "Who'd have thought she had it in her?"

As the weeks passed, I started thinking about the year

ahead—my senior year at Emory.

> The thought of school fills me with terror—fear of
> being faced with an impossible task (that of appearing
> normal and happy and making good grades so no
> one will worry) and fear of never finding a place to
> be alone ... I carry a lead weight in my stomach and
> it hurts ... I would like to simply sit still and close
> my eyes and withdraw from the world, but I am too
> restless for that.

And yet: I knew I was more than this sickness—though
that was an insight that came only sporadically. Sometimes it
came in the form of music, which I listened to like an aphasic
person—mouth agape, struggling to find a word in the coils of
my brain and finding instead a kind of wail. Others had found
that wail too, and transformed it. The "Lachrymosa" from
the Berlioz *Requiem* was my wild grief, the aria from Handel's
Messiah could temporarily dissolve the stone that was my heart.
"Comfort ye, comfort ye my people," sang the tenor, an aching
and sweet melody, "and cry unto her that her warfare is ended,
and her iniquity pardoned." But more than anything, it was the
second movement of Beethoven's Seventh Symphony—the
mysterious and measured theme and the violins in counterpoint,
full of longing.

> I envy Beethoven because he could turn suffering into
> art. He was liberated in every sense of the word. He
> was deaf, he was stout and unlovely, he was lonely and
> he lived most of his life alone—but the music from
> a man who perhaps had the most reasons for being
> unhappy can transmit such a sense of joy that it fills
> my room ... I feel as if I am serving a prison term.
> But his music is like looking through a window of the
> prison cell ... It's a hope that someday I'll be able to
> break out of myself, that I'll be free.

In fact, the opposite was happening. My emotions—my
life—seemed out of my control. Slowly, in ways invisible to

me at the time, the depression was altering my personality, as if a slight deformity in my spine were giving me a permanent limp. The changes were not the symptoms of depression but coping mechanisms for dealing with it, and they built on existing personality traits. I had always been anxious to win others' approval, but now that need became insatiable; I had always been capable of charm, but now charm became a naked willingness to manipulate others to get what I wanted.

I cultivated mentors and father figures, people whose power I perceived as greater than my own. My own father was engaging and jovial, yet somehow remote. I found it impossible to confide in him, and so wanted only to perform—to show him what a good student I was, how many friends I had. But he was impatient with foibles and expert at picking out the one flaw in an otherwise perfect performance. Over the years, as my unsullied report cards became littered with B's in math and science, his comments were always the same: "What about this B?" If he was upset about a B in math, how could I tell him I was losing my mind?

But I was needy for male attention, so I sought it from other men—my boyfriend, my professors, my editors. I demanded Sam's attention. When enough was not forthcoming I directed my anger at his sisters and his mother, who lived in another city. They were too demanding, I said; they wanted too much of his time. My jealousy caused many fights between us, but I could not see how much of the problem rested with me. How could it be? I needed what I needed; to say I shouldn't need so much was like saying I shouldn't breathe so much air. In fact, I was ashamed. At some level, I understood that there was something extravagant about my demands.

The possibility that Sam might leave Atlanta to go to medical school was my most constant, looming fear. I saw other friends deal with separations, even with a boyfriend or girlfriend going to college in another state—and I couldn't imagine doing that. Seeing other people handle it made me feel childish and weak. I lobbied against it, strenuously and surreptitiously, by dropping broad hints about what a good medical school Emory had, right here in Atlanta. The idea that I might have encouraged Sam in his applications to other schools never crossed my mind.

My self-worth was entirely in the hands of other people, but they didn't know it; that meant I had to look out for it, while not letting them know the immense power they wielded over me. In my dealings with my professors, who were nearly all men, I was foolishly ecstatic at their praise, despondent at the slightest criticism. I would leave their offices silently repeating some compliment; later, I would write it down verbatim, and stare at the words, as if by doing so I could own the reality they represented. I was abjectly dependent on what they thought of me. "I'm not the least bit worried about you—you are a writer," my creative-writing professor scribbled at the end of one of my short stories, and I repeated that sentence like a mantra for years. My opinion of myself—the opinion of this defective and possibly deranged person who inhabited my body—didn't count.

That summer, my energies were devoted to culling recognition from my editors. The city editor, Bob, was a rotund, balding man made perpetually snappish by the deadline pressure. He seemed to take a perverse pleasure in telling us interns what miserable cretins we were, how we were unable to construct a decent sentence, much less write a newspaper story on deadline. In our first meeting with him, he solicited story suggestions from us. What would we like to write about this summer? It was a setup. There was an uncomfortable silence, and then another intern—a pleasant-faced young man, scion of a well-to-do northeast Atlanta family, self-effacing and terminally polite— cleared his throat and began to talk. He went on at some length, encouraged by our silence. When he paused, Bob looked at him, deadpan. "That," Bob said deliberately, "is probably the stupidest idea I have ever heard an intern come up with."

I made Bob my special project. Winning the approval of the most curmudgeonly person in the newsroom became my benchmark, the thing I had to accomplish in order to be a "success." Obvious attempts to cultivate Bob's favor, I realized, would only set me up for disaster, so I began by appearing to ignore him. I struck up conversations with editors who sat next to him on the city desk, making jokes and watching to see if his mouth twitched. If I was handing in a story on deadline, I would walk up to the city desk and casually deposit my copy there myself, as if I'd had all the time in the world. (This was in the twilight of the typewriter age, when a reporter writing a story on deadline would bellow "COPY!" and a clerk would snatch it off his desk in "takes," or individual pages, to take to the city desk.) I never complained about assignments, and if I had to ask any questions I did it discreetly. Mostly I avoided asking questions. On primary night, I was assigned to get precinct vote counts in De Kalb County. Not understanding that the only thing that mattered was the total at the end of the evening and whatever messages might be read in their demographic distribution, I breathlessly updated each preliminary count—keeping tabs of hour-by-hour voting surges in individual precincts. Bob never found out about that; nobody did. When I realized that I had been collecting useless information all night, I destroyed all my careful charts and pretended I'd been hard at work doing something else.

After a few weeks, my efforts paid off. Bob called me into his office for a chat.

"Of all the ones we hired this summer," he said, "you are the only one we'd even *think* about hiring permanently." It was, for him, the highest of praise. Later, I told my fellow interns that Bob had been discouraging. "Don't be upset," they said. "He's been telling all of us that we aren't any good." Silently, I exulted. Another stamp of approval. Yes!

At home, I was histrionic, prone to crying jags, silent glowering, dramatic pronouncements about minor crises. My mother asked me to pray with her; it was all she could think of to do. Sometimes I complied, gritting my teeth; at other times, I coldly rejected her suggestion. My sister and I were strangers, even though her room was next to mine and she could hear me sobbing in frustration at night when I couldn't sleep.

"I can tell something's wrong with you," she said to me one day. "I don't know what it is."

"Me either," I said. And then we both turned away, baffled.

• • •

By the time I went back to school for my senior year in the fall of 1976, I was still making weekly visits to my doctor. I had developed a powerful adolescent crush on this fiftyish man with the lumpy nose, who took me so seriously. But, slowly, he was beginning to realize that this problem was outside his competence. He had been sure that a few fatherly chats would help, but they had only made him the new focus of my neediness. He did not want to admit it, but he was defeated.

That winter, he told me our sessions had to end. And then, adding insult to that grievous injury, he said he thought I needed to see a specialist. He had someone in mind. It was a woman, which he thought would help me be more comfortable. Furious and hurt, I reluctantly went to see her.

She was a psychotherapist. I will call her Amanda Mayhew. We were to spend much of the next ten years together.

Amanda was a large woman, tastefully dressed, self-consciously poised, and middle-aged, with a soft drawl that, to my trained ears, bespoke an upper-class upbringing or at least faded Southern gentility. Her office was in Buckhead, a fashionable section of Atlanta. On my first visit, she explained the rules: She could see me an hour a week, on Wednesdays, at an hourly fee of fifty-five dollars. Before we could start, however, she needed me to have a battery of tests, including a general IQ test. Then we would see where we were.

The next week, with the test results before her, Amanda's comfortable maternal demeanor was tinged with concern: she told me she had never seen a patient whose verbal and performance IQ scores showed such a gap, unless you counted the ones who were learning-disabled. My verbal score was exceptionally high, but my performance score didn't match at all; it was in the low range. I remembered that part of the test; it had involved moving nine colored cubes around so that their tops would duplicate various square patterns on a sheet of paper. I had been acutely anxious that day, and I remembered how if I did not immediately see how to solve the problem, I had just sat there, staring at the cubes until the instructor said, "Time's up." Amanda correctly interpreted the disparity in the results as evidence of acute anxiety. "Right now, you're like an airplane flying on one engine," she said. I felt fear and relief: fear that there was something wrong with my brain, relief at realizing that someone had finally noticed. Given my level of anxiety and the trouble I was having concentrating in school, Amanda said, I might be interested in checking into a hospital. But, she added, she was not a physician, and she could not, prescribe drugs. If I thought I needed a hospital, she could refer me to someone else.

I assured her that would not be necessary. The idea of a hospital terrified me; the fact that she would even mention it gave me thoughts of bolting. I could not imagine how I would explain my absence from classes. And my experience with Triavil—which I had ended up taking only for a few months—had convinced me drugs wouldn't help. Amanda, despite my initial reservations, seemed wise and competent, capable of rescuing me. But therapy with her wouldn't be easy, she warned: she foresaw two to five years of intense work ahead of us if I was to get better. Two to five *years?* It felt like a prison sentence.

My mother and Amanda never met, but between them there arose an instant, deep enmity. My mother saw Amanda as a rival who would rob her of my love, and psychotherapy as a tool to destroy every religious impulse she had labored to instill in me. Amanda considered my mother deranged with jealousy. As for me, I saw Amanda with affection that quickly became mixed with hostility; she was a maternal icon of rescue, but there was something implacable about her. She never seemed to come forth with the kind of unconditional acceptance I craved.

In the beginning, in the winter of 1977, my weekly sessions with her were a point of stability, a time when I knew my chaotic feelings would be listened to and taken seriously. Slowly, the depressive episode which had begun the previous spring began to wane. As spring came, and graduation loomed, I felt better— not happy, but at least not preoccupied with thoughts of suicide. Now, I thought, the real work of therapy could begin.

But once this immediate crisis was past, our sessions began

to resemble one long mother-daughter fight. With Amanda, I could act out the rebelliousness I felt toward my own mother. I had never felt free to rebel at home; my mother's need for security was so profound that the usual kinds of teenage rebellion—loutish boyfriends, surreptitious pot smoking, profane music—would have shattered her. Amanda became her proxy. My insistence on continuing my therapy with Amanda constituted the gravest kind of challenge to my mother's authority, though it was one battle I could avoid fighting in person. Instead, I could sit across town, in Amanda's office, and be as insolent, demanding, and bitchy as I liked. Amanda was getting *paid* to put up with me—by my mother, who wrote the household checks. It was, in its way, a beautiful system—a kind of passive-aggressive revolt.

Amanda tried to maintain the proper distance between us, and failed. There was something in her, too, that needed to act out a mother-daughter fight, and our doctor-patient relationship was tainted from the beginning by a distinctly personal element. Some of our battles were epic—scenes of angry tears, slamming doors, furious letters of denunciation on my part, tight-lipped disapproval on hers. "You were one messed-up little girl when I first met you," she told me toward the end of our relationship, with a withering emphasis on the phrase "little girl." Her tone made it clear I hadn't changed much.

She was right. My ego needed constant stroking; my self-esteem was so brittle that the slightest criticism from Amanda felt like a death threat. Yet at other times, it seemed that nothing I could say or do could penetrate her maddening serenity.

> Wednesday, just as I was leaving, Amanda saw my hand, where I had scratched it, and asked, "What happened?" I looked down at my hand. What was visible were only the most minor scratches; most of the marks were hidden by my sleeve.
>
> "I scratched it," I said.
>
> "That must be a very painful way to live."
>
> "There didn't seem to be anything else to do," I

said. "I just sat and watched myself do it. It was very easy. It could have been a lot worse."

"You find it difficult to deal with your anger," she commented, in one of those professional Olympian assessments of the obvious I find so particularly annoying.

"Well, if anyone can think of a better way, I'd be glad to hear it."

"See you next week," she said, and I thought: you bitch.

It was not at all clear to me what Amanda thought my problem was; "depression" seemed the least of it—a mere symptom, not an illness in its own right. Amanda changed her diagnosis several times over the years, but a few stick in my mind. "Hysterical personality disorder" was one of the first—a label I later learned had been very popular earlier in the century, but had since gone out of vogue. "Narcissistic personality disorder" was another; still another, which I think Amanda used mainly to qualify me for a short-lived state aid program when my mother was balking at paying the mounting bills, was "borderline schizophrenic."

But does a personality disorder cause depression, or does depression cause personality disorders? The theory Amanda and I worked under was the the first. If I could begin to understand my disturbed relationship with others, and to repair my sagging self-esteem, the depression which affected me like a persistent undertow would resolve itself.

My mother accused me tearfully of replacing my religion with the false god of psychotherapy. She was right. I had abandoned my childhood church only to find myself in another—one without pews and altars, but one which required no fewer articles of faith. Pills of any kind were a short circuit to that process, as bogus to the psychoanalytic realm as sharkskin-suited TV evangelists were to mainstream religion. "Work out your salvation with fear and trembling," Saint Paul admonished the Christians at Philippi in the first century. Therapy was like that, a form of personal salvation which had to be painfully earned over time. If it didn't hurt, it wasn't working.

After graduation, I moved back home to live with my parents, and took the only journalism job I could find in the Atlanta area, working for a small weekly newspaper on the south side of the city. For the next two years, I waited for life to start.

It stubbornly refused to do so. Sam continued to dodge the issue of marriage. He had failed to get into medical school the first time around, and was busy taking extra courses to bring up his grade point average. I would not consider leaving Atlanta, because it would mean leaving him, my family and friends, my sole sources of emotional security. But despite Bob's grudging endorsement, my efforts to get hired at the *Atlanta Journal-Constitution* were persistently rebuffed. I was seeing Amanda once a week. But therapy, too, seemed to be getting nowhere. There were times in those sessions when I sobbed, undone by the force of some painful realization—only to drive home and pause, my hand on the doorknob, trying to remember exactly which searing insight it was that was going to change my life.

In 1979, two years after we had both graduated from Emory, Sam got into medical school. Unable to convince Emory that he would make a good doctor, he had succeeded in getting into Morehouse, the historically black college across town. Morehouse was just starting its medical school, and it was emphasizing the training of primary-care doctors to work in poor and rural areas. That suited Sam; that had actually been his idea from the beginning, which made him different, to say the least, from most of his whiz kid classmates who were now heading into their third year of medical school and thinking about which high-income specialty to pursue. I admired Sam's persistence and dedication, and I had no doubt he would be a wonderful doctor. I was also increasingly convinced that I was not going to be his wife.

That same year, I rented my first apartment with Necie, the childhood friend whose words—"Be sweet"—as I got off the school bus that day years ago had almost been the last words I ever heard. For a while, I spent weekends with Sam in his rental house on the other side of town. But there were only so many Saturday nights I could stand, watching television in the den while he studied in the kitchen, waking at two a.m. to see the light still on down the hall. As time passed, it was clear that he was growing closer to his classmates than to me. While the intense neediness I had felt during that awful spring several years earlier had abated, it was still powerful; I spent most of my time trying to figure out ways we could be together. I was getting increasingly frustrated with the rut I was stuck in, both at work and with Sam. And yet marriage still seemed the only way out.

Then, in 1980, the weekly newspaper I was working for unexpectedly got a new editor. His name was Charlie Smith. He was the oldest son of an aristocratic south Georgia family whose characters could have peopled a Tennessee Williams play. At thirty-three, Charlie was the veteran of one failed marriage and numerous misadventures with cars, alcohol, and women. I was mesmerized by his sleepy south Georgia drawl, his languid style of sucking on a cigarette, his carefully cultivated James-Dean-goes-to-Memphis persona. Before long, he was writing me poetry when he should have been working and we were exchanging smoldering looks over our typewriters. Those weekends of tepid companionship with Sam couldn't hold a candle to the torrid after-hours gropings with Charlie in the office conference room.

Weeks went by while I agonized and temporized, making assignations with Charlie while maintaining a front with Sam. Finally, I summoned up the resolve to tell Sam I wanted to date somebody else. This didn't mean, I added hastily, that we had to stop seeing each other.

"I am not interested in being one of your many admirers," Sam said shortly. At that moment, we were sitting at his kitchen table. There was a long silence. Then I stood up and left. I had wanted to end the relationship for some time, but there was no way I was going to quit one boyfriend without having another one lined up. Now, at last, I had the opportunity. I felt sad, but also clearheaded, and immensely relieved. No more deception, no more uncertainty.

I immediately went to Charlie and told him the news. He was not overjoyed. One of my main attractions for him had been that I was someone else's girlfriend. He went after women the way dogs chase cars—for the thrill. Having caught one, he wasn't sure what he wanted to do. Neither was I. So we did the next best thing: we broke up—only to get back together the next week. It was the beginning of a six-month off-again, on-again phase of our affair. But I was to have other distractions.

In July 1981, after four years of weekly journalism, editing wedding announcements and covering local city council meetings, my persistent efforts to get the attention of the big newspaper downtown finally paid off. The *Atlanta Constitution* offered me a reporting job. I started work in August 1981.

By then, my father had been dying of cancer for two years.

Doctors had found a malignant tumor in his bladder, probably the result of a smoking habit he had picked up years earlier, in the Army Air Corps. By my first day of work at the *Constitution*, he was in a hospital about a mile away, wasted and weakened by chemotherapy, his hair gone, his skin mottled with liver spots. He was only fifty-nine, and he looked like an old man.

In the evenings, I relieved my mother at the hospital while she got something to eat. My sister's job was to stay at home, take care of my father's mother, who was then living with us, tend to the house and to the horses she kept in the pasture next door. As the weeks passed, and summer waned, it was clear that the end was coming. But death took its time; death was a bureaucrat. Dying in a hospital was something which had to be done by exacting rules. And so when the cancer made it impossible for him to eat, the doctors inserted a food tube in his stomach, to keep him going. Even as the malignant cells continued their invasion into his lungs, they kept up the chemotherapy. I often wondered which would kill him quicker, cancer or modern medicine. The poisons they dripped into his veins made him feverish and delusional. He hallucinated, picking at imaginary objects and quoting, most improbably, bits of Robert Browning's poem "Caliban upon Setebos." One afternoon, my mother and I were standing on opposite sides of the bed, each of us holding one of his hands. And then, for a moment, he came back to us; he opened his eyes and looked at us with something like his old deadpan slyness.

"Say," he remarked, in a tone of offhand curiosity, "do you little girls do manicures?"

He fell into a light coma in early October. I welcomed it, for his sake. By then, the pain had become unendurable. *Go*, I urged him silently, but even then he continued to fight. Sometimes, even in his coma, his eyes were open. But looking into them, I could see no trace of that vivid mind; looking into his eyes was like staring into a bottomless pit. His only reaction to us was when his nurse, Madie, would rub his feet and sing softly, her rich, low voice a river of comfort in that bleak room. Then he would smile—a slow, shy smile like an infant's, a smile unlike the father I loved.

He had left us already, I thought. But one day, my mother and I had stepped out of the room to make some calls on the pay phone down the hall. A few minutes later, she sent me back into the room to get some change from her purse. I was fishing around in her wallet, facing the window, when something made me turn around. It was my father, looking at me.

He had a slight smile on his face. It was not the vacant smile I had seen before. It was *his* smile; behind those eyes, just for a moment, my father had returned. He could not speak, and somehow I understood that. But he didn't need to. The look on his face said everything. It was an instant, just long enough to say goodbye.

"Oh, Daddy," I said, "I am so proud to be your daughter." For a moment we looked at each other, and the love between us was like a tangible, living presence. I could not hold his gaze; the look that he turned on me was so intense it seemed to burn my skin. I buried my face on his chest. When I looked again, the eyes were blank; my father had gone. He died two weeks later, on a gray October afternoon that threatened rain.

My mother was inconsolable, her grief frightening in its abject need. My sister withdrew into her own stony desolation. My own reaction was amazement. I could not, at first, grasp the idea that he was dead, and that life was continuing anyway. At night, I dreamed of hearing the faint sound of a woman's sobs, coming from the end of a long corridor, from behind a locked door. As December became January, my father began to come to me in my dreams—frightening in his health and vigor, because, I kept reminding myself, he was dead now, his presence was alien to the universe. Yet in those dreams, the love between us was as vivid as it had been that bleak October afternoon. I knew he loved me; I knew he had somehow heard me. And then I would wake, and it would be deep in the night, and he was dead.

It was the bitterest winter Atlanta had seen in at least half a century. "FOUR BELOW!" screamed one newspaper headline from that January. It seemed like a portent of doom, the first sign of another ice age. The color of the sky was the color of the interior of my brain: unrelieved gray, not even a faint glow that might have been the sun. It was Emily Dickinson's hour of lead, a paradigm imposed by grief for every serious depressive episode I would have for the next seven years: short days, no sunlight, a pervading sense of abandonment. In January, Charlie left Atlanta for good to go to graduate school at the Iowa Writer's Workshop, and so that, too, was over.

In the space of six months, I had lost three men, including the most important one in my life. This was the utter catastrophe I had foreseen so dimly in those wakeful hours years ago, during that mockingbird spring; this was pure loss, desolate and total. The grief I felt—the grief anyone would have felt—was exacerbated by the extent to which I had depended on those men for my self-worth. It felt like someone had opened the hatch in my spacecraft; outside, the blank universe loomed—cold, airless, and incomprehensible. I was a speck. I barely existed in my own right. Deep in those winter nights, I sat awake, every light in the house turned on, thinking of the pain my father had suffered.

For no purpose, I kept saying, for no goddamn purpose. He was dead and God was silent.

That winter, grief made its acquaintance with depression, its near neighbor. As the months went by, the breathtaking reality of my father's death became a physical hurt, a heaviness in my bones, a pervasive lethargy. I slept long, long hours; when I was awake, I comforted myself with food. None of this alarmed me; I had forgotten what anything else felt like. It was, though I did not know it, the blanketing of depression. It was the Beast, returned in a new form, insinuating himself into my daily life, taking over where grief left off.

The brain changes in minute, anatomical ways every time it learns something—one neuron finds another, connects in a new way. So it was with grief and depression: that winter, the paths traced by those two states were carved into my brain like worn footpaths, merging in the snow.

In 1984, I applied for a one-year fellowship for legal affairs writers at Yale Law School. By then, I had been at the *Constitution* for three years, the last two of which I had spent covering federal court. I enjoyed the work; it was one of the best beats at the paper. But in 1982, the merger of the reporting staffs of the *Atlanta Journal* and the *Atlanta Constitution* had created a deadline schedule that ran virtually around the clock. It was like being a wire service reporter, always rushing from the courtroom to file an update on pay phones, constantly cramming in a new lead before the next edition. After two years, I was burned out. My editor, Jim Stewart, suggested that I apply for the Yale program, and then performed a miracle by arranging for me to stay on the payroll for the year I would be gone. The news of my acceptance came in a phone call I received at my desk late one afternoon in April 1984. When I heard the words I shrieked with joy. *My life*, I thought, *my life is starting*.

My Yale adventure seemed like a good place to stop therapy. It was obviously not getting me the main thing I wanted, which was to transform myself into a desirable marriage partner. Toward the end of that pre-Yale period, I had even begun to doubt the truth of the memories I had of that terrible spring in college. Maybe, I thought, I was just a psychic hypochondriac. *You've pampered yourself enough*, I thought. *Time to grow up*. New Haven, I thought, would mark my new beginning, And so Amanda and I took formal leave of each other before I left for New Haven.

The fellowship, open to five or six journalists every year, put us into the same first-year classes as all the other law students, though we were allowed more freedom than the regular students to choose our courses during the second semester. Yale prided itself on being a school of legal theory and social policy, not a place where you learned the nitty-gritty details of the law. It trained future judges and professors and government leaders; the joke was, if you wanted to actually practice *law*, you had to go to Harvard. But that made it an ideal place for a journalist who wrote about the law. For the first time, I began to catch a glimpse of the outlines of the forest I had been working in.

I promised myself I would not take academic matters too seriously, that I would use my time in New Haven to explore, to make trips to New York, to do more than bury my nose in a book. And to some extent, I did. But I found the study of law absorbing. It was not an ordeal to stay in the library until two a.m.; I actually liked it. That intellectual pleasure helped shield me from the fact that I was acutely lonely. I had chosen to live off campus; I had no fond memories of college life in a dorm. But living off campus isolated me from the life of the law school, and I found it hard to make friends. It was a godsend, then, when about a third of my way through the year I discovered the graduate students' housing complex up the street, home to about a dozen foreign lawyers and their families who had come to Yale to get a graduate degree. Most were planning to return to their native countries to teach. It was a lively, international group, which made its informal headquarters in the apartment of an Australian couple I came to be close friends with. I spent hours there, drinking espresso—"flat black," my Australian friends called it—discussing American culture, and debating things like whether Vegemite should be eaten on toast or loaded into the crankcase of a car.

I returned to Atlanta in June 1985 to create a newly defined legal affairs beat at the *Constitution*. The cast of characters there had changed somewhat, but it still felt familiar and comfortable; I slipped easily into my old world. I had given up my old apartment before I left for New Haven, so now I rented the second floor of a rambling old house in Candler Park. It was a huge place—two bedrooms, two baths, two porches, a living and dining room that ran the length of the house, more room than I could afford. But I loved it. So I placed an ad at the Emory alumni office seeking a roommate. The person who answered was a graduate student in philosophy at Emory named Patti Van Tuyl.

She was a small woman with curly red hair, a few years older than I, immersed in her dissertation on Hegel. We immediately became best friends. Patti called my pursuit of the Right Man "the search for the transcendental object X." She even bought me a wooden block-letter X to remind me that what I was looking for—a person who could guarantee my happiness—did not exist. I often suspected as much, but I wasn't ready to give up on it.

In the meantime, there was my career at the *Constitution*. Because it was in Atlanta, the newspaper was a magnet for reporters all over the South. It also had a liberal reputation dating from the civil rights era, which made it attractive to Ivy League graduates looking for some colorful experience south of the Mason-Dixon line. Uniting us was our relative youth and our hatred for the paper's penny-pinching owners and the executive editor, a hatchet-faced former sportswriter who rarely moved his lips unless he was about to fire someone. Outside a small circle of his cronies, he was thoroughly feared, and his muttered pronouncements were received as holy text whether anybody understood what he said or not. We called him the Prince of Fucking Darkness. When *Constitution* editor Reg Murphy was kidnapped back in the tumultuous 1960s by some madman with an incoherent political agenda, the paper's two fabulously rich-old-lady owners sent the Prince out with several hundred thousand dollars in ransom money packed in a suitcase, with instructions to get their editor back. According to office legend, the old ladies' rationale was that the Prince would scare the kidnapper more than a couple of suits carrying FBI badges, which certainly seemed likely—and if something went tragically wrong, well, the Prince wasn't real popular anyway.

We heard that story from the paper's old-timers. There were quite a few of them, veterans of an age when journalists did not go to Ivy League schools and women in the newsroom were there to write obits or sob stories. Hard news—defined as crime stories or politics—was a man's work. The men who did it were irascible, irreverent, and hidebound. To get along with them you had to be prepared to engage in some verbal mud wrestling. They rarely moved from their desks; years in the business had given them an array of contacts, and they could find out more about a statehouse scandal by picking up the phone and calling ol' Tom in the back room than we could in two days of sleuthing and corridor interviews. Between assignments, they swapped stories and smoked. Anyone who complained was advised to find another line of work—something woodsy and outdoors, maybe as a telephone line repairman. The smoke hung heavy, stinging my eyes and giving me a constant, hacking cough in the winter months. The worst were the cigar smokers, and the worst cigar smoker was a reporter named Monty. One day I stopped by Monty's desk and pointed at the lit cigar in his ashtray. A lazy ribbon of smoke curled upward from it. It smelled like a tire fire.

"Monty," I said. "Did a goat piss on that piece of rope you're putting in your mouth?"

Several people looked up. There was a general rumble of laughter; I had scored a point. Monty drew himself up to his full height, glaring at me through thick eyeglasses. He had shoulder-length gray hair and a beard; when he was mad, which he was at that moment, he looked like the prophet Jeremiah on a bad hair day.

"No!" he bellowed. "*I did!*" Everybody roared. Game, set, and match; I learned to live with cigar Smoke.

Work was my vocation, my social life, my entertainment, my armor against the world. I was Tracy Thompson, *Atlanta*

*Constitution*reporter—a fact I managed to insert into the first five minutes of almost every conversation. My immediate goals were quite modest: to keep up a social life that was so busy I had no solitude or chance for reflection. I cooked fabulous dinners, I spent evenings at Manuel's Tavern, I partied late and hard—almost always with my co-workers. There had been no serious relationships for me since Charlie, a fact which caused me anguish but which I managed to joke about. When I filled out forms and got to the blank indicating sex, I told Patti, I wrote, "Once a year. Usually in the spring." My romantic life was characterized by long stretches of boredom, interrupted by misadventure. My attempts to connect were almost always comically ill-advised. There was the editor at work, who I ended up having a fight with in a glassed-in office, for all the newsroom to see. There was the sweet Jewish guy who told me how his mother went for ritual baths every month after her period; he was really interested in me, if I was interested in becoming similarly Orthodox. (Thanks, but I'll pass.) There was the clerk at federal court who seemed nice until he started complaining about the women in his office. "They will not *obey* me!" he kept saying, and there was a set to his mouth that gave me the willies. And so on. I was edgy, constantly aware that the Beast was at my back. On the occasional Sunday afternoon when my friends were busy and my apartment was empty, the loneliness was a knife in the pit of my stomach.

I had long ago given up the idea that someone might remark on this. Either it was normal, and other people had devised better ways of dealing with it, or I was simply defective in some way, like someone born with a missing limb. Either way, stoic acceptance seemed the only option. I thought I had achieved stoicism, but one day a friend's bluntness stunned me.

"Ever since you've come back from Yale," Jerry said, "there's been a veil of sadness over you."

We were sitting in the lobby at Symphony Hall, during intermission. I protested. No, I said, I *wasn't* depressed; what did I have to be depressed about? I was fine. But later, in the concert's second half, I brooded about what he had said. It was true. As frightening as it was to admit, I did feel quietly despairing. I had no sense of how to define this sorrow, other than my longing to be married—and even then, I did not know where my normal human longing for intimacy left off and something more ominous began. All I knew was that I had not felt any sustained period of happiness or contentment in a long time—not for years. I could think of plenty of happy moments, but that was different. My *life* was not happy. I was living under a shadow. And the more I thought about it, the more it seemed to me that this shadow had first fallen during that awful spring of 1976.

Once acknowledged, the sadness crept in like fast-rising flood-waters. Several nights later, talking to Patti, I began to sob—a racking, uncontrollable crying spell that lasted several hours. Patti was alarmed. The next morning, I did not go to work, but lay on the sofa, bereft of even a mild interest in what the day might bring. In the next room, I heard Patti on the phone, speaking low.

"She's here right now," she was telling someone. "I'm really worried."

I wasn't. This was just another episode in my life, which seemed to be punctuated by these rounds of pointless despair. It was not evidence of illness; it was evidence of the fact that I was screwing up somehow. I just didn't know exactly where the screwup was, much less how to fix it. That was anguish, but the anguish was bearable as long as I kept my mind occupied with other things. The only permanent solution—and, increasingly, I wasn't even sure about this—was the right man, a happy marriage. There was nothing wrong with me that the transcendental object X couldn't cure.

And then an event happened which brought home, brutally, the danger I was in.

I had met Fay Joyce only once, at a hearing at the Eleventh Circuit Court of Appeals in Atlanta sometime in the spring of 1984, at a death penalty hearing not long before the beginning of my fellowship at Yale. My memory of her is hazy—a small woman, with delicate, pretty features and dark, curly hair, dressed in a Diane Von Furstenberg dress with a lace collar, a style very popular that year. She said hello; we talked about mutual friends. Then the hearing started, and we both sat down, doing our jobs.

I had heard of her for years. She was an Atlanta reporter who had left for bigger arenas—in her case, a job at the *New York Times*. That, or a job at the *Washington Post* or the *Wall Street Journal*, was the career move most of us aspired to. Fay was the prototype of those who did it: smart, driven, politically astute. Her career was of interest to me for another reason: we had both started at the same company, a string of free-circulation suburban weeklies based in Decatur. This obscure start, I noted, had not held her back.

In the late fall of 1985, more than a year after that encounter, I heard that Fay was thinking of returning to Atlanta from New York to become the *Constitution*'s chief political correspondent. The move was talked about as a triumphal return, but it was odd. Fay was too young to be thinking about returning to her roots, and it was strange for an up-and-coming writer in her mid-thirties, especially one without spouse or children, to leave the center of the media universe for the green lawns of the Atlanta suburbs. I heard gossip that things had not gone well for her at the *Times*, and this seemed plausible. One of the ways we all coped with not being at the *New York Times* was to tell ourselves that it was a hellish place to work.

The day in December 1985 when she was supposed to start her new job at the *Constitution*, I came into the newsroom, dumped my purse under my desk, and started to take off my coat. My deskmate, Jane Hansen, turned to me.

"Did you hear about Fay Joyce?" Jane said. "She's dead. Shot herself."

I felt icy. I stared at Jane with my coat half off while she told me what she knew: that Fay had failed to take the plane to Atlanta, had failed to show up at the hotel room reserved for her, had not answered phone calls at her apartment in New York. That morning, a building superintendent who had entered her apartment with a passkey to show it to a prospective tenant had found her body in the bathroom, with a bullet in her head.

She had bought the gun on her last trip to Atlanta, at a pawnshop three blocks from the paper, after having a cordial dinner with Frederick Allen, the paper's political columnist. They had talked about Fay's new job and projects they might collaborate on. I looked at Rick Allen, sitting several rows away. He looked grim-faced and ashen. I felt cold all over—cold in my heart, cold in my bones.

Later, I gleaned more details—enough to tell me that Fay had been slipping into a severe depression for at least a year before her death. The Beast had stalked her during the 1984 presidential campaign, in which she was covering Jesse Jackson. She had fought it, had fled it at times, had even once gone AWOL from the campaign trail for a few days. About the same time, she had begun a love affair, which had turned out badly. Friends who saw ominous changes in her behavior either shrugged it off as moodiness or were unable to break through her iron determination to seem "normal." The *Times* had reassigned her to a less demanding job on the real estate page. The move was probably well-intentioned, but Fay had interpreted it as a humiliating exile. The wisest course would have been to take a leave of absence, check into a hospital, and get well. Instead, Fay did what I would have done: she had tried to escape. She had gotten another job. And then, on the night she was to leave New York, she must have realized there was no escape; that this blackness in her mind would follow her wherever she went.

Behind that bathroom door, or in some other bleak room like it, I knew I might come face-to-face with the Beast too. *This*, I thought, *is what waits for you if you aren't careful.* I felt like a soldier in a trench who had just seen the person next to him get blown to bits. It was frightening not to be able to tell people that. Even more frightening was how easily Fay had slipped over the edge. Surrounded by colleagues in the news business who made their living by learning the latest developments in every field, who lived to gather information and disseminate it, she had somehow managed to escape anyone's informed scrutiny—or, at the least, had felt that she could not afford to admit being ill. I knew why. Behind the shock and sadness that I saw on the faces of my colleagues, under the guilt, I also detected something else: embarrassment. *It's too bad*, I could imagine people thinking. *Didn't know anything was wrong with her. She always seemed so normal.* I knew that whatever "abnormality" Fay had suffered from, I had as well. But to say that was out of the question. I had too many years invested in therapy to admit how much I still identified with her.

I tried to shake off the bone-chilling fear, and couldn't. I felt like a person who had received serious, unsettling news about his health—which, in a way, I had. But how could I tell anyone? *I have thought about killing myself too. I have thought about it many times, for years.* Even to sound out those words in my head seemed weirdly melodramatic. Even so, I tried to make my mouth say them. One night, several weeks later, I called my friend Susan, who also worked at the newspaper and who lived nearby. I said I needed to talk; could I come over? Susan was clearing away the dinner dishes when I arrived. I sat down in her dining room, at her ornate, Victorian table.

"What's the matter?" Susan asked.

"It's Fay," I said, and I began to sob. Susan looked at me in fear and bafflement.

"Tracy, what's the matter?" she said. "What's really bothering you? You didn't even know Fay that well."

I looked at her and could not answer. And in that silence I found the worst fear of all.

Chapter Three

Reluctantly, I went back to see Amanda.

I had not expected to see her again, though I sent her cards from time to time. I wanted her to know how well I was doing. To return was an admission of failure. If it had come to this, I thought, it was time to declare surrender, to admit that I was sick. But this grudging admission was not a step toward understanding; it was a badge of shame. If I was sick in the mind, it was not a kind of sickness anyone would want to own up to.

It was the early spring of 1986, and Amanda had moved to a new office, with several new doctors in practice with her. But though the location might change, nothing in her office ever seemed to; it was always the same tasteful sofa and chairs, the same pastel Impressionist prints on the walls. She sat across from me, waiting serenely for me to speak. Her expression seemed to say: *I expected this.*

"I'm ready for drugs," I told her, and that was a sign of my desperation; I had always considered this a remote last resort. "If you can't prescribe them, I want you to refer me to somebody who can." She left the room and returned with a psychiatrist from an office down the hall. He listened to my recitation, and asked me what drugs my internist had prescribed for me years before, and in what dosage. Triavil, I said. I couldn't remember the exact dosage, but I remembered what the pills had looked like, and how many I had taken every day.

"No wonder!" he snorted. "You weren't getting enough antidepressants to cure the blues in a cocker spaniel." He prescribed imipramine, at somewhere around the standard therapeutic dose—about 125 milligrams a day. I left Amanda's office that day with a prescription, an appointment for another individual therapy session, plus a schedule of sessions for a group therapy Amanda wanted me to join. *Back where I started, only worse*, I thought.

After a few weeks, it seemed that the imipramine was helping. My moods stabilized; the constant mental ache subsided. Life seemed to flow more easily—disappointments did not seem as disastrous, loneliness not as terrible. At the same time, at Amanda's urging, I began attending the group therapy sessions once a week, in conjunction with my individual sessions.

The group varied over the three years or so I spent in it, but it averaged around ten or twelve people. With one or two exceptions, none of whom lasted very long, the members were all middle-class women, ranging from their early twenties to their fifties. Our job was to interact with each other, to create some kind of working family unit in which we could hold our behavior up to scrutiny; the sessions were to be an exercise in exploring and changing the behaviors that caused us trouble. Most of those—passivity, manipulativeness in relationships, deep cravings for approval—were in abundant evidence. Since most of the participants had sought therapy in the first place to deal with depression, it seems likely to me now, in retrospect, that these traits in many instances were habits inculcated by years of coping with chronic depression.

Yet, once again, the basic therapeutic assumption was that those behaviors were not symptoms of a problem—they *were* the problem; depression, on the other hand, was a symptom, not an illness. I never heard anyone mention the fact that chronic depression could affect memory, or that there were specific techniques that could assist in unlearning bad habits. If anyone had, I probably would have discounted the information as "gimmicky." After all these years, I was still trying to analyze something irrational, to come up with an intellectual framework for understanding an emotional life that was constantly breaking free of rational constraints. It was like building sandcastles. Each week in Amanda's office, I made slow, painstaking progress; each week, outside her office, those fragile bits of understanding were eroded and buffeted by the currents of real life.

The result was a real-life illustration of the old joke: we had learned from our mistakes and could repeat them exactly. Whole sessions were devoted to exploring which of the women in the room were cozying up to Don, the male therapist, and what they sought in a father figure. Others sessions, in which Amanda and I frequently played leading roles, re-created tensions in mother-daughter relationships. There was a lot of venting. Sometimes it seemed to me like we were each a part of one big human pipe organ, piping the same notes whenever somebody hit us in the right spot. In the end, we learned much about each other's quirks, but not much about how to actually feel better.

Sometimes I felt like some creature caught in a net, thrashing around and unable to get free. I didn't know what the net was, but I knew it was there; I didn't know what was standing between me and deep connections with other people, but that was there too. I felt it distinctly. It was a wall—the same wall I had told my mother about when I was a child. I couldn't get around it, or over it. It was just there.

Years later, Ray Fuller, the scientist at Eli Lilly, told me about an experiment measuring neurotransmitters in damselfish. The dam-selfish were kept in tanks and separated from their natural predator fish by only a glass wall. They thought they were about to be eaten. After a time, levels of certain neurotransmitters in their brains—notably serotonin—showed a marked decrease. It was illustrative in a crude way, Fuller said, of what he and other researchers in brain biology had come to believe: that repeated loss, anxiety, and rejection cause neurochemical changes in the brain. Over time, those changes leave their mark and become permanent, the way waves slowly shape a shoreline.

I look back now and see myself as one of those damselfish. My self-image was rooted in how I thought of myself when I was depressed. I had many friends, but I was still lonely. I wanted psychotherapy to help; I wanted to be as good at it as I had been at my work in school. But I wasn't. Here I was, ten years out of college and still in remedial training for life. One by one, my friends had begun to get married, buy houses, have babies. Wouldn't any normal person have graduated from therapy by now? Even in good times, I thought of myself as having a secret flaw—so I looked for the thing that would make me whole: a career achievement, a man who was smarter and more powerful. Ordinary, decent guys, who felt no urge to get involved in a confined and clinging relationship, I usually dismissed as boring. Once or twice, I pursued men who fit this description, but found they avoided romantic entanglements with me. This I took as further proof of my defectiveness.

And yet, overall, things began to change. The changes were slow and visible only in hindsight. They had begun, in fact, with my decision to apply for the fellowship to Yale two years earlier. But now, in 1986, the changes began to accelerate—though I find it impossible to trace this to any one factor. Age had something to do with it. I was now thirty-one; simply living for some time on my own had given me a degree of emotional maturity I had lacked before, which in turn probably helped me get more from therapy than I had nine years earlier. There was also the imipramine. I started taking it in early 1986 and continued until June 1987, when I simply decided I didn't need it anymore. The dosage I was taking, 150 milligrams a day, was not as high as the dosage another doctor was to prescribe for me later—but it was high enough, and I took the drug long enough, for it to have some effect.

One day I decided, for no reason I could name, that I was going to learn how to swim. This was something that had always terrified me. My dad had tried to teach me to swim, and had failed. His method was to hold me up by the seat of my swimsuit and put my face in the water while yelling, "Okay, now, kick!" Several gallons of water had gone up my sinuses before I persuaded him to let me quit, and the experience left me with a lasting phobia about putting my face in the water. Some years later, my mother had taken my sister and me to the community swimming pool, where the instructor had employed a different pedagogical technique. His method was to get us to blow bubbles for about ten minutes in the shallow end, then take us down to the deep end and have us jump in. If we made it to the side of the pool without having to be rescued, the lesson was deemed a success. From him, I learned how to hyperventilate when I got into water over my head.

Signing up for swimming lessons, then, was a sign of something. I had survived Yale, despite my loneliness; I had even discovered I was not an impostor there. Now I felt ready to tackle other frightening tasks. And though learning to swim might have sounded small to other people, it was a profound experience. It made me, for the first time, confront an ingrained behavior, rooted in a powerful emotion, and taught me how to change it through the deliberate, conscious effort of will, imposed in small increments. It taught me that primitive emotions could be mastered, that it was not necessary to completely understand why you behaved a certain way in order to change that behavior. Later, in another context, that lesson would save my life.

The first step was elemental: I had to put my face into the water.

Whenever I tried, I felt starved for air. The instant my head went below the surface, I felt a powerful need to inhale and fill up my lungs. The thought of exhaling and losing what air I had was terrifying. Whenever I tried, I found myself coming up, gasping and coughing, with water up my nose. No amount of reason or pep talks helped; the only thing that worked was to just do it. Afterwards, I had to spend several minutes calming an impulse to hyperventilate, but when that had subsided I tried it again, this time twice. Then four times. It took a long time for the panic to subside. While the rest of the class was moving on, I stayed off to myself and dunked—20, 40, 75 times. Eventually, at 150 dunks, I was comfortable enough to move on.

Now I had to coordinate breathing with kicking, which we did by hanging on to a kickboard. Then we discarded the kickboards and tried coordinating our arm strokes. Gradually, I realized I was swimming.

The next step was treading water, which proved to be relatively easy. Then, on our fifth or sixth lesson, the YMCA instructor took us down to the deep end for the first time. We were going to learn to dive, he said. The first step was to jump in, feet first, come to the top, and then tread water. Looking at the pool, at my classmates stepping up gingerly to the edge, I felt ready to cry. My chest felt tight. Fear edged at my brain like the cold puddle of water lapping my toes. This was not a skill you could learn in pieces; you either stepped over the side or you didn't. *Just do it*, I said grimly, and willed myself, against all instincts of self-preservation, to step into space. In the instant before my feet hit the water, my heart felt like it would explode. Then there was a rush of water, and then air, and I was treading water, I was not drowning, I was fine. "You okay?" the instructor yelled. Oh, yes, yes, I was okay, I was *better* than okay.

Swimming lessons at the Y also, for the first time, put me with people groping with the same kind of fear, facing it in their own way. It taught me I was not special, or alone. Most, like me, were fighting phobias dating back to childhood. One of my classmates was a young man who had signed up for the Coast Guard. *That*, I thought, was a brave person.

I finished the beginners' course and signed up for Intermediate Swimming. In between lessons, I started trying to swim laps. At the end of six months, I was diving headfirst into the deep end and swimming a complete lap before I had to stop to catch my breath. I had conquered the water; from here on in, it was going to be a matter of getting into shape. It was like opening windows and sweeping out rooms in a musty house. It was exhilarating.

And then, in November 1986, another thunderbolt struck: the Prince of Fucking Darkness announced his retirement.

Even more sensational was the news of who the paper's rich-old-lady owners had offered the job of executive editor to: Bill Kovach, then Washington bureau chief of the *New York Times*. Bill who? I immediately called my friend Robin, who had left Atlanta the year before to work for the *Times* in Washington.

"We just heard about it," she moaned. "He's a wonderful editor. We're just sick about losing him."

We weren't sick; we were delirious with joy. "All my life I've wanted to go to the *New York Times*," one of my colleagues said, "and now the *New York Times* is coming to me."

Days went by, while the office rumor mill ran faster than the presses downstairs. It was a done deal. Well, almost a done deal. They were negotiating over money. No, money was not an issue. Then we heard the deal was off; Kovach was negotiating to have control over the Atlanta newspaper's Washington bureau as well, the owners had refused, and that was that. It wasn't going to happen.

I heard this news at the water cooler, and for a moment I felt, vividly, what Robin must have been feeling a day or so earlier when she said she was "sick." Then, moved by one of those impulses that make no sense, and end up changing your life, I put on my coat and walked out the door.

It was a gray, cold November day. I walked down the block without seeing anyone I knew, turned the corner, and ducked into the grimy little Western Union office, which catered mostly to working-class people who needed to wire cash. What I had in mind was impossible and corny; it was even a little risky, because the Prince of Fucking Darkness was not kind to underlings who were insubordinate or critical. But I felt compelled anyway. I had the *New York Times* address in Washington in my purse, because it was where I mailed letters to Robin. I sent Kovach a telegram. The message was brief, and I did not sign my name; even more than I wanted a new boss, I wanted not to get fired.

"There are a lot of talented people here who want to work for a good editor," I wrote. "Please come."

Two days later, it was official: Kovach had taken the job. For a moment, I felt a sharp, unreasonable joy. Then I calmed myself. Amanda was frequently telling me that I was narcissistic, insensitive to the feelings of others, that I thought every event related directly to me. Now, I scolded myself: *Quit being such a narcissist. He probably never even read it.*

Kovach came to Atlanta and ran the paper for two years. His arrival was not greeted with general elation. Atlanta is a businessman's town, a Chamber of Commerce milieu which does not take kindly to the sort of disrespectful, kick-ass journalism practiced in cities like Boston, Chicago, or New York—which was, of course, the sort of journalism Kovach was interested in. Atlanta sees itself less as a part of a larger world than as a regional capital—"Capital of the New South" is its slogan—and foreign news or big-picture stories about national trends only served to remind the city's leaders that they were simply big fish in a medium-sized pond. Some people started calling us the Southern edition of the *New York Times*, and that was no compliment. Bo-ring, they said, looking at Sunday stories that were twice the length they used to be; *bo*-ring, they said, their eyes glazing over at in-depth pieces about places they had never heard of in Africa. The old-timers muttered darkly about Yankee carpetbaggers. Well-known columnist Lewis Grizzard, who had been a protégé of the Prince dating back to the time they were sportswriters together, resigned with a flourish one night in a bar, bought several cases of Dom Perignon to celebrate, then changed his mind, came back, and tried to put the champagne on his expense account. I don't think so, Kovach said, and Grizzard had to ante up himself. He was incensed; this was not the good ol' boy code he knew. Eventually, Grizzard stopped coming to the office, preferring to file his columns from home rather than deal directly with Kovach and the corps of *Times*men he had brought in. The *Journal-Constitution*, that venerable Southern institution, was being remade in the image of the Gray Lady of Forty-second Street.

It was a doomed enterprise. To ask somebody like Kovach to run a newspaper owned and published by such deeply conservative Chamber of Commerce boosters was like inviting H. L. Mencken to go to work for George F. Babbitt. But for a while, it was exhilarating. Unlike the Prince, Kovach liked being in the newsroom, liked talking to us. "Good story," he would say briefly in passing, and his praise was remarkable in a corporate culture which had allowed initiative to go unrewarded for years. Unlike the Prince, Kovach made eye contact with people when he talked; he made jokes and laughed at other people's jokes. He was, in short, human. A craggy-faced man with prematurely white hair, he had a twangy eastern Tennessee accent that often made people forget that he was, in fact, the son of Albanian immigrants. There were rumors that he had a violent temper, which I suspected was true; growing up with my father had given me extensive experience with people who masked their ferocious depths under a veneer of charm. I liked him, but I would not have liked to cross him.

His arrival, and the personnel changes he began to make in management, quickly had a discernible effect on morale. People stopped taking two-hour lunches and spending great chunks of the day emailing messages to their friends. The number of whispered conversations—people surreptitiously trying to line up job interviews at other papers—dropped precipitously. Suddenly, there was work to do; we had a paper to put out.

In the past, reporters had tended to steer clear of certain topics for fear of writing about them in a way that might offend the Prince. It wasn't so much that he had an array of sacred cows—it was just that he was so enigmatic, and so occasionally-ruthless, that nobody wanted to run any risks. Once, some reporter had referred to the paper's belated attempt to cover a small scandal at Georgia Power, a scandal some had hoped to ignore, as "covering our ass." He found out the Prince was displeased when he got a phone call telling him to come back to the office and clean out his desk. The Prince was a big fan of the University of Georgia, and a fervent Bulldogs supporter. It was not unusual for readers to take complaints about a story directly to him and to get an apology which the writer of the offending piece would find out about later. When my friend Jane misspelled the name of a south Georgia county, the Prince had ordered the paper to run a correction that referred to the "ignorance" of some of his staff. Jane found out about it when she opened the paper that morning. Investigative reporting had been possible, but only by the most determined and resourceful; we had failed to recognize our chance to be the first newspaper that wrote about AIDS. According to one story, the reporter who covered the Atlanta-based Centers for Disease Control was told the Prince had no interest in some disease that only affected a few gay guys. That may or may not have been true, but nobody was brave enough to actually go to the Prince and ask.

Now there were interesting things going on all around: a series on discrimination by Atlanta banks against blacks who applied for home loans; firsthand reporting on the famine in the Sudan; some incendiary editorial cartoons by a new person Kovach had hired, Doug Marlette; an investigation into the state's foster care system; a series about how indigent black defendants fared in a rural judicial circuit in east Georgia.

The last effort was mostly mine, though a colleague, Larry Copeland, helped to report and write one of the five stories. I had embarked on the project in the summer of 1987, and it had taken me four months to research. The stories ran in December 1987, andone told the story of an impoverished young black man whose white court-appointed lawyer had pleaded him guilty to manslaughter without bothering to research the case or interview a single eyewitness. If the lawyer had done so, he would have discovered that the wife of the shooting victim was willing to testify that the young man had shot her husband in self-defense. After the case came to public attention, the Georgia Board of Pardons and Paroles ordered the young man's release.

In March 1988 there was more news: the rumor mill had my series on the short list for a Pulitzer.

I had never paid close attention to the Pulitzer announcements before. They were like the Nobel Peace Prize—interesting, newsworthy, and just about as likely as a Nobel to be a matter of personal significance. But on that day in March 1988, the newsroom was wired. Nobody was doing any work; everyone was glued to a computer terminal, waiting for the Associated Press to move the names of the winners. At a little past noon, Kovach came in the newsroom, with Marlette in tow—and it was official: Marlette had won, for editorial cartooning. It was the first Pulitzer the paper had brought home since 1961. There were four runners-up from Atlanta in other categories, including my series, in the category of investigative reporting.

"You were robbed," growled my boss, Sonny Rawls, but I was overjoyed. Seven years earlier, when the *Constitution* had hired me, I had mentally outlined my career goals. One had been to get a Neimann fellowship for journalists at Harvard, and I had managed something comparable by going to Yale. The other had been to win a Pulitzer, though this had seemed so unlikely that I had never told anyone. Now, I had almost done it—and in truth, almost winning was, at that moment, preferable to winning. Success was frightening, unpredictable; it might carry me away from the cozy harbor I had created for myself in Atlanta. At least this way I could tell myself I was good enough to win, while avoiding the risk of change that winning entailed. Locked inside my modest ambitions, I felt a sweet and dizzy elation.

The end of the Kovach era came exactly two years after his arrival—in November 1988. I was sitting at my desk when an e-mail message flashed on my computer screen. It was from my editor: "Bad news: Kovach just quit."

Even more stunning was the reason: an ancient bit of office intrigue, the old dispute about control over the paper's Washington bureau. Kovach wanted it; he argued that the Washington bureau was poorly run, and that he could do a better job. That morning, for whatever reason, the subject had come up again in a discussion Kovach was having with the publisher, who had backed the bureau's longtime chief. And this time, thwarted again, Kovach had quit—blown up in one of his infamous rages and walked out of the publisher's office without another job to go to. Looking at those words on my computer screen, I knew instantly: *This means I will have to leave Atlanta.*

A group of us formed a delegation and drove over to his house to try to talk him out of quitting. When we got there, he was sitting in his living room with his wife, Lynne, and it was soon apparent that he was fixed in his purpose, as inflexible in his way as the newspaper's owners were in theirs. "I am either going to make this work or fly it into the mountain," he had told the *Washington Post* two years earlier, when news of his hiring had broken. Now, I felt like one of the plane's passengers, staggering out of the wreckage.

After a while people stood up, preparing to leave.

"You know," Kovach said unexpectedly, "I almost didn't take this job. But one of the things that changed my mind was that I got several anonymous telegrams from you people while I was still in Washington." I felt my face get hot.

"One of those was from me," I said to him, in the general murmur of people getting their coats and edging for the door.

He grinned. "Yeah," he said. "I thought so."

I let a few weeks go by before I called him up again. We met for lunch at a downtown cafe. "I have decided I don't want to stay at the paper anymore," I said.

"I'm glad to hear you say that," Kovach said. "Let me talk to some people."

A few days later, my phone rang. An unfamiliar woman's voice identified its owner as a recruiter for the *Washington Post*.

"We would like to talk to you."

Kovach's phone call to Ben Bradlee had been well timed: the *Post* had an opening for someone to cover federal court, the same beat I had covered for the Atlanta paper. I sent them my clips, and went through the *Post's* agonizing interviewing process—two trips to Washington, each for day-long meetings. On my first trip, I was ushered into Bradlee's office, a glass-enclosed space with a panoramic view of the *Post's* newsroom on one side and the *Post's* parking lot on the other. Bradlee was exactly like his pictures, only more so—gray-haired, with a big booming voice and a chest to match. He had the aristocrat's habit of saying exactly what came into his head; clearly, this was not a man who worried about offending people. He asked me why I'd had a co-author on one part of my series about the rural judicial system. I explained that I'd needed help with the interviews on that part, because some of the people I needed to talk to were older black men who had been taught by bitter circumstance not to talk to white women.

"Yeah," Bradlee said, grinning at me. "And you *are* rather white."

"Real, real white," I agreed, grinning back. "Pale, even." Looking at Bradlee's splendid winter tan, I thought briefly about the weirdness of the American caste system, in which skin that is dark chocolate makes a person "black," while skin that is too pale makes someone else a "redneck prole." Len Downie, Bradlee's managing editor, sat off to one side during this exchange, looking vaguely dismayed at this display of bad taste. At that moment, Bradlee made me think of Tigger in *Winnie-the-Pooh*—pure brashness. "Hi!" he seemed to be saying. "I'm a Boston Brahmin! Who are you?" I liked him.

Another long day of interviews followed, and by the end of that I was almost convinced that they didn't want me—but no: the *Post's* federal beat was offered to me a few weeks later. There was never any doubt I would accept their offer, but the leave-taking was wrenching. It was like stepping off a cliff, a worse feeling by far than learning to dive into the deep end. I wondered if this was what had happened to Fay Joyce. Had she been seduced by the offer of more prestige and more money? I had heard many times that the *Washington Post* and the *New York Times* were snake pits where only the strong and cunning survived. Could I survive? Could I move to a completely new city and find my way? In Atlanta, at least, I had my support system. My friends were there, and so was Amanda. I had been back in therapy for a little over two years now, going to group once a week and to individual sessions with Amanda roughly once a month. I wasn't taking imipramine anymore—I had quit taking it after less than a year, having arbitrarily decided in the summer of 1987 that I didn't need it anymore—but since then I had felt more or less stable. Even so, it was a purely theoretical stability; I had never put it to the test, and I didn't want to. And still: there was this opportunity, which would probably never come again. I agonized so long over the decision that finally Patti—who was no longer my roommate then, but still a close friend—lost patience.

"You are the only person I know," she said, "who could turn a job offer from the *Washington Post* into a major personal tragedy."

And so, in April 1989, a moving van came and emptied my apartment. A few days later, I packed up my car. The back seat was occupied by a large cat carrier containing Ralph and Alice Kramden, my tabby cats. The front seat was occupied by my sister, whom I'd persuaded to help me with the driving. I had fantasies that we'd make the trek up the east coast enjoying one long sisterly confab, but in fact she hated cities and city driving—hated anything, in fact, that forced her to deal with strangers. She had returned home after college to live with our parents, and never left. Now she was thirty-five, working as a hospital lab technician, and I had the distinct fear that I was abandoning her, that she might never venture beyond the tight little orbit she had created for herself—an orbit even narrower than the one I had created for myself, and which I was now leaving with such ambivalence. My fears about her turned out to be unjustified; within the next two years, she would move into a place of her own, move into a better job, and marry a wonderful man. But at the time, I was afraid, and guilty at what I was doing to her. She was afraid and guilty too—afraid of the city we were going to, guilty at not wanting to give the help I asked her for.

We made the trip mostly in prickly silence, with Ralph and Alice waking from their drug-induced drowsiness at intervals to yowl in protest from the back seat. We drove into Washington late on a Sunday afternoon, across Memorial Bridge. Before me, the Lincoln, Jefferson, and Washington monuments loomed, white and sepulchral; traffic was quiet and the city seemed to doze, looking slightly golden. I had reached a milestone. This was either the Big Time or the Jumping-Off Place. But I had no idea which.

Chapter Four

Pierre L'Enfant envisioned Washington, D.C. as a European capital of stately avenues and monumental edifices—and to some extent, it is. Swarming around the feet of those downtown monuments are armies of workaholics—bright, ambitious, former high school nerds whose nerdiness has finally paid off. Official Washington, unlike New York, does not value artistic insight or style, traits which might allow for a certain creative moodiness. It values power, and for the legions of players who populate its corridors—lawyers, lobbyists, Capitol Hill staffers, and journalists—power is created by the assiduous, daily application of smarts. It has little interest in, or tolerance for, mental frailty.

Federal court was housed in a nondescript beige building within sight of the U.S. Supreme Court, literally and figuratively. On my first day of work in the building, a jury convicted Oliver North. It would have been terrifying, except that the *Post's* national desk had exclusive claim to that story and I was officially assigned to the metro staff. I not only wasn't going to write that story, I wasn't going to get near it. I spent my first day at work feeding tidbits and quotes to the main writers.

But it would not happen again, I promised myself. My new boss, Mary Jo Meisner, told me that one of my missions was to reclaim the big stories on the federal courthouse for the metro staff. National stories would, of course, run in the national section—but it would be me, not somebody from the national desk, writing them, or most of them. I had parachuted into the middle of one of the *Post's* legendary turf wars. This was a new level of play. No longer was there merely deadline pressure to get a story, to make sure no other news organizations got it first;

now I also had to make sure my own colleagues didn't steal it.

So I ran. I darted like a rabbit through the courthouse corridors, barely stopping to talk to people I needed to get to know, frantic at the thought I was missing something on another floor. I ran to catch cabs on unfamiliar streets. I bolted to catch subway trains, racing down escalator stairs in feet blistered by the new shoes I'd bought in honor of my new job. I was terrified at the thought that I might fail. My send-off in Atlanta had been large, rowdy, and full of good feeling. "You'll always have a job here," my editors told me as I left. Which was unthinkable, of course, for one reason: that was the scenario that had killed Fay Joyce.

Most of the time, I did not think about her; I focused on thoughts of specific work-related catastrophes which could happen. But at four a.m., when I awoke with visions of failure at my job, I thought about her, and I wondered if I was headed down the same path. Filled with vague dread, I would lie awake for hours. During the day, I ran.

It was an exceptionally torrid summer, even by Washington standards, and I spent most of my time in the courthouse pressroom, a prisoner of the irrational notion that I would miss a story if I so much as left the building for lunch. The east wing of the National Gallery of Art, with wondrous treasures, was across the street, but I never went there. At the end of the day, when the heat had diminished a little, I collapsed in front of the television in my stuffy little ground-floor apartment, in a row house on a shady street in Woodley Park.

I had rented it in a hurry, noticing only the terra-cotta tile floor in the kitchen and the tiny fireplace in the living room, overlooking the fact that the apartment got almost no sun. It was small, with a bathroom only slightly bigger than an airplane lavatory and a "sun room" that looked out onto the back entrances of several restaurants facing Connecticut Avenue. The alley was frequented by rats who dined on restaurant garbage. I had also overlooked the lockbox my landlord put over the thermostat to prevent anyone from lowering the temperature below 78 degrees. That, he explained, was to prevent the 1950s-era air-conditioning unit from overloading. It didn't work. The indoor temperature hovered around 80, except when the condenser blew out, when it went up to around 90. On good days, when the unit was working, I learned I could cool things off by turning on my blow dryer and aiming the hot air directly at the thermostat, through the slats of the lockbox. That undoubtedly hastened the demise of the system, but I didn't care; the whole thing needed to be replaced anyway, and in the meantime I could at least cost my tightwad landlord a small fortune.

It was a miserable time, but I had expected to be miserable; that was what moving to a new city was all about, I thought. And though I had friends nearby, it was soon apparent that Washington did not operate on the same informal standards as Atlanta. In Atlanta, I would have dropped by a friend's house on my way home from work and expected to be asked to stay for dinner. In this city of workaholics, dinner parties were a form of after-hours networking, lined up weeks in advance. People did little spur-of-the-moment socializing of the kind I had always used for comfort and relaxation. Dating was a fantasy; I had left behind no serious relationship in Atlanta, and all the men I met in Washington seemed to live behind their desks.

And so the Beast began his stealthy approach.

Except that to describe it as "stealthy" isn't quite accurate; the Beast, in my mind, was never a sentient being, with malice towardme personally and a method to hunting me down. I thought of it as more of a runaway train—one of those horrifying visions from my childhood, when I thought this huge, metal locomotive would bolt from its tracks and head toward me. It was mindless, it was unnatural. It was crazy. Now, as if that distant whistle were sounding, I was afraid.

Once, years before, I had taken an aerobics class in an un-air-conditioned church gymnasium in the middle of the summer. Intent on following the steps and determined to keep up with everyone else, I had one night worked myself into a state approaching heat stroke. I realized I had passed my limit only when I looked around to see the class was ready for the next dance and I was still wandering aimlessly. "Tracy?" people were saying, looking at me oddly. "Tracy, are you okay?"

This time, not even odd looks could rouse me. The first symptom, clear only in retrospect, was the loss of concentration.

Two weeks after I started at the *Post*, a federal grand jury handed down a major drug indictment, naming twenty-six people in an alleged conspiracy to import cocaine into the District from Colombia via Panama. It was a three-day wonder of a story, and on the day the indictments came down it led the paper. Late that afternoon, after covering the press conference, I found myself on deadline, trying to read a thick indictment. Indictments are like jigsaw puzzles, or stories told out of sequence: in paragraph A, person B commits act C on a particular date. The same date and event might be mentioned twenty pages later, in connection with Person X. Making sense of this is difficult, but I had done it often. Sometimes it was even fun, deciphering the real story behind the legalese. But this indictment made no sense.

Sensing trouble as the clock inched toward five p.m., my boss, Mary Jo, dispatched another reporter to help me. Her name was Elsa Walsh, and she looked at me with bafflement.

"Here," she said. "When I read these I put yellow Post-it notes on things I may come back to." *She thinks I'm an idiot*, I thought. I did not blame her. Every time I read a paragraph and went on to the next, I forgot the paragraph before. What good would yellow Post-it notes do? Twenty feet away, Mary Jo sat at her desk, waiting for my copy to start coming in, clearly fretting at the delay. I shuffled through pages, wrote a paragraph, shuffled through some more, changed what I'd written. Finally Elsa said, "Here, let me make a copy of this." In a few minutes, she was back with her own copy of the indictment, which she skimmed through, marking important dates and underlining names. Somehow, between the two of us, the story emerged— not a triumph of fine deadline reporting, but at least accurate and more or less in on time. When the next day's edition of the *Washington Post* landed on my doorstep, with my name on the front page for the first time, I felt no sense of accomplishment. I knew I had not done the story alone; I was beginning to suspect I couldn't. And yet, it did not occur to me to say this to anyone, or to ask for help. I was sure that if I could just gather my wits, if I could just find my goddamn car keys, things would start to get better.

A few weeks later, during a break in some hearing at the courthouse, I was interviewing a lawyer connected with the case. Notebook in left hand, pen in my right, I asked him his name. He told me. I looked at the page, started to write, realized I had forgotten what he'd just said. Pretending I hadn't heard, I asked him to repeat himself; he told me his name again. A blank. I asked the third time. Finally, letter by letter, I got it down.

"Bad day, huh?"

"Yeah," I said. More irritating proof of my stupidity. It was as if I had left my brain in Atlanta. More and more, I spent my days in a state of anxious irritation because of blunders like that. I wasted enormous amounts of time going back and forth from the courthouse to the *Post*, having forgotten some crucial file; I left my car keys at the office; I went to the grocery store without my wallet. It was enraging. At the worst possible time, I was being blindsided by my own ineptitude. I wondered what Amanda would say, but our years of therapy made it possible to guess. This was a secret wish to fail, she would say—an expression of some kind of repressed hostility, some device I'd come up with to ensure that I'd have to go back to Atlanta and be near my mother. I assumed that was true. On the other hand, my hostility didn't *seem* repressed; anger felt ready to boil out of the pores of my skin.

I was a psychic sleepwalker, going through the motions of wakefulness without the self-consciousness that attends normal wakefulness, only vaguely aware that something is wrong. This is not denial; a person who is drunk may protest that he is sober, but he at least knows, at some level, that he has been drinking. A person who is slipping into depression cannot know the changes going on in his brain. It is impossible to understand that you are getting sick when the hallmark symptom of that sickness is the loss of feeling.

Almost all feeling, that is, except anxiety. That was constant. At night, to keep the jitters under control, I kept a glass of white wine at my right hand. Two glasses would put me to sleep; then, about four a.m., I would wake up, rigid with tension. There was no mockingbird outside my window this time, only the roar of the antique air-conditioning unit in my bedroom closet. Otherwise it was an eerie repeat of the terrible spring of 1976, my junior year at Emory: hours of hot, vacant darkness, lying in bed and looking at the ceiling, waiting for morning to come. Weekends were blank stretches of time which I filled with shopping expeditions when I could find a friend, or with obsessive housecleaning. Sometimes I went to the office and manufactured things to do. A lot of people did that, I noticed. In Atlanta, that would have been a sign of severe social deprivation; in Washington culture, where it is a mark of status to have to work on the weekend, it was a perfect cover for misery.

I began to lose weight. Women in my family have always been pear-shaped, and since puberty I have battled the Curse of Alta Mae (the label came from a particularly unfortunate picture in the family album of a female relative, wearing a 1920s-style flapper dress with a large rosette pinned to her ample haunch). When I arrived in Washington I was a size 12. Soon that dropped to a size 10, and even those clothes started to feel loose. That was fine with me. If I could be slim, I thought, perhaps I would be attractive. Maybe, if I had an acceptable body shape, someone would at last find me worthy of love.

And then a most amazing thing happened: one day a friend in the newsroom said, "I know someone who said he would like to meet you."

The formality, the old-fashioned propriety, of his approach was a big part of its charm. He was British by birth, raised in Canada, twelve years older. A university professor with two children, his wife had been killed in a car accident two years earlier. He was a neighbor of my newsroom friend; we had met each other in passing a few weeks earlier when I had dropped by her house for a drink and he had been returning a yard rake. My friend had watched as he dealt with his wife's death. She described their happy marriage, his grace under the worst of pressures, his courage in confronting his grief, and his strength in comforting their children. He had taken a sabbatical after her death, rented out their house and moved to Montreal with his children for six months to take up a temporary teaching post while his parents, who lived there, helped take care of the kids. Then he had come back to Washington to resume his life of teaching and consulting. His name was, I will say, Thomas McCrary.

All the glowing descriptions were true. But what my friend could not have known was the intensity of Thomas's need to find a wife. Once, a year or two after we met, I was helping him clean up his study when I came across a scrap of paper on his untidy desk. It was a list of women's names, some crossed out. I knew, or had heard of, all of them; it was a list from his dating days, all women who were single and unattached, and from the looks of it he had been methodically going down it, name by name. Not surprisingly, most were crossed off; Thomas had exacting standards. He was not looking for a beautiful woman, he once told me—characteristically, he didn't care how that sounded—though obviously a woman who was unattractive or fat would not have gotten his attention. The most important attraction, he told me, was mental: "There is a level of intellectual companionship I find absolutely essential."

Our first date was in August 1989. He presented himself at my door—a well-dressed man in his mid-forties, of average height, wearing a dark business suit of a severely conservative design that contrasted—as it was meant to—with a silk tie of daring color and design. For the first few moments, he seemed awkward, but then one of us made some wry remark and I heard a quiet chuckle, and instantly I thought: *This guy is really sure of himself*—which was, of course, exciting. We walked across the Duke Ellington Bridge to Adams Morgan. I was wearing a flowered cotton dress with a low-cut neckline. It was a balmy evening. I felt tingly and alive; at that moment, the loneliness and fears of the past few months seemed like a dream. We sat down at an outdoor table at a restaurant and ordered wine.

"Tell me about your life," he said, and somehow that slight variation on a banal phrase—"Tell me about yourself"—seemed infinitely promising.

"What do you want to know?" I countered.

"I can't think of anything I *don't* want to know," he murmured, looking at me. Thomas's concentration, when he chose to focus it, was almost palpable, and at that moment I almost thought I could hear the air between us humming. It gave me a kind of energy I had not felt in weeks. I talked about myself—my Southern family, funny stories about my Tennessee relatives. Dinner came. Then, remembering the social conventions, I said, "Tell me about your children."

He did, with warmth and detail. He spoke, too, of his wife, and of the shock of her death. His youngest child, Peter, had been only three then. Once he had asked Peter what he remembered of his mother. Peter had said, "A lady in a red coat."

We sat in silence for a moment. My eyes felt hot.

"That makes me want to cry," I said.

"Imagine how it made me feel," he said. And then, simply, looking straight at me: "It's been very lonely."

Killer loneliness: I knew what that was—but I did not say so. That was the old me, who had such intimate knowledge of loneliness. The old, needy me was not the person I wanted to show Thomas—not on a first date, not ever. She was whiny, clinging, desperate; I hated her. I wanted to be the person he saw before him—and who, at that moment, I *was*: self-possessed, confident, attractive, warm, a woman who sipped wine and told funny stories well. A bird trapped in a dark room will fly toward the first patch of light it sees. I had been in a dark room a long time; my heart was that bird. At the evening's end, he took my hand and said urgently, "I want to see you again."

"I think that can be arranged," I replied, attempting to be coy. In fact, I could not imagine how time would pass between that moment and the weekend.

We spent it together, with his children. Within a month, he had asked me to move in with him. I agreed, instantly. "I want to marry you," he said. At the time, I did not hear the shade of ambiguity in his words: *I want to marry you* meant *Will you marry me?* "I will marry you," I said.

He was in love with me; he told me so. It was almost frightening, this intensity of feeling—so different, he told me, from any love he had known before. He felt lost in it, intoxicated, disoriented. And so was I. For despite what was to follow, at the beginning I was intensely in love. The world seemed transformed; the city that had seemed indifferent to my presence now seemed enchanted, because he was in it. His mother's family had been from Cork, and to me Thomas seemed Irish to his bones—the pale skin that resisted the sun, the too large nose, sharp blue-gray eyes that could light up with amusement. He loved stories of human foibles, the dumber the better; he clipped newspaper stories about bungled robberies, burglars who lost their car keys, drunks who mistook a police intercom for the speaker at a drive-in hamburger joint, and kept them in a file labeled "The Criminal Mind." He was fierce in his passions and at odd moments prone to sentimentality, a trait he tried to hide. He could be pugnacious, yet he was capable of having a brawling good time. He taught me the words to "Finnegan's Wake" and courted me extravagantly, introducing me to a city I had not known: Shakespeare at Arena Stage, jazz at Blues Alley, Dionysian nights of beer and blues at Wolf Trap.

We talked about a wedding the following April, followed by a honeymoon in Paris. Work, friends, my old habits—all disappeared. I felt electric, drunk with exhilaration. He seemed much older to me, with an established man's estate: a house in an affluent neighborhood in McLean, two children, a solid career. He was casually sophisticated. We met powerful people at parties, who spoke to him as an equal. In his presence I felt more powerful myself. His own self-assurance was evident, not as an obvious boast but as a simple statement: *I am smarter than almost everyone I know.* If someone that smart was attracted to me, I was surely smart too. I had thought so, but there had always been an element of doubt. Now, nourishing myself on Thomas's ego, I felt free.

His children were then six and nine. Peter was a tadpole of a boy who had just gotten his first barbershop buzz cut, in anticipation of his first day of first grade. Melissa was dark-haired and chubby; from pictures, I realized that she resembled her mother. The two of them regarded me with friendly skepticism. Already, they had seen several girlfriends come and go. But if they had doubts, Thomas did not. He included me in their bedtime rituals; together, we read them bedtime stories, and at his urging I kissed them good night. Thomas wanted me in his life, there was no doubt about that. We were floating on a hormonal tide, the sexual chemistry of love that is as intoxicating as champagne.

And for us, just as nourishing. A month went by, six weeks. Then, subtly, the high began to wear off. It was a while before I noticed, but Thomas had begun to pick up on signs that all was not well with me. I had never known how disrupted my sleeping patterns were, but Thomas, a light sleeper, told me I got up three or four times a night. He found my tossing and nocturnal ramblings wearying. When he mentioned it, I shrugged it off. Then, one morning in late October, we were driving in to work together, when I remarked that this being-in-love business was feeling stressful.

"For some reason, I just want to burst into tears," I said. We were rounding Dupont Circle; he was driving. In an odd way, I went on, I wasn't feeling sad, just not as euphoric as I had the past couple of weeks. And there was this wall of tears right behind my eyes. It didn't occur to me that this was strange, or significant.

"That is a classic sign of depression," Thomas said. "That and your sleeping disturbance is worrying."

"What sleeping disturbance?" I said. I protested: it was nothing, It was just "stress," that was all—that all-purpose word people use when they don't know what's really bothering them. It was also true enough: moving to a new city, taking a new job, entering into a new relationship—one with two children attached—was certainly enough stress for anybody. I told Thomas he was overreacting.

I had gradually come to recognize that the word "depression" had two meanings—one medical and one vernacular. The medical sense meant a serious mental illness, and that was clearly the way in which Thomas was using the word. My application of the word to myself fell somewhere in between. Maybe depression was an illness, but in my case it was occasional and benign. Whatever was wrong with me was more than just occasional disappointment or frustration with life—but, whatever it was, I was *not* mentally ill.

Yet with Thomas's remark, a new fear was born: maybe this affair did not mark a new phase in my life after all. Maybe I was still defective. And maybe Thomas was about to notice.

But there was also another problem: the issue of control.

Thomas wanted me in his life. But he wanted *only* me—not my furniture, not relics from my past life, and especially not my friends, whom he considered provincial and boring. My attachment to them was, he said, like refusing to give up the old high school gang. "Leave your old life behind," he urged, and despite my increasing fear, I tried. But when we talked about what furniture I would bring with me to his house, somehow the contents of my dim little apartment seemed newly precious. The coffee table I had bought for ten dollars in a flea market for my first apartment, the dining room table purchased with the money I had earned from my first free-lance magazine piece, now seemed part of me. To him, they were just inconsequential and ugly. Even worse were reminders of old relationships—a piece of jewelry, a book, a poster. There was one poster he liked well enough—a print of a Degas ballerina, bending over to lace her shoe. I loved it too. We talked about where to hang it. But there was a problem: it had been a gift from Sam. I put off telling Thomas this for as long as I could, then confessed. We were in my apartment at the time. He looked at me, amazed. I would *lie* to him, keep a memento from an old lover and hang it on a wall in his house?

"You would *do* that to me?" he said.

"I'm sorry," I said, miserably. Without a word, he went to the wall, took the poster down and put it out the back door, next to the garbage can in the alley.

"What are you going to do with it?" I asked. He stared at it for a moment, then kicked it hard. The glass shattered all over the parking lot; the poster crumpled.

"That worked," he said grimly. And that was that. I was forgiven; we would talk no more about it.

A month after we met, I was supposed to go back to Atlanta for a party Patti was throwing to celebrate completing her doctoral dissertation in philosophy. I had promised her before I left that I would return for it. My normal inclination would have been to get Thomas to go with me; I wanted him to meet my friends. But that would have meant leaving the children for a weekend—two days of the week they looked forward to because they could spend time with Thomas. Besides, Thomas did not want to meet my friends. Nor did he want me to go either. "Why?" he kept asking. "Why are you clinging to your old life?" The week before the party, I called Patti to say I would not be coming. The disappointment I heard in her voice was a painful rebuke. But it was okay, she said; she understood.

"That," Thomas said soberly when I told him, "was a very close call."

I wrote to my mother to tell her that I was moving in with Thomas. She responded in a vitriolic letter, telling me that if I did so, he and I would be living in sin and, worse, leading little children into sin; I was condemning myself to an eternity in hell, which was clearly where Thomas belonged already; she would not be responsible for the catastrophe I was creating. I had not expected her to be pleased, but her rage took my breath away. I had never fully realized the rigidity of her worldview, these barriers she had erected between the respectable life she had found for herself and a childhood of poverty. Marriage was the sacred token, the only pathway to the carnal realm; sex outside of marriage was "shacking up," something only poor, trashy people did—and now her daughter was doing it. To her, it must have seemed proof, after all these years, that her tainted past could not be escaped. At the time, though, I could not analyze her reaction; it seemed frightening to me, and wild, another unbearable pressure in a situation which already had several. I gave her letter to Thomas, who read it in silence. "Well," he said evenly when he was done, "this woman will never set foot in *my* house." This woman? *My* house? My stomach felt like lead. That night, as he watched me from across the kitchen table, I called her. I tried to appease her, to placate and plead. He listened in growing fury and astonishment. When I hung up, his reaction was ferocious. He had expected nothing less than a stern ultimatum: Apologize for this letter, or I will not speak to you again.

"Where is your *loyalty?*" he demanded, incredulously. That was a question I asked myself, lying beside him that night, thinking furiously while he slept. I was fighting off a terror that felt a lot like nausea. Was this going to be the cost of this new life I had longed for—to discard my past like old clothes, to cut myself off from my family? Surely not, I told myself. I was overreacting; he was overreacting; my mother had certainly overreacted. In a few days, everybody would calm down. Besides, I did need to be more independent of my family. It would all blow over, I told myself; somehow, it would be all right.

Back at my apartment, newspapers piled on the doorstep, mail accumulated unread, bills went unpaid, and the red light on my answering machine blinked with messages I feared to return. To my friends, it was as if I had disappeared from the face of the earth.

But to question this, or to give up the idea of being with him, was unthinkable. If there was tension in our relationship, it had to be my fault. Thomas had been happily married, for more than a dozen years; there was ample evidence that he and his wife had been absorbed in each other. All I brought to the table was a track record of failed relationships. Yet I had a powerful urge to bolt. I couldn't figure out why the one thing I had always wanted—a husband and a family of my own—was so terrifying. One night I confessed this to Thomas.

"It's not that I don't want to be with you and the kids," I said. "I don't know why I am so frightened, but I am. Isn't that strange?"

I had hoped he would give me reassurance, "To me, too, it is remarkable," he said. He was sitting at the kitchen table, looking at me sadly. *I will not fail at this*, I thought grimly.

And so we set in motion a vicious cycle: everything that betrayed my underlying depression, Thomas noticed. Whatever he noticed, I met with evasion, lies, and subterfuge. The deception was all the harder because Thomas wanted access to every corner of my mind; true intimacy, he said, consisted in having no secrets, none at all. He wanted to know every detail of my past, the name of every lover, the story of every romantic misadventure, no matter how painful. He wanted it all, every scrap; in fact, he felt entitled to it. And every failure of mine to tell the whole story about something, he took as evidence of deception. He was asking for a full accounting of events I did not want to remember; he was asking, in fact, for an admission of something that I could not admit to myself—that for years my life had been shadowed by the Beast.

Under those circumstances, it was impossible to be anything but dishonest. After a while, it seemed that all my attempts to be authentic were turning in on themselves, making me into a kind of liar I'd never been before. Caught in a web of half-truths and omissions, I kept apologizing for what I was doing, and I kept right on doing it. The more I lied and apologized, the angrier he got. The angrier he got, the more I began to fear him. The more I feared him, the less self-confidence I had, and the less I could imagine being without him. I kept evading and apologizing; his anger mounted, and began to take on a tinge of sadism.

Increasingly, I felt like a zombie, moving through each day's set of tasks, returning at night to a house where I had just a few of my things shoved into a drawer here, a corner of a closet there, trying to help Thomas be a parent to two children I barely knew. October became November. I still had not really moved in; the talks we had about subleasing my apartment and buying an engagement ring somehow got shelved. My attempts to express warmth toward his children were unconvincing; even when I felt warmth toward them, which was seldom, I couldn't show it. My cats, on the other hand, were different: they were mere furry creatures who needed no interaction and simply accepted an occasional cuddle. To me, they were more like children than Thomas's children were, a fact which did not escape his notice.

"Is it possible for you to be a little warmer toward the kids?" he asked me one night. "If I see you ignoring them and picking up the cat one more time, I don't know how I am going to be able to stand it." And, on another occasion: "You have three people here who really want to be with you, and you are keeping us at arm's length." I felt guilty. I vowed to do better. And I also felt angry. *What's the matter with wanting what I want?* I thought. *Why can't I just be myself? Why do other people need so much attention from me?*

What began to enrage him the most was my remoteness, my zombie face—this blank look I had. It closed him out, which was the one thing he could not bear; to him, overt hostility would have been better. We could be watching television, having a meal, driving down the road, when he would say, "You're doing it again." The zombie look was, in fact, the mask of depression, a clinical symptom known well to psychiatrists. But the creeping emotional numbness I was falling into made it impossible for me to know when my face assumed that expression; all I knew was that suddenly, like a kamikaze plane diving out of the sun, came Thomas's anger. I felt like Ingrid Bergman in *Gaslight*, trying to please a fiercely possessive, inscrutable husband and slowly going nuts in the process.

Any little thing could bring the tension to a head. One Sunday afternoon, I was feeling itchy and anxious. Thomas was at work in his study; there was a lecture he had to give at a conference coming up soon. Melissa, the nine-year-old, was doing something on herown; Peter was ragging the two of us, and occasionally Thomas, to play some board game with him. I wanted to read the paper, so I would send Peter to her, and she would refuse him, irritably. He shuttled back and forth, trying to get somebody's attention. From the outside, the goings-on might have looked like a comfortable family Sunday. To me, the confinement was intolerable. The noise from the football game on the television set in Thomas's study was infuriating; every time the crowd yelled, I twitched; if I had to put my paper down to play one more game of checkers or Chutes and Ladders with Peter, I was going to scream. The whole weekend had been spent on chores and family errands—a trip to soccer practice, lunch at Hamburger Hamlet, a game of putt-putt. Normally, I liked to shop on weekends, or have long brunches, or maybe just sleep late, but those things were out of the question. *All this is for the kids*, I thought, aggrieved. *What's in it for me?* Outside, the daylight was going fast. I wanted to get outside, and I wanted to do it before Peter realized what I was up to and suggested throwing a football in the front yard, which he was dying to do at every opportunity.

"Does anybody want to go for a walk?" I asked. In a functional family, this suggestion would hardly have been worth noticing; after a weekend of tending to kids and errands, any adult in the house would be entitled to a break. But in this family, there were three kids: Melissa, Peter—and me. The reason Peter was nagging everyone so much for attention, the reason he and Melissa were fighting more than usual, was that Thomas was paying some long-overdue attention to his lecture, leaving Peter and Melissa to me. Melissa and Peter, temporarily deprived of their father's attention, were getting only grudging notice from me. The only person I wanted attention from was Thomas, and he was busy. Everything was out of kilter.

When I posed my question, Thomas came out of his study and called a time-out. We convened a family conference around the dining room table, to work something out.

One fact was immediately clear: nobody wanted to go for a walk. I had known that, and was secretly relieved. "Fine," I said quickly, getting up from the table. "I'll just go by myself."

Before I knew what was happening, Thomas had stood up, crashing his chair to the floor. The children scattered, knocking over their own chairs in their haste to get out of the room. Thomas grabbed me by the shirt collar, and I found myself with my back to the wall. His face was only inches from mine, ugly with anger.

"You have taken your last walk," he said, still gripping my collar, and there was menace in his tone. *"Do … you … understand?"*

"Don't you manhandle me!" I yelled. He let me go and

stalked out of the room.

Stunned and humiliated, I tried to figure out what had happened. It was as frightening and incomprehensible as if a visitor from another galaxy had just knocked at the door. Thomas's reaction had been extreme; he had to be reacting to something. But *what?*

After a while, the children came back into the kitchen, acting as if nothing had happened. I was sitting at the kitchen table when Peter scooted up beside me on the bench in the bay window. He sat on the windowsill, propping his feet on the table. His face was serious.

"Hey, sport," I said, trying to pretend that all was well.

"I'll go for a walk with you," Peter said. "Do you wanna?"

"No, thanks," I said. "I changed my mind."

I began to lose faith in my own perceptions. It was as if I were standing in front of a mirror which was gradually getting distorted;eventually, what I saw bore little relationship to reality, but the change had been so slow that I had no idea where the distortion began. I knew I was not happy. But I *had* to be happy: here was this wonderful person who said he loved me, who wanted to give me everything in his life, including his children, who asked only that I share my life with him. How could I not be happy? If I felt unhappy, it was only because I was so immature, because I had no idea of what the responsibilities of married life and parenthood would be like. Anyone in my position would feel pressured. So if I felt unhappy, it was only due to the pressure I was under—and that had to be normal. If I looked at it that way, my unhappiness was proof that I was, at last, becoming normal.

I steeled myself to accept some things with blind belief. If my perception of something clashed with Thomas's, mine had to be wrong. Every reaction, every innocuous encounter with another person, was now suspect. How would I know when a man was flirting with me? Thomas was of the opinion that all men were obsessive sexual predators, and though that trait might be tamed it was never absent; I thought men and women could have platonic friendships. How would I know when I should fight for my point of view in a disagreement with my boss? Thomas's style was ultimatums and direct confrontations; mine was to avoid conflict. How would I know if my old friends were bad for me? He thought the way I depended on them was unhealthy; I had always considered them an essential source of emotional sustenance.

With the same desperate energy I had felt trying to read Saint Augustine's *Confessions* in college years before, I renewed my efforts to stifle my raw emotions. I became obsessively eager to please him. But it was all wrong. I was like a deaf person on a dance floor: all I could do was to copy what I saw. My blank refusal to admit I couldn't hear the music was turning Thomas into someone ugly and mean.

One night I was working on a story on deadline when Thomas called me from his car phone. Peter had a severe stomachache, he said; he was on his way home to take him to the emergency room. This was unusual. Peter was never sick; he was unusually stoic for a six-year-old. But I was distracted: I had a story to finish and an editor standing over me, waiting impatiently to talk.

"Okay," I said to Thomas. "Talk to you later." I hung up. About ten seconds later, Thomas rang up again, his voice cold with fury.

"I don't want you to come over tonight," he said. "I will handle this on my own."

Belatedly, I realized I had failed, again. But I wasn't worried about Peter; I was terrified for myself. I had done something which might cut me off from Thomas—an error as catastrophic as if I were a scuba diver who had lost his breathing apparatus. *You are so fucking self-absorbed*, I thought, sick with self-loathing. I was a disgusting, selfish bitch. It was an image of myself which Thomas's fury did nothing to disturb. I began to apologize, once again; and once again I placated Thomas, and persuaded him to detour by my office so that I could go with him to the hospital. I typed something into the computer, told my editor I had an emergency and would check with him before the second edition, and bolted for the elevator.

Peter's stomachache turned out to be not appendicitis, as Thomas had feared, but an intestinal virus. We made it back to Thomas's house that night at nearly midnight. But the emergency room doctor wanted to double-check Peter's white blood count before he went off his shift—so I got up at five-thirty a.m., woke Peter up, and took him back to the emergency room. I wanted to prove to Thomas that I *could* shoulder responsibility, and to make a peace offering for my blunder of the evening before. It didn't matter; in his eyes, the damage was done.

Before, I had slid into depressive episodes relatively unnoticed; now I was doing it in the face of an exacting, excruciating scrutiny. I knew things were drastically wrong, but I still did not think of myself as actually sick. I thought of myself as incompetent, selfish, and screwed up. For his part, Thomas was clear about the fact that I was suffering from depression, and he understood that it was an illness. He just couldn't believe that finally, now that he had met a woman he was really interested in, she turned out to be sick. I think he hoped that one day the episode would disappear as mysteriously as it had come. In the meantime, he found the experience acutely painful. "I can't be with you today," he might announce abruptly as we were meeting downtown for lunch. "You're being buzzy again." That was his way of describing my jerky eye movements and oddly tense body language when I felt acutely anxious, which was almost all the time; the increasing anxiety was a major symptom of my depression. He understood that; at times, his anger would subside as quickly as it had flared. "You can't help it, I know," he would say, with pity. "You're sick." I felt like a drowning person, watching the rescue helicopter appear, then unaccountably move away. I *had* to get well. I gave myself deadlines for getting well. They passed, without result.

In mid-November, at Thomas's suggestion, I made an appointment with a nearby psychiatrist, who prescribed a gradually increasing dose of imipramine—the same drug I had taken for a year, starting in 1986. Back then, I had never taken more than 150 milligrams a day. Now I moved up over several weeks to 275 milligrams a day. In addition to the medication, I saw this doctor—a woman recommended by some friends of Thomas's—once a week. But these sessions, unlike my sessions with Amanda, were perfunctory, thirty-minute visits; I felt unable to talk freely because exposing my life meant exposing Thomas's as well—and he was adamant that this was to deal with my illness, not his life. He wanted as little involvement with psychiatrists as possible, he said; psychotherapy was a bogus enterprise. When it came to depression, he said, drugs were the only thing that worked—but most doctors didn't know that.

In this, I think, he was half right. Certainly all of the doctors I had ever been to in Atlanta seemed to have an antidrug bias—or, at the least, seemed to consider antidepressants more or less like dietary supplements, potentially helpful in rare cases but something most people could do without. The psychiatrist I saw in Washington was conversant with drug treatment. Since I had seemed to respond to it before, her decision to prescribe imipramine was in keeping with conventional medical wisdom, which held that whatever worked before should be the first remedy tried in case of a relapse. This time, however, the effect of the imipramine was minimal, even at a much higher dose—a phenomenon which, I later discovered, has a name: "discontinuation refractoriness." A drug that has good effects the first time around, and is discontinued, sometimes has little or no effect if the patient resumes taking it. At the time, researchers at the National Institute of Mental Health were just beginning to document this effect in manic-depressive patients who were resuming lithium treatment after a hiatus; there was no evidence to think it might affect people like me, who suffered from depressive episodes without any manic symptoms.

In theory, imipramine could profoundly affect the way I perceived reality, but it could not alter the way I was *reacting* to it. That required some exertion of conscious thought—and that, in turn, required putting thoughts into words. But the more my doctor tried to engage me, to get me to talk about this relationship that was obviously making me so unhappy, the more

I resisted. The problem wasn't Thomas, or Thomas and me, I told her—the problem was *me*. I could tell she was skeptical, and that only made me more confused.

For the first time in years, I resurrected my journal:

> DECEMBER 7, 1989: I talked to Patti last night and felt better; but then what she says so completely contradicts what Thomas says that I have no idea right now what's true … I don't want to face the kids. I am so ashamed I failed their father.

> DECEMBER 8: He's angry and hurt and he lashes out at me, and either he's nuts or I am doing something so awful to him that I can't see what it is. I don't think he's nuts. But nothing seems rational right now … I couldn't give up control over my life to him. He says if you love someone, you do—it's a mutual thing. That sounds reasonable. He says it should be easy…. What if the problem here is that I'm just unable to love? What if what I call love is really just getting what I want?

The journal entries were one form of something I was doing a lot of: compulsive note taking. My emotions were so jumbled and intense that, at some level, I knew they didn't make sense. But it was inconceivable that my moods might be dictating my perceptions, instead of the other way around. I turned to the other alternative: my perceptions had to match my moods. And that required note taking—because keeping track of the "real" perceptions was difficult: I tended to forget what they were, and because they didn't actually match reality, I kept having to fix them in my mind, to remind myself of what the "truth" was. I wrote short notes to myself constantly during the day, at odd moments at work, on the subway, sitting in court waiting for a hearing to start. After a day or so, feeling ashamed at the thought that somebody might find them, I would throw them away.

As my depression grew deeper, the "reality" I was keeping track of grew more and more distorted. It was a phenomenon I was to recognize much later, in the scribbled notes left behind by White House counsel Vincent Foster before his suicide. In those notes, I could clearly hear the agonized voice of a mind struggling to reconcile its perceptions with the immense pain it felt. ("Here, ruining people is considered sport," wrote this highly successful lawyer and counselor to the President, whose career was anything but ruined. And, later, in what must have been a highly uncharacteristic tone of recklessness, the flat statement: "The FBI lied.")

And so it was with me. In one undated scrap of paper that survives from that period, I found in my own jagged handwriting: "Lost self-confidence—wondering if old self-confidence wasn't based on an illusion."

And: "His children basically don't like me ... They find me cold and ungiving ... If I'm this cold, perhaps I shouldn't have children."

And: "If I'm a charity case, I don't want to be with him. Better to be alone."

But no amount of analysis could stop the inevitable unfolding of events. One night in early December, Thomas said with finality, "I think you should pack your things and go home." That weekend, we agreed, I would come back while he was out of the house with the kids, and remove the rest of my belongings.

Here, finally, was visible proof of the defectiveness I had tried all my life to hide. In September, I had told my friends I was getting married; now I was getting kicked out of the house. What hope was there, if not even a man who had kept his family together through a major tragedy could stand to have me around? No alternative explanations, not even the intrinsic self-pity of that question, occurred to me. In less than three months, this fairy-tale love affair had crashed and burned. I was left with my old companion, the Beast.

It was Christmastime; from the pressroom in the federal courthouse, I saw the tree go up in front of the Canadian

Embassy next door, watched night after night as dusk fell and the traffic flowed down Pennsylvania Avenue, a glittering red and white river of cold misery. I worked, or tried to—but like a machine whose circuits are slowly winking out, my brain each day found a smaller and smaller focus. I thought the same thoughts over and over again; on Tuesday, I re-created the work I had done on Monday. I had passed up the chance to cover a big drug trial in favor of working on a project I thought more interesting. It was an idea born out of my experience at Yale, about the degree to which class-action lawsuits challenging the running of various city agencies—the jails, the food stamp program, shelters for the homeless—had resulted in federal judges taking over the functions of city government. My editors agreed to this, and pulled my colleague Elsa Walsh away from what she was doing and assigned her to cover the trial. It was a decision that caused the maximum amount of inconvenience for everyone. Elsa was in the last stages of planning her wedding to Bob Woodward, the former Watergate reporter who was now a senior editor at the *Post*. Covering the trial meant that a hectic period in her life became downright frantic. Day after day, she sat in the courtroom painstakingly taking notes on the testimony, using breaks in the trial to dash back to the pressroom to make phone calls to the caterer, the florist, relatives.

Meanwhile, I was realizing I'd made a bad move. As harried as Elsa was, she kept getting into the paper with fascinating tales of the city's drug underworld, while I sat in the clerk's office, slowly reading the same court documents over and over, trying to gather my thoughts about this major project I had so foolishly promised my editors. Years later, cleaning out some old files, I found a memo I had written to my editors about that idea. To my surprise, it read clearly, marshaled a lot of disparate facts in support of a single, coherent argument, and made a case about federal court intervention in city government that was later the subject of a reform commission report; a couple of years after that, the same story, updated, was written by my successor at the federal court beat, and ran on page 1. I had been on the right track after all. But I couldn't discern that at the time. I could barely complete a thought, and when I did manage to write a complete paragraph, I forgot it almost immediately.

I don't know when the idea of suicide first occurred to me. In some ways, it had been in the back of my mind for years. Yet, oddly, I would never have thought of it as an option. It was the perceived *lack* of options—the final, unacceptable solution to a grave and insoluble dilemma. I had always thought of it in the same way: If *all else fails, if I have nowhere else to turn, I can do this*. There had been isolated moments—for instance, that long-ago episode with the aspirin bottle—when that option had seemed to present itself. But those had been impulsive and relatively short-lived. The episodes of depression which had produced them had never been so intense as to rob me of a sense of their transience.

This was different. This was bleak, grinding despair—day after day of it. I thought of the friends I had said goodbye to in Atlanta, the great things they had expected of me. Now it had come to this: the institutional tan of the bleak hallways of the federal courthouse, a newsroom where I had no real friends, a gray city of marble and snow and impersonal edifices. I couldn't go back to Atlanta; I could barely bring myself to admit to anyone that yet another love affair had gone sour. Thomas and I talked on the phone every day—long, bitter conversations full of recriminations and pain.

"I offered you total devotion," he told me in one of those conversations. "You offered me shit."

And yet, even at this desperate point, there were still moments of pleasure, when Thomas and I put our trouble aside for an evening and helped the kids do their homework, or piled up with Peter and Melissa to watch a video. When I first met Thomas's children, I had viewed them as rivals, conversational interruptions, and impediments to whatever it was I wanted to do. Now, as Thomas and I drifted apart, I belatedly began to discover they were individuals with charm and humor; it was a tribute to their power that even at this low point, they could lift me out of myself for a few hours.

Melissa loved snow and believed in magic. Every evening after dinner, she retired to the porch to talk to her elves. She had an incantation that was guaranteed to ensure enough snow to clog the roads and close school for a day—but to be effective, it had to be chanted, at high-decibel level, for at least half an hour. "Hey-yonna, ho-yonna, please make it snow-yonna," she intoned, walking from room to room and flapping her arms. It was hard to carry on a normal conversation, but her exuberance made me grin. Peter trailed in her foot-steps when he was not immersed in his own world of costumes, drawing, and comic-book heroes. Once, when he was supposed to be taking a bath, I found him dawdling in his room, intent on some problem.

"Hey, sport," I said. "You're supposed to be in the shower."

"Okay," he said. "But first I have to find my basketball."

"What are you going to do with a basketball in the shower?"

"I don't know," he said, looking surprised at my lack of imagination. "I just never tried it."

Christmas came. Thomas and the kids left for Montreal to visit his parents, leaving me behind. "This is goodbye," he said as they left, but neither of us believed it; both of us were incapable of actually severing the relationship. I went to Atlanta and called him every day, hoping to hear in his voice some softening note, some clue that he might be able to forgive me for my failure. Instead I heard bitterness and longing. He wanted to salvage something from the wreck, even though his common sense said it was hopeless. Even when we were at our best together, he found my most superficial traits maddening; my ingrained Southern habit of being polite even to people I did not like or was angry at he described in one word: "phony." There was some truth to that. And yet his characteristic bluntness could be caustic, even cruel. Once I brought over the wrong vintage of wine for dinner. Thomas looked at the label and sighed. We were standing on the deck, in front of the children. "You can drink this shit, because I won't," he said, handing the bottle back to me, and then he added, with withering contempt: "Someday, you will learn that competence counts."

My craving to please him, my constant shading of the truth, about whatever—why I was fifteen minutes late, what my boss had said at lunch that day—brought out the worst in him. "You have made me angrier than anyone I've ever met," he told me once. And on another occasion, he said, "Emotionally, we are a bad match"—a statement which was as good a summary of what had gone wrong as any.

The new year came in the middle of that hard winter, a season of gray slush and evenings that started in midafternoon. Thomas returned from Montreal with a pronouncement: he was ready to resume dating other women—though, he added, he would not rule out our getting back together at some point. It was a pathetic crumb of hope; any healthy person would have given up. I refused. And despite his words, Thomas kept in constant contact; he called me at least once a day, sometimes three or four times. We often met for drinks or dinner. He wanted to be rid of me; he could not let me go.

Things were out of control.

There is a pounding noise somewhere. It's insistent. It's been going on for a long time, maybe for hours; I can't tell. I have to find it. But somehow gravity has turned sideways; every time I try to stand, the walls slope down. There is another noise—a loud thump. Again. It's dark. I realize the thumping noise is me, falling down. Gradually, part of the bedroom wall comes into focus. I have to stand, walk, somehow find the pounding noise. My face is cold; there is an icy wind in my face. It's because I am at the front door, and the winter night is rushing in. Thomas is standing there, looking like death. He pushes his way through, into my apartment, goes into the kitchen. I'm standing, swaying, in the living room, my hands over my face. None of this makes sense—except that I remember going for a drink with Thomas sometime—hours ago? Was it today?—and then he was taking me home. I wanted to stay with him, but he said no. "I have a date tonight." I remember his saying that. Now I am in bed again, and Thomas is standing at my bedroom door. I speak to him. I cannot see his face clearly—the light is behind him—but he shakes his head: No. On his face, I think that I see disgust.

The next morning, I knew I had not dreamed it: there was an empty vodka bottle, several empty wine bottles, on the kitchen counter. Thomas must have found every ounce of alcohol in the house and poured it down the sink. I remembered the evening before: drinks after work, the flirting between us, the sexual tension, then his casual hurry to leave. His bald words: "I have a date tonight." Why had he said that? It was deliberate cruelty. I remembered getting out of the car like a person whose bones were broken, thinking only that I wanted to go to bed, even though it was only about seven-thirty. I had taken my nightly dose of imipramine, and to make sure I slept, I had washed the pills down with a tumbler of vodka. Then I had put on my pajamas and gone straight to bed. All I wanted was to sleep, to escape my misery for a while.

On my right leg, there was a bruise that covered my thigh from hip to knee.

Thomas called that morning while I was at work. I knew he would.

"I called you," he said. "You kept picking up the phone, but you wouldn't answer." He had panicked, gotten in his car, driven to my apartment and pounded on the door. It had been nearly midnight.

I realized that I had almost killed myself. Thomas's haggard face was imprinted in my memory: more fear there than I had ever seen in anyone's face. He almost had a suicide on his hands; he must have known people would say he had driven me to it. The thought of that, the damage that would do to his reputation, had made him frantic. The funny thing was, I had not been thinking about dying. It would have been suicide, just the same, but all I had wanted at the moment was oblivion. There was no thought, although I well understood that drinking alcohol with imipramine was not a good idea, and no planning. Just: *Give me peace.* A lot of people, I realized, must end their lives that way. Not caring was sometimes all it took.

So he feared the damage I could do to his reputation. But

he also loved me. I think it was, by that point, against his will, but there it was. There was a bond between us, a strange kind of friendship which had not even existed at the beginning, but which had grown stronger for all our conflicts. At some level, we both recognized that the other was struggling, in anguish, trying not to drown. Even if he had wanted to end all contact with me, he didn't dare. And so we clung together, locked in a macabre dance of pity, need, and torment. "I am not abandoning you," he said. But I didn't want his compassion. I wanted his love. I was in sole, blind pursuit of it.

I stopped going to the gym, hiding my bruised leg. Thomas and I never spoke of that evening again.

One day in mid-January, in midafternoon, the city desk called me at the federal court pressroom. There was a hearing starting in just a few minutes across John Marshall Plaza, in D.C. Superior Court. Bart Gellman, who usually covered superior court, was tied up on a story. I was needed to cover for him.

It was a sentencing hearing in a case that had been widely publicized a year earlier—the infamous nanny murder. It was every parent's nightmare come true. A couple in upper northwest Washington had hired a nanny to look after their nine-month-old daughter, their only child. They had done all the things parents were supposed to do: they had interviewed the nanny in person, they had asked for references, they called the woman she described as her previous employer and checked her out before hiring her. The nanny had worked in their home for one week when in a fit of anger, because the baby would not stop crying, she struck the infant's head repeatedly against a wall, severely fracturing her skull. The baby died the next day.

The couple could not have known who they were hiring, because the nanny had lied to them. The name she gave them, Linda Johnson, was not her real name; under her real name she had a lengthy criminal record in her home state of Louisiana, a record that included a charge of criminal neglect of children. Charged in the Washington case with first degree murder,

Johnson had later entered a guilty plea to manslaughter. Now she was due to stand before Judge Henry Greene for sentencing.

It was a wrenching case, made more so by the fact that the parents of the dead infant were sitting in the courtroom, holding tightly to each other's hands and struggling to keep their composure. Then Linda Johnson entered the courtroom from a side door.

She was in her early forties, slightly pudgy, and her face bore the marks of recent tears. She sat down at the defense table without looking at the couple behind her, and the hearing began. It lasted for nearly ninety minutes. When it was all but over, and the judge was ready to pronounce sentence, Johnson was asked to stand. Did she have anything she wanted to say on her own behalf? the judge asked her.

Johnson stood, seeming to lean against the table for support. Then, for the first time, she turned to face the couple whose daughter she had killed. Her face was contorted; tears ran down her cheeks.

"I would like to say to Amy and Larry Banker, I'm sorry for what I did," she said. Her voice was cracked, and it held a pleading, desperate tone. "I never meant to hurt Jamie. I never meant to kill her. I lost control. I lost control. I never meant to hurt her."

She sank back into her chair and sobbed. I looked at the parents. Lawrence and Amy Banker were both weeping quietly. Lawrence Banker held his wife's hand tightly, looking at the floor. But Amy Banker—visibly pregnant with the couple's second child—was looking directly at the woman who had killed her baby. She was shaking her head silently, and what she was thinking was clear to any observer: *No. This I will not accept.*

Both Johnson's defense attorney and the prosecutor scrambled to their feet, and there was a small flurry among the spectators. In legal terms, what Johnson had just said was enough to cast the faintest tinge of doubt on her guilty plea, since the law requires a judge to reject a criminal's guilty plea unless the accused admits to every element of the crime. Now, Johnson had just tried to weasel out of a crucial ingredient: intent. She had made the whole thing sound like a freak accident.

After a few moments of listening to the lawyers, it became clear to me that this was a legal battle that had already been fought, when Johnson officially entered her plea two months earlier. Everyone—the prosecutor, the defense attorney, the Bankers themselves—wanted the guilty plea to stick; no one wanted a trial, with gruesome medical testimony and autopsy pictures. And so, after a few minutes of wrangling, Judge Greene decided: Enough. He would accept the guilty plea and pass sentence. But before he did, he had something to say.

"I see a very, very strong strain of self-protection," he said, looking at Johnson, who was still crying. He noted that Johnson had given the police three different versions of events before she told the truth about what had happened. "She took steps to save her own skin. She saw what had happened, she understood the consequences … She began a virtual campaign of deception."

And then he pronounced sentence: the maximum possible for manslaughter under District of Columbia law—fifteen years to life.

It was right on evening deadline, a gray and rainy January day. I walked across John Marshall Plaza to the federal courthouse pressroom to file my story, close to tears myself and chilled to the bone, though not by the weather. In Linda Johnson, I had glimpsed myself.

"At issue in the hearing," I wrote on my computer, conscious of the scant half hour I had to file the story, "was a question that goes to the heart of every accused criminal's guilty plea: Did Linda Johnson accept responsibility for her act?"

Did I accept responsibility for my actions?

This felt like a dangerous question. It was not a question about what made people act the way they did, nor was asking it a way of taking on an inappropriate burden of guilt. People did what they did for many reasons. I had heard a brief version of Johnson's life in that courtroom: raised in dire poverty, abused as a child, uneducated, virtually unemployable, knocked about by life. She had been dealt harsh blows; she had many reasons to be a bitter and unhappy woman. But still: there had been a moment when she had held the baby in her hands, had shaken her violently, had knocked that tiny infant's skull against a wall. She had done that, in anger, repeatedly. She had done it. And yet—

Everything she had said in court, everything that I saw in the legal papers I had before me, showed a woman who could not, or would not, make the final, fatal connection between her action and its consequence. What she had said instead was spelled out in the legal papers, only a small part of which I had room for in the story.

"I wasn't aware of what the crying was doing to me," she had said at the hearing the previous November, according to those papers. "Your Honor, I never wanted to hurt the baby. I never intended to hurt the baby … I wasn't aware of what the crying was doing to me subconsciously. I wasn't even aware of it. I guess all of this was going on all week with her, the fussing and the complaining and not eating. Maybe it was building up inside of me. I don't know. Maybe that is what made me lose control. All I'm trying to say is that when I shook her I just lost control. I wasn't aware of what I was doing, and I am so sorry. I am sorry to the Bankers. I am so sorry. God knows I am."

Here was remorse, and something else: self-pity. *Consider my pain instead of the pain I caused you*, it said. *Look at my reasons!* It was human, it was entirely understandable. But it was not honest. There would have been at least some scrap of human dignity in confronting this horror, looking it in the eye—in saying, *Because I did this horrible thing, that thing happened. The act speaks for itself; nothing I say or do will ever atone for it. I alone take responsibility.* That was something a grownup could say. The other voice was the voice of a child.

I saw this clearly, as I had never seen it before, and for the first time I applied it to myself. There were reasons for why I was behaving the way I was—ample reasons, entirely understandable reasons, reasons which were in large part out of my control. And yet my behavior was causing consequences. I had done things that caused pain and terror in other people. More important, my actions had just the other night almost killed somebody—me. These consequences were happening before my eyes; they were real. And this mattered. At some point, somehow, I would have to take this fact into account, or forever be the pitiful kind of person I had seen in court that afternoon.

But no sooner had this thought formed than I was overwhelmed, as Linda Johnson had been, by remorse that was so mingled with self-pity I could not tell the two emotions apart. I had filed my story, and now, clearing off my desk, I put my head on it and started to cry. It was hard, so hard to sort this out. I didn't know who I was crying for; I just knew I felt like crying.

The friends I had cut off contact with in the fall tried periodically to get in touch with me, but I seldom returned their calls; even if I had not felt the humiliation of having to admit to them that I had failed at yet another relationship, I knew that Thomas did not like them, and I wanted to be the person Thomas wanted. I knew I was inflicting enormous damage on them; these were people who keenly felt my sudden indifference. But it had to be that way, I thought.

The old Tracy had never been good enough; so I would remake myself into someone who was. It was not the first time I had made this promise to myself: over and over again, sobbing over some abortive love affair, I had said to myself, *I want to* change *my life.* It was the reality of depression I wanted to change, but I had not known that. Then, as now, I simply knew I wanted my life to be profoundly different. I wanted that so much I was willing to put my future into one bleak and unsparing formulation: *Change your life or die.*

Change your life or die.

But all my attempts at change were being thwarted by the Beast. The Beast, in fact, was the very thing I was trying to change. But he was much stronger than I. The Beast had me in a viselike grip, forcing my gaze away from him and toward one tiny point in the universe: Thomas. If I could change my life, I could save that relationship. I could be with somebody; I could have a home and family. I could be a normal person. If I failed at that task, I could not live. And as the weeks passed and there was no sign of any renewed warmth from Thomas, I knew I was failing.

I began to plan my death one night in early February. I had come home, poured myself a glass of wine, and was sitting in an armchair in my living room when the thought came into my mind: *Well, that's it.* The room was quiet; I had had the news on earlier, but the television was off, the phone was quiet, and on this day there was not even a blinking red light on my answering machine. It was Thursday night, and in the back of my mind the weekend loomed, a two-day space of blank time that I had no idea of how to fill. In a strange way, it was that thought which snapped the last tiny thread in my mind; it was one more task, one more thing to do, on top of a burden that had already grown intolerable. Something had to give, and the half-formed thought came to me that perhaps there was a way I could avoid the weekend, not just this weekend but all weekends to come. For the first time in months, I felt some energy. I got up and went into my study.

The actual means of death was simple: pills and alcohol. I had learned—had I not?—how easily it could be done. I had another bottle of vodka on hand, and a newly refilled prescription of imipramine: lots of pills. I had looked up the dosage once in the*Physicians' Desk Reference*, and found that the amount I was taking nightly was near the maximum recommended adult dose. The *PDR*also went into some detail about toxicity and contraindications, the main one being that imipramine had a heavily sedating side effect even in normal doses, and was dangerous to use in patients who were acutely suicidal. It would be a simple thing to triple or quadruple the dose—or better yet, just take the rest of the pills all at once and swallow them with vodka. I had read of people doing it.

But it seemed important to leave things in an organized fashion—apartment tidy, papers in order, a will written, letters to friends dispatched. I was especially worried about my cats. I did not want them to wind up in an animal shelter, so I wrote a letter to a friend down the street, asking her to adopt them. Then there were my journalism awards, which I wanted to send to my mother. I gathered them all up, found an old packing box, and put them away, with a note on top directing where they should go. That left the letters, which took hours to write. I found myself trying to explain, and to apologize, without thinking too much of the reality they represented; if I thought about reality, I would not be able to go ahead with my plan—to the extent I *had* a plan.

Even at this stage, my preparations were like strapping on a parachute in an airplane that was about to crash; the whole time I was preparing to hurl myself out the door, I clung to the hope that something would happen at the last minute to forestall that terrible necessity. And it was necessity I felt—not hostility, as psychiatric texts would say, or vengeful rage, or a desire for attention. This was done in secret, out of a need to alleviate pain which was as implacable as thirst.

I was like someone in the last stages of cancer. I had a body that had outlasted my mind's ability to endure pain, and now I faced the possibility of opting out. But there the similarity ended. A terminal cancer patient considers the prospect of suicide with all the mental equipment he was born with. I was living in a twilight zone between rational thought and irrationality. My choice was a rational response to a set of irrational perceptions, the inevitable result of all that note taking I had been doing.

This is one of the least understood aspects of depression, this tenacity with which severely depressed people cling to the very perceptions that are most distorted. Doctors can attempt to reason with their depressed patients; people who have never been depressed can simply dismiss this behavior as "crazy." To the person who is depressed, it seems just the opposite: it is a way to *keep* from going crazy. Perceptions and emotions simply have to match, at least in some rough way; there is something in the human brain that categorically rejects the preposterous idea that it might be home to emotions which simply erupt, divorced from external stimulus. It flees that alien possibility straight into a never-never land of absolutes. "I will be alone forever," the brain tells itself instead. "This pain will never end."

That is what I told myself—and at the same time, I

postponed my leave-taking that evening, hoping still for some clue, any other option. I went to bed well after midnight and slept soundly for the first time in several weeks. The next morning, I got up, showered, dressed, and went to work as usual—for what reason, I could not say, except that not going to work would have seemed abnormal, and I was still deeply attached to the idea that I must try to seem normal. I have no recollection of anything I did that day, until late in the afternoon.

It was about four o'clock, on a gray afternoon which had not seen the sun. I was sitting at my terminal in the pressroom at the federal courthouse, typing another in that unending series of notes to myself.

"Right now I am thinking I want to die," I had just typed. "I am ashamed of that. I feel it is a weakness." I was sitting there, looking at those words on my screen, when, without conscious thought, my hand went to the telephone and I dialed Thomas's number at work.

"It's me," I said, diffidently.

"Yes?" I could hear irritation in his voice. It was a bad time of day to be calling; he was leaving his office for class. I paused, not knowing how to say this. A long moment passed.

"I am in serious trouble."

He understood instantly.

"Where are you?" he asked. I told him. "Stay there. As soon as I can get away, I will come and get you. Don't go anywhere. Do you understand?"

"Yes," I said.

Then I hung up and waited for the next, unimaginable thing to happen.

Chapter Five

"I've talked to Phyllis," Thomas said, as soon as I got into his car, referring to my psychiatrist. "She thinks you should be in a hospital. So do I. Why don't we go there right now?"

I was shocked and ashamed. This was not the kind of rescue I had been hoping for; this was more like an abduction. Despite the harrowing evidence of the past few weeks, I was certain I was not sick. Maybe Thomas was trying to call my bluff; maybe he thought I was trying to manipulate him. But no: unlike other times he had accused me of manipulation, he did not seem impatient or disdainful. He seemed concerned, detached, purposeful.

I protested, but only weakly. My craving for Thomas's approval ran so deep that it conquered even my shame; I was willing to consider anything he asked me to do. I had, moreover, no ideas of my own, or at least none I thought he would consider. (*Take me to your house*, I wanted to say. *Let me hide there. I'll catalog your books, I'll clean up your study, I'll do anything.*) And I was exhausted. For the first time, I realized why Thomas had coped so effectively with his wife's death: disaster management was the ultimate form of control. He was good at it because he believed completely in his own intellectual superiority. I was not so blinded by love that I had not noticed his arrogance, how often he alienated people. Still, there was something admirable about the way he could look catastrophe in the eye.

We were by now on Massachusetts Avenue, headed toward Suburban Hospital in Bethesda. I was sure they would dismiss me as a hypochondriac. If they admitted me, I was sure it would mean the end of my career at the *Post*. Not that they would fire me; I knewbetter than that. I thought they would just treat me with pity—probably shift me into some make-work job and quietly encourage me to find a lower-pressure job somewhere else. Since I had nowhere to go but Atlanta, that would mean going back home, a failure. Faced with the same prospect, Fay Joyce had put a gun to her head—a decision which, at that moment, seemed very logical.

Yet I did not want to die; I wanted to be out of pain. Sitting in the passenger seat, I began to rationalize. Assuming I could check in secretly, a hospital might be a good place to rest, to turn off the ceaseless voices of recrimination and self-loathing in my head. A private room, maybe a garden to walk in. This idealized picture began to take shape: maybe the psychiatric ward would have nice decor, not like actual hospital rooms, but rooms that would open onto this garden—a subtle acknowledgment that we were special, fragile people with "mental" problems that were somehow superior to gross physical things like kidney stones or a broken leg. Maybe there would be other writers there—poets and artists who, like me, had been too sensitive to live forever in the real world. (This notion, vaguely based on the stereotype of the mad genius, did not track with the shame I felt at being thought "mentally ill." But the contradiction didn't occur to me.) The garden, in my imagination, would have a small pool, goldfish, a small fountain; there would be the peaceful sound of running water. People would treat me with gentleness and sympathy. They would leave me alone and let me sleep. That might not be so awful.

It was well after midnight before I surmounted the emergency room bureaucracy at Suburban Hospital, made more chaotic than usual that night because of a car crash earlier in the evening. When we signed in, the admissions clerk had asked me what the problem was. Before I could speak, Thomas said, "Suicidal depression." The clerk had written it down without expression. After an hour or so, a doctor came to ask me some cursory questions. Was I thinking I wanted to die? *Yes, but*—Had I thought about how I would kill myself? *In a way, but*—After that it seemed a foregone conclusion that I would be admitted. At ten-thirty, while I was waiting to be assigned a room, Thomas had gone home to the kids.

Now, late at night, a nurse's aide, a middle-aged black man, escorted me out of the din of the trauma room. We walked and walked. Obviously the psychiatric wing was far away from everything else; that might be a good sign. The halls were dark; everything was quiet. Finally we reached an elevator, and went up to the top floor.

"Wait here," said the aide, and walked over to the nurse's station. It was a dimly lit bank of desks in the middle of a large, dark room, where a nurse sat writing something. Another nurse, a skinny man with a pockmarked face, was wandering around. Neither of them looked at me. I was in some kind of activities room, mostly bare of furniture. Drab walls, green fluorescent light. There were tables and chairs pushed into a corner, a jack on the wall where a telephone had been. Industrial wire mesh covered every window. On the bulletin board I saw valentines and a schedule of activities. The next day's activities said, "Cut out and make valentines." Like kindergarten, I thought. I walked over to a counter, where a stack of brochures was lying out. "How to Open a Bank Account," said one.

At that moment, the horror of mental illness became physical. It meant *this*: an existence in ugly space, the mind fettered by drab walls and wire mesh, life reduced to childish make-work and getting by. The room I stood in was a vivid expression of the psychic isolation which had dogged my life, which I had fled from and waged war against with long hours at the office, the never satisfied craving for tokens of achievement and acceptance, a frenetic social life. Now, despite all my efforts, I was about to be locked up with a bunch of drug addicts and schizophrenics, the pathetic flotsam of life, people whose hands shook and who pissed on themselves and who made valentines to remember the lovers they would never have. Was this what people saw when they looked at me? Was this what they would see from now on? *No.*

I turned. The burly nurse's aide was walking toward me. He had some paperwork in his hand, and he was about to tell me something.

"I have to leave," I said, before he could speak.

"I can't let you leave," he said.

"I have to leave."

"Talk to the nurse."

She was still bent over her paperwork. "I have to leave," I repeated.

She looked at me. "We understand," she said. "It's very traumatic—"

"No, you *don't* understand," I said. My voice must have held a note of hysteria. "I have to leave. I do not *belong* here. I have to get out of here. Can I make a phone call?" No, she said; patients were not allowed to use the phone after a certain hour.

"I don't belong here," I said. "I'm not a patient."

She paused. Maybe it was the desperation in my voice, maybe it was some bureaucratic logic in what I had just said—she still had not filled out all my forms—or maybe it was simply that I was about to cause trouble and it was the middle of the night. Whatever the reason, she said to the nurse's aide, "Let her make a phone call." He pulled the telephone out of a metal filing-cabinet drawer and plugged it into the wall jack I had seen earlier.

"This is against the rules," he said.

I called Thomas, who had just gone to sleep.

"Don't make me stay here," I said. I was crying.

"Just stay tonight," he said. "I'll come get you in the morning."

His voice sounded kind; he wasn't even angry I had awakened him. I took a breath, trying to calm myself. "Okay," I said, and hung up.

For a few moments the nurse puttered around with her paperwork. The room was dead and silent. It was ugly, so ugly. Where would they put me? Where would I sleep? Would I have a roommate? Would it be somebody who would let me sleep? Would I *want* to sleep, locked up with crazy people? I could not stand this, not for one night. And I had to act quickly. At any moment, they might take the phone away.

I redialed. "I'm sorry," I said, in panic. "I can't do this. You have to come get me. *Please.*"

"It's okay," he said. "It'll take me a few minutes." I hung up.

"You'll have to sign this form," the nurse said. I looked at it. It said something about checking out "AMA"—against medical advice. I signed. In ten minutes, Thomas's car pulled up outside. At his house, I fell into his bed and into a dreamless sleep.

Morning came, a bitter and windy February day. I awoke late, in a state of profound apathy. The house was quiet; the kids had long since left for school. Going to work seemed out of the question. Yet somehow I hoped we could forget the previous day's events, could contrive a way to resume the facade of normal life. But that required energy, and I had none; I felt as inert as a turnip.

Thomas, however, had no trouble thinking of what to do. As soon as he thought someone would be in his office, he called to cancel his appointments and classes for the day.

"I'm having to take today off," Thomas said. "I have to deal with Tracy. She's suicidal, and we're checking her into a hospital." I noted he didn't mention my last name. So he would have spoken of me before; the people in his office knew who I was. Obviously they did not think of me as Tracy Thompson, writer for the *Washington Post*. To them I was just some unstable woman Thomas had unfortunately gotten mixed up with, an object of pity or scorn. This was humiliating. But somehow I could not work up much feeling about it.

Thomas was businesslike again; seeing him shower and get dressed, I could have imagined he checked his women friends into psychiatric wards every day. I showered and dressed too, and after stopping to eat a late breakfast we drove to the hospital—this time, Georgetown University Hospital. It was a quiet Friday morning, and the wait was considerably shorter than it had been the night before at Suburban. After about fifteen minutes, a bearded young doctor called my name, and Thomas and I went back to an examination room. I sat on the table; Thomas sat on a chair beside me, holding my hand.

"Why are you here?" the doctor asked me. This was a more open-ended question than the ones I had faced last night. I told him a few things that had happened in the last few weeks, leaving out the incident with the vodka and the imipramine but telling him about the suicide note, the letters, packing up my things. Even as I was talking, the events did not seem real to me. I felt an urge to disclaim them, to add, "But this is silly, forget I said it." When I stopped, the doctor paused, looking at me carefully. He must have noted my pallor, the death-mask expression on my face, the one Thomas called my zombie face.

"I think you should check yourself in for a few days," he said.

This time, I knew, there would be no backing out. I still didn't believe I was sick. I was defective, but that was another thing; medicine couldn't cure that. There were no words for the hopelessness I felt about my defectiveness. It was the same feeling I had known years before, confronting the scars on my face after the car accident: there was something wrong with me, it was visible and humiliating, and there was nothing to be done about it. But if people had to find that out for themselves, I was, for the moment, willing to let them experiment on me.

Thomas was still holding my hand, and now he squeezed it.

"It's the best thing," he said, watching me closely. "Don't you think?"

"Okay," I said. The doctor left the room for a moment. Thomas looked at me.

"That was a highly sanitized account you just gave, I must say," he remarked. I felt ashamed. I was lying again. But frequently my descriptions of myself did not seem like lies to me until after the fact, when Thomas challenged me about something—and even then, sometimes, I knew he was wrong. But I had learned even on those occasions that protests only made him angry; he considered it a disgraceful form of weaseling if I didn't immediately confess. Besides, his judgment of me, harsh as it often was, often held some grain of truth. I was good at shading the facts, presenting myself in the best possible light. I did it reflexively, all the time. It was an old habit of self-concealment, dating back to those days in adolescence when I hid my spells of rage behind closed doors, afraid someone would find out how screwed up I was. Over the years, the habit had grown all-encompassing, into a need to cover up the most minor of transgressions. If I was late for an appointment because I had dithered over what to wear, I wouldn't apologize for being late—I'd just make up a story about how a terrible traffic jam had held me up, how my tardiness was not my fault. I was constantly having to deflect situations that might bruise my fragile sense of myself.

I held Thomas's hand for as long as they let me—through the admissions office, upstairs on the elevator and down the hall into the ward itself, which looked depressingly like every other hospital ward I had ever seen. They showed me where my room would be. I held his hand as I walked back up the hall with him to the outside door, and finally let it go as the door closed between us with a heavy, electrical click, locking me inside. Then they took from me all my belongings, everything that remotely looked like a sharp object, every pill, even my compact mirror, and led me to my room, where I sat on the bed and looked out at the pale winter sunlight on the bare trees across the road.

If there is a God in this universe, I thought, *it is not anyone I have ever met.*

I found myself a character in an Ionesco play, surrounded by people with no discernible connection to each other, a dozen plot lines arbitrarily twisted into a motley strand. I took notes; it was the only thing I could think of to do.

> Alice is my roommate. She is an attractive woman, red hair, fiftyish, British, works in a downtown consulting firm … She is a manic-depressive who came here after a severe manic episode. She is allergic to lithium. It's her third week on the unit; they're trying to find medications to treat her illness that won't make her vomit or swell up, as lithium does. I like her.
>
> Akmal is a Saudi Arabian, a tall, burly man with black hair and a booming voice. His eyes dart around the room, but he does not look anyone directly in the

eye. He spends his time on the telephone. Seems hostile, paranoid.

Pearl is an older black woman, Southern accent, very sweet and slightly addled.

Kevin. A student here at Georgetown. Taking some kind of medication that makes his eyes puffy; he wanders around looking doped, shuffling around. Is that what they're going to do to me?…

Hugo … A hard life. Alcoholic, wears big thick bandages on both wrists, walks around wearing two hospital gowns to cover his nakedness.

Bob. Very withdrawn. Spends most of his time in his room. Explains that his girlfriend is pregnant, he thinks. He doesn't know for sure. Also doesn't know whether it's his baby or her ex-husband's baby. Seems slightly proud of this mixed paternity question.

Luisa. Big, blowsy blond woman, married with kids, has at least three boyfriends. "They all know I'm married, I know they're married," she explained. "I know they ain't sleeping with anybody but their wives, and besides, we use condoms." She is also a manic-depressive … She tried to kill herself a week ago with sleeping pills and booze. As she was losing consciousness, she called a friend. 'Take care of my kids,' she remembers saying. The next thing she remembers is looking at a fireman at her front door …

Frank is a Mormon, a fat guy who just seems incompetent to handle life's complexities. He had to send his son to a drug rehabilitation center; he and his wife were getting evicted from their apartment because their son was disturbing the neighbors with his drug gang friends … Talks frequently about God and prayer. Amiable, when he's not sobbing.

Arlene. An old lady. No lights on upstairs. Periodically, she stands in the hallway and bellows, "I WANT TO GO HOME!" She does this so regularly that in my mind I call her Old Faithful.

This was no loony bin of the sort I'd seen in movies. There were a couple of patients whose thoughts seemed disordered and strange, not to mention the old lady who yelled in the hall. But for the most part we were just a collection of sad people, each of us sad in our own way. There was the desperate sadness of Luisa, with her multiple lovers, and the pathetic, resigned sadness of Pearl, who had come from a homeless shelter and would go back there when she was discharged. Hugo was a gregarious man who told me that he had gone home from work one day, gotten drunk as usual, then undressed, got into the shower and slit his wrists. His landlord was about to evict him. By chance or design, Hugo was in the shower when the landlord showed up to serve the eviction papers. By then, he had almost bled to death. "They hauled me in here bare-ass naked," he said cheerfully. He had the look of a man who would swap jokes with his executioner.

A day or so after I arrived, there were two newcomers: Lara, a pretty university student who had also tried to slit her wrists—though not with the same zeal Hugo had shown—and a white-haired man in his eighties who was a retired surgeon. Their diagnosis was the same as mine: severe depression.

"Thin old man," I wrote in my notes of the doctor. "Shuffling walk. Alternates between walking the halls and lying in bed. Can't sit through group … Flashes of his former self come through unexpectedly. Coming up to me and Lara—young things, I suppose we are to him—he gives a playful nose tweak in midair, just to get our attention, then an engaging grin. 'How're you?' An hour later, despair has settled in again."

Were these people really ill, the same way that having diabetes or a brain tumor made you ill? I was willing to admit some of them might be. The doctor, in particular, seemed to be in the grip of something almost palpable; watching him was like watching a landscape under fast-moving clouds—light one moment, darkness the next. Alice described herself as ill, and was commonsensical about it. She had gone into a manic phase while planning a reception at the consulting firm where she worked. Gearing up for the big event, she had started working longer and longer hours until she was staying up all night. Nobody could convince her this was unusual, she said. Her husband brought her to the hospital after she had gone four days without sleep. To me, she was like a diabetic who had suffered a severe insulin reaction; the whole issue was medication management. I found myself playing a semantical game in my head: the doctor was "sick," and so was Alice. The nature of their illness might be unclear, but its existence was obvious and physical.

Then there was Akmal, who paced the halls muttering to himself and glaring at anyone who crossed his path; I had no idea what was the matter with him, and I wasn't sure the staff did either, since none of them spoke his language and Akmal's English was poor. He might be a paranoid schizophrenic—but then, he was locked up on a mental ward in a strange country with no family or friends around; who wouldn't be paranoid? Other patients seemed merely pathetic stereotypes: Frank, a religious zealot; Pearl, a homeless bag lady; Hugo, a drunk. I had nothing in common with them. If I identified with anyone, it was with Lara; in her I could see myself, fifteen years earlier, overwhelmed by college life, swept along by chaotic emotions. But Lara and I weren't sick, I decided; we were just afflicted with the same curse in love.

Clearly, I didn't belong here, and I thought that fact must be obvious. Still, it was a relief to be told what to do, to forget about the pretense of normality. Depression had sapped my energy for months, and the physical toll was obvious. My face was thin and pale, my clothes hung on me. Mentally, I felt as if I'd been walking around for months dragging a lead weight on each foot—and now I had given up; now I would just lay myself down in the middle of the road, and rest. The doctors had decided to keep me on imipramine, but to supplement it with lithium, taken three times a day. The combination made me drowsy, a side effect I seemed to share with most of my fellow patients; people were always nodding off in the dayroom or shuffling around in a zombie walk. For the first few nights, I lay down, my mind as vacant as a television test pattern, and fell asleep instantly. It was easy to slide into the institutional routine.

I wanted to, after all. I wanted to be anonymous. My mother and sister, both in Georgia, were sick with worry about me, but I was adamant: they were not to come up, I did not want them here. My sister called Thomas at work. "What have you done to her?" she demanded. He told me about it later; he thought her effrontery was mildly amusing. I understood the code: my sister tended to get belligerent when she was frightened. But I did not call her back.

I had been on the ward for only a few days when the arrival of a new patient disrupted my carefully arranged definitions of who was sane and who was sick.

Her name was Loretta. I never knew her diagnosis. She arrived on the ward late one afternoon, just before dinner. She was in her early thirties, all bones, with red hair and stark white skin. Once she might have been beautiful, but now she looked like a famine refugee. She arrived at dinner wearing an opulent green silk dressing gown and when she smiled at us her mouth looked like a bleeding wound. There was a witchy look in her eyes. She scared me. I wanted nothing to do with her.

That night, just before eleven p.m., I went to the nurses' station to get my pills. Loretta was in the hallway, curled up in one of the tattered easy chairs next to the telephone, about twenty-five feet away. I caught a fragment or two of her end of the conversation, enough to realize that she was earnestly trying to persuade the person on the other end to come get her. Her tone was placating and reasonable, quite a contrast to her haggard expression and those scary eyes. The scene struck me as ironic. I was clearly out of place on a mental ward, but this sure looked like the right place for Loretta. Maybe there was some inverse rule of thumb, I thought: the harder you found it to get out, the more you needed to stay. Then, behind me, I heard a crash.

I turned. Loretta had hurled the telephone against the wall in a fury, smashing it, and was running toward the nurses' station, headed for the exit at the far end of the hall. She couldn't have gotten out—the door was locked—but the thought struck me that she was going to hurl her body at it or maybe try to put her fist through the glass. I moved to get out of her path. Somebody yelled, "Loretta, no!" and then four or five staffers were out in the hallway, blocking her. Seeing them, Loretta threw herself at one of the nurses and wrapped her hands tightly around the woman's throat. The mass of people went down, the nurse on the bottom and Loretta on top of her, strangling her. Several of the male staffers wrenched Loretta's hands away from the nurse's throat, and one of the men got her by the arms and held them behind her back. Even so, it took two more people to completely subdue her. The strength in that thin body was frightening and unnatural.

The commotion had brought almost everyone to their doors.

"Clear the hall, please," somebody said, and then the incident was over. Holding the little paper cup with my pills in it, I edged back down the hall as the nurse Loretta had attacked leaned against the wall, gasping and shaken. My roommate, Alice, poked her head out of our door. "Goodness," she said cheerily. "Thought all my things had fallen out of the cupboard." She padded back to bed and pulled the covers over her head. I couldn't fathom her lack of curiosity. A few minutes later, through a crack in the door, I saw two hospital security men escorting Loretta down the hall. She was walking quietly. I couldn't see her hands, but the way she held them in front of her made me think she was in restraints. They put her into an isolation room at the end of the hall. It had double doors. I heard voices in there, and after a while, I heard both the doors click shut. And then the screams started.

Loretta screamed off and on until I fell asleep. After a while her screams existed as wordless background noise; in my exhausted state, I probably could have slept through antiaircraft fire. The next morning I awoke at seven to hear the rattle of the breakfast cart and the subdued bustle of nurses making rounds to check vital signs—and Loretta, still screaming. Several people said she had kept them awake most of the night. As the day wore on, the screams became not less intrusive but more so. In the intervals of silence, we found ourselves listening for them, unnerved by the respite. The sounds coming from that room were enough to make a rational person start thinking about irrational things, like the existence of demons. To cover our uneasiness, some of us grumbled. Others made jokes.

That afternoon, we were asked to clear the hall again, and they let Loretta out to use the phone. It was right outside my room, and I could hear everything. Sitting cross-legged on my bed, I took notes.

"I want to come home, Mom," she said. Her voice was ragged, hysterical. "I want to come home with you guys. I'm dying, Mom … Don't leave me! I'm trying to do this on my own. I can't make any phone calls. I can't even call work to tell them where I am. Don't leave me in the hands of strangers! …

"Are you coming? Let me give you directions …

"I can't be put in a room like that. You're not allowed to raise your voice. You can't wave your hands because you're out of control. It's bizarre!"

Late that afternoon, two hospital security guards arrived, along with six or seven other people I had not seen before. I glimpsed Loretta walking down the hall surrounded by people, like an inmate on her way to the electric chair. I never saw her again.

This was my first close-up view of someone who fit the classic definition of crazy, the image of *Jane Eyre's* madwoman in the attic. But the most significant fact about Loretta was my position in relation to her. I was her peer, in the eyes of the world. No matter how different I felt myself to be from her, the outside world classified us both, for the moment, as mentally ill. By coming here, Loretta had confronted me with this fact. Now I shared her taint, as unmistakable as the smell of poverty, as obvious as the itch of lice.

In her hysterical pleading, I had heard echoes of myself, that night at Suburban. That point of similarity was deeply disquieting. I was thinking of this hospital stay as voluntary, but what if it wasn't? What if somebody decided I couldn't leave, even when I wanted to? Like everyone else, I was relieved that Loretta was locked away from us. But it was a brutal thing to see.

Impossible not to feel a chill of fear at her protests—impossible not to think about the horror of being thought insane when you weren't. Or worse, being insane and not knowing it. How *would* you know if you were insane? I had resigned myself to going along with the program in this mental hospital with the comforting thought that I really didn't belong here. But Loretta hadn't thought she belonged either. Maybe just *thinking* you didn't belong in a mental institution was proof of being crazy. How would you know?

Sometimes, when I'd made him really angry, Thomas would say to me, "You are *insane*." Once, in a particularly nasty moment, he had called me a pathological liar. I had found both accusations unanswerable—the first because I thought it might be true, the second because a pathological liar would, of course, deny being one. To both, I had reacted with automatic defensiveness. *No, I am not a pathological liar. No, I am not insane.* True, I felt defective. I was convinced of my defectiveness down to the marrow of my bones. But being defective still held the implication of moral responsibility; defective as I was, I could still say that my mind was my own. That was the special curse of my condition, in fact: it was somehow my *fault* that I was defective.

But to be insane meant I had literally lost my mind—that I had abdicated all responsibility, that nothing I saw or did was necessarily connected to reality. If so, I had lost my only real asset; my brain would then simply be a diseased organ. Yet to eliminate the disease would eliminate everything I thought of as me. Those were my choices: the assumption of total moral responsibility, or mental obliteration.

Yet—I clung to this thought—there were undeniable differences between me and Loretta. Loretta might pass herself off as rational on the telephone, but anyone who saw her demeanor, anyone who had looked into her eyes or witnessed her attack on the nurse, would have concluded that there was something classically "crazy" going on here; she was not at the moment legally or morally responsible for her actions. Yet I *was*. My attempts to gloss over some of the things I had done were tacit proof of this; nobody tried to duck a responsibility they did not feel. So if Loretta and I were both "insane," the moral implications of insanity had to be more complex than I had thought.

"We're all relieved when she leaves," I wrote. "She is a symbol—a true madwoman. What we could all become, and may yet become. There are no guarantees."

And, for the time being, I put her out of my mind.

My crisis had been ill-timed. There were major events happening on my beat. The mayor, Marion Barry, was indicted by a federal grand jury on charges of cocaine possession a few days after my admission—a legal development everyone had expected since the electrifying news of his arrest on cocaine possession charges the previous January. It was the biggest story on my beat in many years. I watched the news conference outside the federal courthouse—my courthouse!—on a television in the nurses' lounge, straining to see who was there from the *Post* newsroom, feeling guilty and worried about not being there. My sudden absence at such a crucial moment was, I later discovered, the topic of hot gossip in the office. Lots of people wanted a piece of the Barry story, and now here it was, headed toward me like a high fly hit to my spot in center field. And I wasn't there.

But I also felt relieved. I did not feel like covering a major news story. If I had tried to carry on much longer in my distracted state, I might have made some blunder which might have harmed my career as much as being in a psychiatric ward was going to, and more publicly. Thomas had talked to my boss, Fred Barbash, and told him where I was, and Fred had immediately sent me a handwritten note of encouragement and support. I appreciated the kindness behind that gesture, but did not for a moment believe the words. Fred wanted them to be true, I felt sure; maybe as far as he was concerned, they *were* true. But the stigma of mental illness was real. I could not imagine a greater humiliation than what had befallen me. Fred's letter made the worry more tolerable; now I knew, at least, that people at the *Post* would not openly sneer at me. But I was still sure my career was going to suffer; the only question was how much.

By day three or four, as my physical exhaustion abated, my

old anxiety began to return, that familiar itchy hum in my head. Out my window, I saw people walking around in light jackets. The weather was unseasonably warm for February, the sky clear. It looked like spring might be coming early—and every passing day must, I was sure, have been increasing the gossip about my whereabouts. I was still on suicide watch, which meant that someone checked on me every fifteen minutes, twenty-four hours a day, coming into my room at night to watch me sleep. I had no privacy. I might have consented to this imprisonment, but it was starting to feel onerous.

> FEBRUARY 10: We had group therapy this morning: me, Akmal, Pearl, Hugo, Kevin, Luisa, Alice, Frank, and two other female nurses. A poor display. Four of the eight patients were nodding off from their medication. The leader of the group was a young nurse with large eyes and a long blond braid. She sounded like the computer program "Ask Hester"— the one that simulates psychotherapy by keying in on stock phrases.
>   "You seem to feel that——"
>   "You haven't mentioned——"
>   "Where does that feeling of——come from?" All asked in the same detached tone. She seemed distant and bored. I talked a little. Much rambling, no therapy. I'm very tired.

> FEBRUARY 13: Bright sun, blue sky. I'm dying for fresh air. I haven't left this fifty-foot stretch of hospital corridor in five days. Feeling antsy and anxious. At group, talk drones on, nobody says much. I sit and think of all the groups I've been in. What good is it?

Every day brought new reminders of the indignity of my position. One day, it was a new patient named Jay, a middle-aged man who had clearly not bathed in weeks. He said nothing, sitting morosely on the outskirts of groups—far enough away to signal his separateness, close enough to smell. Luisa sniffed conspicuously.

"Is there a soap shortage around here?" she asked loudly.

"Hush, Luisa," Pearl said mildly. Jay seemed oblivious.

The hospital staff were, for the most part, nice people. I sensed that some were wary of Thomas's obvious influence over me. Butthey kept a respectful distance on that subject. They seemed to like hearing me talk. Several of them told me I was "articulate." I wasn't surprised they thought so; compared to the tortured syntax they used in group therapy every day, anybody who could speak in short, clear sentences must have sounded like Winston Churchill to them. "An encounter with another person need not be a conflictual one," was one gem from one group therapy leader; I had written it down afterwards, with a note to myself: "Have to get more of these." The therapists and interns came by my room, drew me out on the subject of the car accident, my fundamentalist religious upbringing. The attitudes about the latter seemed one-dimensional to me. They grasped quickly that hellfire-and-brimstone preaching went heavy on the notion of sin, and that telling people they were sinners made them feel guilty. That, they thought, was bad. But what about moral responsibility? I asked. I could see that to them my question was only more proof of pathology, of my morbid and irrational sense of guilt. But maybe guilt wasn't all bad, I said; maybe sometimes people did things they *should* feel guilty about. Maybe I had. But no, they assured me. Guilt was a negative emotion. Guilt was an obstacle to mental health.

I gave up; I had no energy for this argument, especially when delving into it was obviously convincing people I was even sicker than they had thought. But our talks were evidently interesting to someone. One day I was asked to be the guest at grand rounds, so all the psychiatric residents could hear me talk. I pretended reluctance, badly; in fact, I was thrilled. (*Look at her—outstanding in every endeavor!*) But then some important doctor came up with a scheduling conflict, and the event was canceled. I was crushed.

In addition to the nursing staff, various outside therapists came in to hold sessions. Attendance wasn't mandatory, technically, but sitting out the sessions counted as evidence of noncompliance, which in turn was considered proof of continuing severe illness. I attended faithfully, ever the teacher's pet. As a hardened veteran of group therapy, it never occurred to me that these sessions might seem odd to the uninitiated—until one day, when my group had to meet in the nurses' lounge for lack of any other available space. We wandered in, one by one, at the appointed time. A nurse's aide had picked that spot for her lunch break, and was sitting in an easy chair eating a sandwich and watching a soap opera on television. Absorbed in her soap, she didn't notice as more and more people came in the door and sat down. Then the psychiatrist came in—a genial, gray-bearded man whose name I forget. To signal that it was time for group to start, he turned off the TV. The nurse's aide looked up, startled, to find all eyes on her. The expression on her face said, *Oh my God, here I am in a small room with a dozen crazy people.*

"Should I leave?" she asked, with her mouth full.

"Well, we don't know," I said. "Is there anything you would like to share with the group?" *Pfffft*—she was out of there.

The psychiatrist looked at me. "Obviously, *you're* feeling better," he said. "You're getting your sense of humor back." What he didn't realize was that my sense of humor had never entirely left; jokes had always been a way to express rage or pain. The comedians I had found funniest, like Jackie Gleason and Jonathan Winters, were adept at transmuting anger into humor, and my father had been no slouch in that department. I thought about saying this to the psychiatrist, but didn't. He would only have asked me what emotion *I* was feeling at the moment, which was that given the choice, I would have been right behind the nurse's aide. I could foresee the tedious colloquy that would follow. *Why do you want to leave? What are you avoiding?*

The group therapy sessions were helpful only in that they gave us something to do. Short of having a therapist assigned to each patient, I couldn't think of any other way the hospital staff could fill up our day. In the group sessions I'd been to in Atlanta, there was at least a core of people who came to know each other, and sometimes our growing familiarity spawned a useful insight or two. Here, the staff was trying to conduct group therapy with a constantly shifting cast of characters, all of whom might as well have had little cartoon balloons over their heads that said, "I'm the one who doesn't belong here." Trying to get us to "relate" to each other in group was like trying to teach a bunch of scorpions to sing around the campfire. It was pointless.

How pointless came home to me on the day I watched live television coverage of Nelson Mandela being released from prison after twenty-seven years as a political prisoner. An art therapy session was about to start in the dayroom, where I was, but I insisted on making everybody wait. I hadn't even realized the release was about to happen; I had been in the hospital at that point for a week, and had not read a newspaper or watched a news broadcast in that time. I hadn't missed the news, which was unusual for me. But this morning, when the networks interrupted a rerun of *I Love Lucy* for live coverage of Mandela's release, I felt interested. Here was a reminder of a world outside this rather sterile haven I had found. I regarded it with a kind of wary interest, the way someone recovering from the flu might eye solid food.

"Wait," I said. "I have to watch this."

They indulged me. At first nobody else was interested. But then people began to wander over to the television. We saw a large crowd lining both sides of a road—and then, in the distance, there was clapping. After a moment or two, Mandela appeared, walking down the road, smiling and waving, holding his wife's hand.

"Okay," I said. "That's all I wanted to see." Someone turned the television off, and there was a scraping of chairs as everybody gathered around a table in the back of the room, where the therapist had laid out a bunch of string and a collection of beads. At that moment, it struck me that my colleagues at the *Washington Post* were at work in Johannesburg and Washington, crafting the first rough draft of a historic moment. And I was in a mental ward, a prisoner of the ultimate cliché—stringing beads.

Actually, once a person lost all semblance of pride, stringing beads was not so bad. It was soothing, in a mindless sort of way. Other forms of "therapy," however, seemed silly.

> After lunch we have Movement Therapy ... We sit in a circle and while relaxing music plays we extend our arms to be "aware of other people's space." Next we stand up and bouncier music comes on; we are asked to "let your body tell you how it wants to move." Then we go around the circle, and each of us is asked to introduce a new movement. At intervals the movement therapist asks us whether we would like to talk about the emotional meaning of those movements.

> "Are we trying to kick something away?" she asks Jay. "Yeah," he says, bored into a coma, clearly thinking: Whatever ...

> [That night] we have Relaxation Therapy. A middle-aged nurse named Evalina comes in with some schematic drawings of the human brain that look very familiar. Suddenly I realize I've seen them, or something very like them, in my seventh-grade biology textbook. She talks for a while about creating new "pathways in your brain's circuitry," which one is allegedly able to do by thinking really hard about something. To illustrate her point, she gives each of us a piece of paper which has a circle divided into fourths by two intersecting lines, like the cross hairs of a rifle. On the circle, where twelve o'clock, three o'clock, six o'clock, and nine o'clock would be, there are the numbers 1, 2, 3, and 4. Then we get a washer tied to a string. She tells us to dangle the washer by the end of the string with our elbows on the table and hold it over the intersection of the two lines in the middle of the circle. Then, she says, think very hard about "one-three, one-three, one-three." The result of this exercise is familiar to anyone who has ever played with a Ouija board, but it impresses the group a lot.

> "I can't wait to get home and show this to my

kids," Luisa says. Then somebody hauls out the tumbling mats and we all—or most of us—lie down on them while Evalina turns out the light. Akmal, a good Muslim, makes tracks for the door: none of this immoral business of men and women lolling about together for him. Hugo, who has been complaining all week that he can't sleep, settles down on the day-room sofa. Evalina starts talking soothingly of white sand on a beach, the waves lapping against the shore, etc., a spiel interrupted only by increasingly loud snores from Hugo.

Obviously, I had to get out.

It was possible to get off the ward the same way I'd done it at Suburban—"against medical advice"—but I ruled that out. I didn't want Thomas to accuse me of sidestepping anything. This time, I wanted to follow the rules, whatever they were—at least in form.

At Georgetown, the first step was getting off suicide watch. That meant writing a self-evaluation and presenting it during the morning group therapy session. The self-evaluation was supposed to include a detailed account of how you had come to be admitted to the hospital, and a list of steps you planned to take to prevent a similar situation from recurring. Then the plan was put to a vote. If it sounded viable to a majority of the patients, you graduated from suicide watch to acquiring limited pass privileges to get off the ward. First, you would be allowed off with a staff member, then with a family member, then with a friend, and finally alone. Getting a personal pass to venture off the ward alone, with a time set for your return, was the last step before discharge.

To me, the self-report sounded like the old television show *What's My Line*—the object being to come up with something the audience would believe, whether or not it was true. I waited for a day or so, knowing that too dramatic a recovery would look suspicious, then wrote my self-evaluation. Coming up with the right words was easy; after all, I used words for a living.

The next day, I read my plan during morning report, and was rewarded with a unanimous, if listless, consent. Pending a doctor's signature on my chart later, during rounds, I was on my way home.

I called Thomas, expecting he would be pleased.

He was not. He was angry. Why had I not discussed this with him first? Had I talked about it with the doctors, or anybody on the staff? Why not? Why had I simply dashed something off so quickly? Did I actually mean every word of what I had written?

The last question was the stumper. I couldn't even remember everything I'd written, much less whether I meant it. My self-congratulatory mood evaporated under his merciless scrutiny. In tears, I promised him I would make things right. He was unconvinced. I was lying again, he said; it was hopeless for any sane person to talk to me. Nobody could believe a word I said.

I was furious at him—but saying so was out of the question. I still needed Thomas more than I feared him. I knew that if I told him how angry he made me, it would be the last straw. He would simply cut me off; he had come close to doing that several times already. Better to be the sick one, the person who lost every argument, than to be alone.

But there was something else that made me bury my anger, for the time being: Thomas could confront me with some truths about myself that nobody else had been able to get me to look at before. He could be brutal about it; I even wondered if he took a sadistic pleasure in pointing out my evasions and inconsistencies. I hated him for that sometimes. And yet: I wanted to be different. I wanted to be a healthy person. I was willing to undergo torture, if necessary—and I thought then that it was—if that was what it took to find my way out of this maze.

That night, at the evening group session, I made an announcement. The self-report I had read that morning had not been sincere, I said; I had written it just to qualify for pass privileges. But since then, I had realized how wrong that was, and now I was ready to mean it, every word. Would that be okay?

A circle of people looked at me in silence. Hugo, with his drinker's nose; Jay, with the terrible body odor; Lara, looking embarrassed; Pearl, looking addled as usual.

"I'm not so sure Tracy is ready for privileges," somebody said. I felt my face flush. These people were judging *me*?

"I think we should put this to another vote," said somebody else. This time, it was unanimously rejected.

I was furious. How had I landed in this humiliating mess?

Back in my room, I thought about who to blame. The most obvious culprit was, of course, my parents. From them I had learned the paramount importance of stifling emotions: the more authentic and deeply felt, their example had taught me, the more dangerous—and the more important that they be stifled. And I could blame my culture, while I was at it. My indoctrination as a Southern female had taught me there was no benefit in real honesty when something more comfortable would suffice. Better to keep quiet—or, if you had to talk, to say something that someone wanted to hear, something that might get you what you wanted. This approach to life didn't actually ban honesty outright; what you meant to say and what the other person might find pleasing could occasionally coincide. But the main thing was to say what was necessary, or socially acceptable, or expedient. Now I had done just that, and where had it gotten me?

Then I decided the real culprit was Amanda. All parents had faults; everyone was a product of his culture. Amanda, however, had been a supposedly objective observer. Her job had been to cure me, or at least improve me. Yet she had never forced me to confront the truth about myself; she had never warned me of what would happen someday when my garments of deception slipped and some unwelcome truth revealed itself to the world.

But after a while, I realized this theory, too, was flawed. I remembered my tears, my furious defensiveness whenever Amanda said anything even remotely critical; I remembered how much effort I had expended over the years in putting up a good front for her, too, in my all-consuming need to win the approval and admiration of everybody I knew. Amanda might have been too personally invested to be a good therapist for me; she might have been mistaken in her assessment of what my problems really were. But anyone would have found it difficult to penetrate the steep defenses I had erected around my fragile ego. My problems may not have been entirely of my own making, but I had found the solutions so difficult because I had been so immature. And still was, apparently.

For years, in fact, I had devoted considerable energy and enterprise to the act of appearing normal. My zeal in imitating health grew in direct proportion to my shame at knowing there was something wrong with me, even though I lacked a clear idea of what that was. This way of living had worked, in the short term. I had fooled a lot of people for a long time; I had even, at times, fooled myself. But the costs had been steep: years of tumbling in and out of depressive episodes, years of unhealthy dependence on the approval of others, of a ravenous emotional neediness which had threatened to consume every man I had tried to get close to, and which had doomed me to long periods of loneliness and isolation.

So the real culprit, then, was me.

You brought this on yourself. It didn't matter how I had learned this behavior, or from whom, the fact was that I had lied. And I would have continued to lie if Thomas had not challenged me. It seemed to confirm his most devastating assessment of me: maybe I *was* a pathological liar. Could you be one and not know it? Worse, I had been judged and found wanting by a group of people I thought myself superior to. I felt overwhelmed with shame, paralyzed by the thought that my emotional defects were matched by even bigger moral defects. This self-laceration was typical depressive behavior: though I was closing in on a realistic view of myself for the first time, I was seeing with a histrionic intensity. I was like a person wearing distorting glasses, who couldn't navigate without wildly overcompensating for every curve in the road, real or perceived.

That night, I called Thomas again. "If this is the way I am, if I can't change, I don't want to live," I sobbed. He said nothing, and in that silence I heard agreement.

Yes, his silence seemed to say. *You would be better off dead.*

I awoke the next morning with a grim determination to

regain my moral standing in the ward—a standing perhaps perceived by nobody but me, but vital all the same. I would be a model patient. I might no longer be able to claim innate superiority, but I would by God earn it. I would be the hardest-working, most insightful patient in the history of psychiatry; I would qualify for the Psychiatric Hall of Fame.

During all those years of therapy with Amanda, my grandiosity had made my faults appear more glaring and more horrible than anybody else's; a clear-eyed view was impossible, which was all the more reason to avoid looking. Now, I decided, I would no longer try to avoid looking at my flaws, I would search them out. In fact, the more I found, the better: in a perverse way, being able to detail all my flaws would be proof of the superiority I craved.

I was like a monk who aspires to God by praying more devoutly, abasing his body more, fasting longer. I would chronicle and change my defects through sheer force of will. It was, in its way, another experiment in performing—this time, not to win the group's approval, but Thomas's. But I was to discover that it didn't matter. My monkish self-abasement did have one benefit: for the first time, I started thinking critically, and without self-pity, about my behavior.

I began by shutting myself away in my room and drawing up another self-evaluation. This time, I thought carefully about every word.

Why was I here?

Because there was something wrong with me.

What was it? Some innate defect, something I had no control over? It was simple to think so—I had always thought so—but no: I also considered myself to be morally responsible for my actions. That meant the truth was more complicated. I was here because of *something I had done*. I had planned a murder of myself. And I had given thought to this often before. The latest crisis was only one in a series, the true extent of which I had never fully told anyone.

Just as important as that was the way I had done it. I was impulsive. I did things without thinking of the consequences.

Not only had I planned to kill myself, I had almost succeeded weeks earlier through *lack* of planning.

For the past few months, I began to realize, I had been blundering out of control, as oblivious to peril as a sleepwalker crossing the freeway. And it could happen again. At some point it probably would, if I didn't own up to what I had done. My self-destructive behavior was particularly deadly in light of how impulsive I was. It was what led me to abuse alcohol and the imipramine on that frightening night, not to mention all those other evenings when I had sought a milder form of anxiety relief with a few glasses of Chardonnay. My impulsiveness was the major reason I had been caught trying to weasel my way off suicide watch; no sooner had I thought of a scheme than I had put it into effect. Now I simply had to start *thinking* about what I was doing. The worst deceptions were the ones I perpetrated on myself.

And they took several forms. As an exercise, I began to catalog them.

To begin with, there was outright lying. I didn't actually do this very often; when it came to public honesty, I was conspicuously honest. Even when I was earning only a hundred dollars for a free-lance magazine article, I had scrupulously reported every dime on my income taxes; I went back to the grocery store cashier if she gave me five dollars too much in change. I had, until now, considered this the sum total of honesty.

But recent events showed me that there were other means of deception. For instance, denial—simply not admitting the reality of something I had done or said. The night of the not quite accidental overdose was a clear example. When I put lying to myself alongside impulsive and self-destructive behavior, it was a wonder I was here.

Also, there was selective amnesia—picking out one remark someone else made, out of many, and using it to justify something I wanted to do in the first place, or using it as evidence of some "absolute" truth. Once, during a quarrel, Thomas had insulted me: "There are times when I wonder about your intelligence." Later, he had apologized; he'd been angry, he said, and had found himself saying something he didn't mean. I understood how it was possible to blurt out words and instantly regret them; I'd done it myself. Yet months later, I was still nursing the memory of that remark, using it as incontrovertible evidence of Thomas's true feeling about me. If anyone had accused me of nursing a grudge, I would have denied it.

This behavior went hand in hand with failing to speak when I had something to say. That constantly got me into trouble. I couldn't get angry without something setting off a long colloquy in my head. *I'm angry. But maybe I shouldn't be. Maybe I'm just making too much of nothing. It pissed me off but if I say so I'll look silly and supersensitive. I'll just keep my mouth shut.* My sense of outrage would go underground and fester. Later, if I was lucky, I might get a chance to make the offender suffer. "You seem quiet. What's wrong?" *"Nothing."* It was a very Southern-belle skill, this business of hiding hostility behind a smile, a razor hidden in a bouquet of flowers. But wherever I had learned it, I was good at it. Both tactics—selective amnesia and allowing old anger to fester—were ways to obtain the status of victimhood, while foreclosing for others the option of making amends. Being a victim was a very handy weapon, all the more effective for being covert. No matter how much your actions hurt somebody, you could always say you hurt worse. Being a victim meant never having to say you were sorry.

Then there was simple evasiveness. When Peter's soccer banquet came up and Thomas couldn't go, I had bought two tickets: one for Peter, one for me. The truth was, I didn't want Melissa to go. Peter and I were buddies, but Melissa refused to join my fan club. When she found out about the tickets, she howled: Why had I left her out? I reacted with righteous defensiveness. "It's a boys' soccer banquet. I didn't think you *wanted* to go." That had made her even angrier. *What a brat!* I'd thought at the time. Now her reaction made more sense. She was a child, but she was not stupid; she knew instinctively I was avoiding her, shutting her out of her little brother's big night. I'd met people with hidden agendas before. I remembered in particular an editor in my past, a woman who had tried to curry favor with *her* boss by making drastic revisions in a long article I was writing about the death penalty. Not only had she not improved my writing, she had told me she was only doing it to help me. My reaction to her had been the same as Melissa's reaction to me: anger and distrust.

That left the last question: How would I deal with the next crisis?

Honesty. It was that simple, and that hard. For one thing, I did not want to risk another public humiliation. I was more frightened of that than I was of being honest, even though honesty was frightening in itself. But it would be worth it if I could avoid placing myself in a position to be criticized again. In that sense, honesty could be a way of exerting control over my life; if I did a better job of keeping tabs on my true motives and feelings, no one else could blindside me by revealing them. Having to constantly check up on my own motives was a painful prospect. But the searing memory of that circle of suspicious faces was even more painful. Better to inflict pain on myself than let other people do it.

So I wrote my safety plan. I would deal with the next crisis, I wrote, by admitting what was going on—first to myself, and then to someone else. If I ever again felt like killing myself, I would call someone and tell them. Immediately. And then, because I was impulsive, I included a corollary promise: that in another crisis I would not allow myself to be alone, not even for an hour. If it meant going to a hospital emergency room or roaming the aisles of a twenty-four-hour supermarket, I wrote, I would force myself to be in the company of other people until better help arrived. I would do that no matter who I had to call, no matter how much it damaged my confident, in-control image. I would ask for help, even if it made me feel pathetic.

I kept my new plan to myself for a day—not for effect this time, but to convince myself I really meant it. This time, it was a harder sell. I was learning that it isn't so easy convincing people you are no longer a liar. That hurt my pride. I'd never had to work to convince anyone of my honesty before. In fact, I felt entitled to a presumption of moral integrity. For a moment, I was resentful. But then I realized: *The harder I work to persuade them, the less they will believe me. They'll just have to see.* That was frightening. Now I had forced myself to follow up my words with actions. But I could not afford to fail.

> FEBRUARY 14: Valentine's Day on the psych ward. I read my new safety plan, which is endorsed by the group, though less enthusiastically than the first time. For a horrible moment, I wonder if I'm going to get any support at all—if I'll be a prisoner for another week. But it flies. And this time, I can say I mean it.

It was the first step in a long journey, and my motives for setting out were less than noble. But long journeys don't have to start with noble motives. They just have to start.

Things began to change after that, in ways that weren't immediately apparent. I still kept notes, but my fellow patients began to seem more like human beings to me, and less like observational phenomena for my notebooks. I wrote less—it is difficult to reconstruct some incidents from that time, for that reason—but started talking to people more. For the first time, my journal shows I had begun to take an interest in my surroundings.

> Physical description of the unit: one long hallway, seventeen beds, including isolation rooms. Floor is white institutional tile, walls beige, furniture hospital institutional—except for the dayroom, which features two cheap, uncomfortable sofas, a piano, and a small sink and stove in the corner. Over the piano is a hand-lettered sign with the Alcoholics Anonymous prayer: "God grant me the serenity to accept the things I cannot change, the courage to change the things I can, and the wisdom to know the difference." A variety of house plants on the windowsills. Flowered curtains. A refrigerator which holds mostly cans of soda and,

in the freezer part, ice cream ... In the hallway, there
are two phones, one at either end. Beside each phone
there is a cheap easy chair with torn plaid upholstery
in shades of brown and beige.

I also began to notice interesting commonalities—the most
obvious one being that hardly anybody slept at night. No matter
what hour I was up, I had company. Sitting in one of the two
easy chairs in the hallway, I could see Hugo, a lumbering white
apparition wearing two hospital gowns and fat gauze bandages
on his wrists, on his way to the dayroom to watch TV; he was
a fan of old *Star Trek* reruns, and any rental movie, no matter
how saccharine or dull, got his rapt attention. Usually there
was at least one other person in there with him; when I passed
by, I could see two or three dark figures, huddled in the dim
light of the electronic box. I could hear its low murmuring,
mingling with the voices of the nursing staff doing paperwork
at the nurses' station across the hall. If I stood in the hall for
just a few minutes, another door would open. Sooner or later,
somebody would enter or leave almost every room. It was like
watching a French farce performed underwater, by sleepwalkers.
At morning meetings, a member of the nursing staff sat down
with all of us to review the previous twenty-four hours. Usually
the chart notations began with a summary of how each of us
had slept. Very few of us got more than two or three hours of
uninterrupted sleep.

Listening, I remembered Thomas's comments about how
troubled my own sleep was. I had thought he was complaining
simply because I woke him up. Sleep disturbances, I had read,
were a classic symptom of major depression. I had filed that
away in my mind without thinking much about it. Now, I was
seeing a whole room of people, as varied a lot as I could imagine,
mostly suffering from "mood disorders"—and none of us were
sleeping normally. Here was a physical expression of something
I had thought of as abstract.

Another detail was disruptions in appetite. We seemed to
fall into two groups: those who didn't eat at all, and those who ate

incessantly. I started out in the first group but quickly switched to the second. At that point, I had never heard that depression can manifest itself in eating too much as well as in eating too little. On some nights, the patients made a communal dinner, using groceries brought in by the staff. One night Hugo made a salad with a dressing several of us took an inordinate liking to. I had seconds, and thirds—only to discover later that Hugo had flavored the dressing so heavily with garlic that anyone who ate it reeked of garlic for days, sweated garlic out the pores of his skin. Thomas pointed this out to me on one of his visits. I had hardly been aware of it; to me, the salad dressing was simply the first thing I had eaten in a while that I could actually taste. The return of my sense of taste was the very first physical difference I noticed after I started taking lithium, and it was noticeable within the first two or three days. The effect was like color gradually seeping back into a sepia portrait. Once my sense of taste returned, I found that I craved sweets, especially chocolate. I wasn't alone. The staff kept a large plate of brownies and cookies in the dayroom for general consumption, and it had to be constantly replenished.

In every visit, Thomas would bring me the latest fruits of his research expeditions. He had been haunting the medical sections ofbookstores, looking for up-to-date writing about depression. I wouldn't have bothered. Over the years, I had picked up books on the subject, and they seemed to fall into two major categories: either pop psychology—how-to manuals for psychic repair—or books filled with psychoanalytic theories that quickly began to sound like the hairsplitting interpretations of religious doctrine that had bored me silly in church as a teenager. The first had seemed too simple, the second too obscure.

This time there was a difference. Thomas was finding an unexpected bounty of research about the link between moods and specific chemical brain processes. These books weren't warm and fuzzy, and none of them mentioned things like narcissistic disturbances in toilet training. Depression was no longer the province of peppy self-help articles in women's magazines and pipe-smoking guys in cardigan sweaters. Now it was a subject for chemists, neurobiologists, even medical historians.

One book in particular caught my interest: *Melancholia and Depression: From Hippocratic Times to Modern Times*, by Yale University psychiatrist and medical historian Stanley Jackson. I did not begin reading it in any coherent way—my concentration span was still short—but opened it at random and read what interested me. On the first page I found an arresting passage.

"Accounts of this clinical description have been traced in approximately two and a half millennia of medical writings," Jackson wrote. "While there have certainly been variations in the content of this clinical disorder, there have been both a remarkable consistency and a remarkable coherence in the basic cluster of symptoms."

One of the most extensive descriptions was written in 1602 by a Renaissance expert, Felix Platter, dean of the medical school at the University of Basle.

"Melancholy, which is named from black bile is a kind of mental alienation in which imagination and judgment are so perverted that without any cause the victims become very sad and fearful," Platter wrote. "They have solitude and flee the company of men ... Just as these disorders just described, of grief and fear do not produce the same effects in all, but pervert the mind less in some and more in others, so it happens that even though they keep a continual hold on those whom they have invaded, still they have in turn their periods of aggravation and remission."

Nineteen years later, Robert Burton reiterated this observation in *The Anatomy of Melancholy*: "Fear and sorrow make it different from madness ... fear and sorrow are the true characters and inseparable companions, of most melancholy." Yet, Burton added, "in all other things [sufferers] are wise, staid, discreet, and do nothing unbeseeming their dignity, person or place." They were, in other words, dedicated to appearing normal.

I realized I had been working with an outmoded set of assumptions. One was the vague idea that Sigmund Freud invented depression, that it was a purely twentieth-century phenomenon. Another was that it was a sign of spiritual decay, the penalty exacted for estrangement from God. The two concepts meshed; as a child, I had been taught in Sunday school that estrangement from God had been getting worse ever since the nineteenth century (the finger of blame here had pointed directly at Charles Darwin). The idea of depression as a definable illness, documented for millennia, was new.

I mentioned my discovery the next day to Thomas.

"Yes," he said matter-of-factly. "You have a noble disease."

"Depression" was a word I'd used since I was fourteen, but its very familiarity had obscured its meaning. People thought they knew what it meant, when in fact it encompassed layers of ambiguity. A person might say, "I am depressed," and mean, "I had a fender bender on the way to work," or he might mean, "I am going to buy a gun and shoot myself." The second meaning was now coming into focus for me, peeling off from the first like two pages stuck together. It was disorienting, like finding out that the parent who kissed you good night had an evil twin who was a paid assassin. "A noble disease." A disease, I thought, was something caused by a germ. But the dictionary definition was broader—"a condition of the body in which there is incorrect function resulting from the effect of heredity, infection, diet or environment; illness; sickness; ailment."

Depression, then, was a kind of disease, an illness. I'd even said that myself on occasion. But even that had not clarified the confusion; illness was another concept that had layers of meaning. There was illness that was caused by something you could see, if only under a microscope, like the bacterium that caused tuberculosis—or it was something whose effects were visible, like cancer. Then there was another kind of illness, as in, "God, she's a sick person," "How sick," "This is a really sick idea." The second kind carried the weight of moral blame. There was an element of choice involved—or, if not choice, some residual notion of original sin. Charles Manson and Jeffrey Dahmer were sick, but that kind of sickness no one would willingly claim. That kind of sickness deserved to be cast away from society. When I had glibly said that depression was an illness, it was more the second kind I'd had in mind.

But what if depression was an illness of the first kind? Then it would be an incorrect functioning of my brain. I could say, *There is something wrong with my brain.* That was a different thing from saying, *There is something wrong with me.* The second was self-pitying; the first was a simple, factual statement. It was a subtle nuance, easy to miss. But as I grasped that difference— and it was slippery, I kept losing it at first—other doors began to open in my mind:

Depression is an illness. I am sick. I need to be here not because I'm defective, not because I'm a moral leper, not because I've fallen from grace or turned my back on God, but for one simple reason: because I am sick.

But there my thinking stalled. So I was sick. But this was my *brain* I was talking about, not my gallbladder or my kidneys. It had some mysterious property called "consciousness." It produced behavior, the sum total of which was somehow *me.* If I wanted to say simply that my brain was sick, I could stop there and disavow responsibility for that sickness—but if I did that, I would be giving up my idea of autonomy in the world. I would be simply a product of some chemical abnormality in a lumpy gray organ between my ears. I would be a creature led through life by the promptings of that organ, as subservient to its messages as a dog chasing cars. The thought of that deeply offended my ego.

For most of my life, I had thought that whatever it was I called "depression," it was something I was responsible for. I had based years of work in psychotherapy on that assumption and felt enormous guilt when therapy produced no lasting results. Was the alternative simply to walk away from the idea of personal responsibility altogether, to say simply, "I'm sick, I can't help it"? I didn't know, but it seemed to me that if the first approach was too simplistic, its opposite might be as well.

Where that left me, I didn't know.

Days passed. I kept on reading in the Jackson book. He got into much more detail about bilious humors and medieval medicine than I was interested in, so I skipped to a section entitled "Melancholia and Depression in the Twentieth Century." I could not absorb it. "Melancholia consists in mourning over libido,"

Sigmund Freud had written, but this made no sense to me: why was Freud so focused on sex? This was of merely academic interest to me, anyway: I hadn't had any libido in so long I had forgotten what it felt like. I suspected Freud was probably saying something more, but I couldn't muster the energy to puzzle it out. As my friend Patti would have said, Freud did not "speak to my condition."

"As to how a clinical depression came about, [Edith] Jackson thought that a diminished self-esteem was the essential feature," Jackson wrote. No shit. An essential feature of extreme physical pain was that it hurt. Here we were, back to the psychoanalytic closet again. But what did this *mean?*

I found the beginnings of my own understanding in a section that dealt with an aspect I had not seen anyone address before: the effect of depressed people on those around them. It seemed to echo a lot of what Thomas had been telling me for months—that depression did not just make the sufferer sick, but depleted the energy of everybody in his vicinity. This was not a popular point to make; it was hard to say anything about it without sounding callous. My own reaction had been intense guilt, and then self-pity: how dare Thomas point this out, when I was so miserable? There had been a touch of sadism in his readiness to remind me of this at every opportunity. And yet, I could not argue; I knew it was true.

But then I found this quote in the Jackson book, from Alfred Adler. Depressed persons, Adler had written, "will always try to lean on others and will not scorn the use of exaggerated hints at their own inadequacy to force the support, adjustment and submissiveness of others."

Yes, I thought, immediately recognizing the plaintive, infuriating helplessness of my father's mother, that chronically depressed woman whose credo had been never to do for herself what she could con others into doing for her. (*Would you wash my hair? Would you trim my toenails?*) Her pain had been real, almost palpable. But she had used it as a weapon and a snare; nobody in the family had escaped unscathed. I had done that myself, as far back as high school, with my anything but casual mentions of how many Sominex I took. And though over the years I had learned to conceal my real problems at all costs, I had never hesitated to keep the world informed about the moment-to-moment developments of every minor headache or back sprain. Which was ironic: I always found it extremely annoying if someone else did the same thing to me. *Quit whining!* I would think.

I read on. What I found next came from someone named Jules Bemporad, in a citation dated 1978. Here was a description of depression different from anything I had read before, and it resonated.

"Depression is not merely a group of symptoms that make up a periodic illness, but … it is a practice, an everyday mode of interacting," Bemporad had written. "Any interference with this type of functioning leads to an outward appearance of clinical depression in order to coerce the environment into letting the individual reinstate his usual interpersonal behaviors. The major pathological elements in this specific way of life are manipulativeness, aversion to influence by others, an unwillingness to give gratification, a basic sense of hostility, and the experience of anxiety."

I underlined this. The words sounded harsh, but there was something familiar lurking in that passage. "An everyday mode of interacting." That was exactly what I'd been searching for—a sense of this illness not just as a chemical abnormality, but as a chemical abnormality that produced *behavior*. Here was something I might actually be able to work on, and change. "Manipulativeness." What I had done with the phony self-evaluation might fairly be called manipulative. "An unwillingness to give gratification." Not exactly, I thought—not unwillingness but inability, or maybe some combination of the two. Someone who is desperately afraid his own needs won't be met is not apt to think too much about the needs of others. I remembered my initial resentment of Thomas's children, how I had begrudged every time we had gone to a kids' movie instead of some adult movie I wanted to see. Even worse: I remembered seeing my own sister sobbing at the death of our father, how I had stood there, not giving her so much as a gesture of physical comfort. I had been thinking: *Who will comfort me?*

"Aversion to influence by others." This seemed wrong; if anything, I was too open to influence, especially Thomas's influence. On the other hand, submitting to his influence had entailed discounting, sometimes brutally, the influence of others. "The experience of anxiety." God, yes. "A basic sense of hostility." Even that was familiar. There were my spells of rage, hostility directed at myself. There had also been times I projected my own hostility onto other people. Melissa had once made two drawings, one for me and one for Thomas. He put them up on the refrigerator, and one day I noticed mine was gone. "Who took my drawing down?" I asked accusingly, and Thomas had gotten angry. It turned out that the housekeeper had accidentally knocked it off. I had to admit my first thought had been that Melissa had done it, to show she didn't like me.

Alice had gone home about a week into my stay; her doctors had finally found a dosage of lithium that did not send her straight to the toilet to vomit. She had left without saying goodbye, but on my bed I'd found a dime-store valentine, which had touched and surprised me. My new roommate was named Heather. She was a beautiful college freshman who was putting herself through school by competing in beauty pageants. She had glossy black hair, a taut little body, and a bright, perpetual, phony smile. She did not talk to anyone, and if anyone spoke to her they got only a vivacious, vacant "Hi!" in response. In group therapy that evening, somebody asked her why she was on the unit.

"I get angrier than other people sometimes and I came here to identify the problem and see how I can fix it so I can get out and go home," she said. *Big* smile.

She attracted a steady stream of visitors—other students, mostly male, who huddled around her bed at the other end of our room and carried on long, earnest conversations. Bit by bit, I got the outline. She had a boyfriend who had wanted to break off the relationship. There had been a scene in the boyfriend's kitchen. Heather had seized a butcher knife and lunged at the boyfriend, then turned it on herself and made a gesture at slashing her wrists. Friends had brought her to the hospital. The boyfriend was nowhere in sight.

In those conversations, Heather's visitors tried to tell her that it was best to end the relationship, or at least back off. Let him go, they said, but she would not be deterred. At the same time, her manner with her male visitors was provocative and flirtatious. She craved admiration, that was clear.

"Heather," I heard one of her friends say, "don't run after him. You'll never catch him that way."

She laughed prettily. "Yes, but I can run pretty damn fast!" I wanted to slap her.

Which brought me up short. What Heather was doing, I recognized, was an extreme form of what I had often done myself. She was a needy person who camouflaged her neediness with charm. She was so needy she was blind to other people and how they felt. I never heard her mention her boyfriend's name; I never knew how long they had been together, how they met, or what he did. She never spoke about missing him; she never even admitted the attack with the butcher knife, much less expressed any remorse. This boyfriend was simply an object that promised to fill up a black vacuum inside. And, having been threatened with the loss of that object, she had reacted with the same kind of rage a person would use to fight an attacker. What he wanted, I deduced, hardly mattered. There was a cold calculation about all this I found appalling.

But it also seemed oddly familiar. I remembered myself in college, trying to talk Sam out of applying to certain medical schools he might have gotten into, trying incessantly to steer him toward marriage. I didn't stop to think about whether either of us was ready for marriage; certainly, I didn't care when he said he wasn't. I just *needed to be married*. I needed it for my self-esteem. All my subsequent relationships had held some element of that. These were love affairs which did involve love, but which also provided me with an emotional fix—always transitory, never quite enough, always holding the tantalizing possibility that enough might be found, if I could just find the right buttons to press. The thought of what I had to offer a man—of what any man who called himself my husband had some right to expect from me—had never crossed my mind.

It sounded cold; it *was* cold. Yet Heather seemed to have many friends. Not only was there the constant stream of visitors, but the phone rang incessantly with calls for her. Inclined as I was to judge her harshly, I had to admit that she was, in many ways, an attractive person. I was struck by the loyalty of her friends, and by her desperate eagerness to be appealing. Here was a person for whom no number of friends would ever be enough; no amount of admiration could ever fill the hollowness inside.

That, too, seemed familiar. Over and over, my friends had proved their loyalty to me. In the months I was with Thomas, I had cut myself off from most of them—and yet several of the people whose calls and letters I refused to answer had called or written or visited when they heard I was in the hospital, offering love and support. A couple had even offered to come stay with me for a few days when I went home. Clearly, there was something about me that was likable, worthy of love. Yet I had always discounted the love they offered. What I really wanted was their admiration.

Finally, there was the intense reaction Heather seemed to arouse in me. I couldn't stand to be around her. I could see the sadness behind her facade, the desperation, but all I felt was anger. *Get real!* I wanted to yell at her. It was similar, in a way, to the kind of rage I had felt at my grandmother, when I was a child—only Heather provoked it not by her helplessness but by her phoniness. With my newfound practice of ruthless introspection, I found myself asking a new question: If being around Heather affected me this way, could that explain some of the fierce anger I seemed to provoke in Thomas?

Then there were Thomas's children.

In their relations with me, I saw reflections of my own ambivalence. Melissa didn't know whether she liked me, or feared me, or held me in disdain. Only Peter was uncomplicated and easy, ready to run to me on the playground when he'd hurt himself, or leap on my back like a monkey when I was bending over to pick up my shoes. But as my relationship with Thomas had deteriorated and my depression grown more intense, even Peter had grown quiet and withdrawn. He was falling behind in school. Melissa had become dependent and clingy with Thomas, ready to burst into tears at almost anything. It wasn't my fault that I was sick, but it wasn't theirs, either.

Melissa said as much. One night, Thomas had come by the hospital to bring me another book, and had left the kids in the van outside for a few minutes. When he came out, Melissa leaned over the driver's seat from her perch in the back of the van and said, "It isn't fair, what she's doing to you." He reported her remark to me later. If he intended to induce guilt, it was not guilt toward him that I felt. Thomas, at least, had started this whole affair; he had sought me out and kept coming back even when he said things were over. He was an adult. He had gotten more than he'd bargained for, but at least he exercised some choice. His children had none. And now I was beginning to see how deeply disruptive my presence in their lives had become.

By now, I was well into my second week on the ward, my fifth day of freedom from suicide watch. I had in that time moved up the ladder to acquire an outside pass, which meant I could leave the ward accompanied by a friend. It was a weekend afternoon, a dreary day in the dreariest month of the year, and Thomas arrived after lunch in the van, the kids in back. The status of our relationship was unclear; he seemed consumed with concern for my welfare, yet he had the distinct air of a man who was just doing his duty. I had the sense that our affair was like a bowl of crazed glass; it wasn't possible to tell just by looking whether the cracks were now part of the design or whether the whole thing would shatter, given a nudge. I didn't dare broach the subject. I just took what he offered, gratefully. Today, we were all going to a movie.

> FEBRUARY 18: I'm feeling not so great about this afternoon. Thomas is sick with a cold; Melissa clings to her father and will barely look at me. We go to the movies … It's hard; I keep having to lay aside my ego

here, and pay attention to these children as carefully as they paid attention to me. I am not used to it, and I am not good at it. Not being good at something hurts my fucking pride.

On the way back, I manage to get Melissa to talk to me a little. She's in her customary position, wedged in between Thomas's seat and mine in the van … Little by little, we start talking about the ward, and the people she'd noticed there. I'm amazed (I always am) at the vast amount of data she collected on her brief visits. She asked specifically about Hugo, Frank, and Alice. We talk about manic depression and depression in general. Thomas joins in once or twice as we're driving down Wisconsin Avenue, but mostly it's me and Melissa—the first conversation we've had all day.

We are at the hospital. I say goodbye to Thomas and the kids and jump out, and suddenly I want to cry … How to convey the isolation caused by this disease, the sense I felt the other night of wasted years, wasted opportunities?

That moment stays in my mind: a February dusk, chill wind against my light sweater as I stood in the parking lot watching the van drive away. In my memory (though I know this is not true) the van is lit up, like the pleasure ship from that dream of many years ago, and it is getting smaller and smaller. The family I want, the husband, the sense of belonging, normal life—those things all seem to recede with it too, denied to me for reasons I can't understand. Before I went back inside, I turned my face to the brick wall and cried.

It was tricky, this business of equating marriage with normal life. On the one hand, there was the reality I could see all around me, of people locked in an unhappy marriage, or embittered by one that failed, adults still carrying psychic scars from the wars their parents had fought. My own parents' marriage—a long and happy one—had included its share of arguments and frosty silences. And my ideas about marriage had changed a lot in the years since college; having lived for a decade on my own, I now found the idea of marriage as a kind of social necessity for nice Southern girls vaguely silly, as quaint as the idea of a "nice Southern girl." But marriage was still the most powerful symbol for me of health, of connectedness, of a life fully lived. It was not the only route to such a life, but it was the route I wanted—and in that, no matter how many brave declarations of independence I read in women's magazines, I knew I was not wrong. Yet over and over, I had been thwarted. I kept choosing the wrong people, or the wrong people kept choosing me, I couldn't tell which. It seemed to me that throughout my twenties I had carried an invisible mark on my forehead which could be read a mile away by men who were emotionally healthy and available. "Stay away," it said, and they had. Then when I attracted a man who was clearly interested in marriage, I had driven him away.

I wanted a connection I couldn't have; I did not understand or value the ones I did have. It was a story I saw again and again in the ward. "Only connect!" E. M. Forster had written, but we hadn't, or couldn't, or never had. There was the doctor, lost in his personal torment, or Heather, grasping for superficial symbols of connectedness, or Luisa, looking for it through sex. It seemed to me the basic definition of any mental illness, this persistent, painful inability to simply *be* with someone else. It might be lifelong, or it might descend like a sudden catastrophe, this blankness between ourselves and the rest of the world. The blankness might not even be obvious to others. But on our side of that severed connection, it was hell, a life lived behind glass. The only difference between mild depression and severe schizophrenia was the amount of sound and air that seeped in.

One day after group, I was sitting in the dayroom, idly watching television, when Hugo sat down beside me. He was still wearing his two hospital gowns, front to back and tied together. The makeshift toga came only to his knees, exposing his stumpy, hairy legs. The thick white bandages on his wrists had gotten considerably smaller. He was in his fifties, I judged, with a face like an aging prizefighter, and thick glasses. Altogether, he was an unattractive sight. But I wasn't going to win any beauty contests myself: it was weeks since I had worn any makeup, the steady diet of brownies was padding my rear end, and my hair looked like I'd had an accident with a threshing machine. It was almost lunchtime; outside, in the hallway, I could hear the conversations of the nursing staff and the cafeteria crew, the clatter of the cart that contained our trays. People were killing time, waiting for the trays to be distributed. Pearl was sitting in her usual spot, next to the piano. Hugo and I sat on opposite ends of one of the dayroom's cheap blue sofas, two ugly people stuck together in a ward for the defective, and somehow it was clear from the deliberate way he walked over and sat down that he had decided to talk to me. It was our first and only real conversation.

Hugo had on his mind something he'd brought up in group that morning. He'd called it "the monkey on my back for all these years," referring to feeling responsible for his little brother's death. He had said that in group, and people had rushed to reassure him that no, of course he was not responsible. Now, having started to tell the story, he felt compelled to do it in detail, to finish it.

It had happened when he was five or six, he said, living in a working-class suburb outside New York. His little brother was a year younger, the natural son of the man Hugo knew as his stepfather. The younger child was a pest who followed Hugo everywhere. It was Hugo's job to watch him. Hugo longed for affection from his stepfather, but the man doted on his natural son. To Hugo, he was cold. Hugo despised his brother with a child's pure hatred.

One day the boys were in the front yard playing. A truck was coming down the street. Hugo remembered his little brother chasing him; he remembered making a conscious decision to dart across the street just in front of the truck.

"I knew I would make it, and I knew he wouldn't. The next thing I see is his brains all over the pavement." He looked down at his wrists. "I don't remember anything for seven months after that, okay? I asked my mother, 'How long have I been like this?'"

He sat there, an ugly, aging alcoholic who had never married, his hands in his lap, palms up in an attitude of uselessness. I don't remember what I said. I think it was something like, "I'm sorry," or, "It's okay." What could anyone say to that?

"I've never told the whole story to anybody before," he said. Then he got up and wandered away.

So why did you tell it to me? I thought. But slowly, over the next day or so, I began to realize he had given me a gift. Trapped behind my own glass wall, loathing my own isolation and contemptuous of others in the same trap, I only wanted escape. I wasn't really interested in anyone else's pain, except to criticize it, as I had with Heather, or observe it like some weird phenomenon. But hearing Hugo's story, I had for a moment entered somebody else's isolation. And in that moment, as simplistic as it sounded, he had offered me a fragment of that thing I craved: connection. I had only wanted it from people on the other side of the glass. Now it was as if out of dozens of people trapped with me inside that glass cage, one had stopped, turned to me, and said, "I am caught too. A connection with me may seem worthless to you, but it's the real thing. It's yours if you want it."

I left the ward two days after that encounter. Altogether, I had been there for only two weeks. My doctors were skeptical; several urged me not to rush things, to stay another couple of days or even another week. *Sure*, I thought, *you guys know I have health insurance, you know somebody will ante up*. In fact, I didn't want to listen; my compulsion to leave the hospital so soon was, in its way, another defensive rear-guard action against admitting how much trouble I had been in. I was itchy to get out and get back to work, to try to find a new definition for "normal life"—and maybe make everyone forget I had fallen apart this way. And so I prevailed: in the end, they signed me out.

But my two weeks inside Georgetown's psychiatric ward had not been wasted. I had found two things there. One was the beginnings of a rudimentary and sobering understanding that I was dealing with a real, physical illness, and that it was called depression; the other was that tiny fragment of connection. The day I checked out, I hurriedly stuck a yellow Post-it note on the glass over the nurses' station; I didn't want to deal with Hugo face-to-face. "Goodbye, Hugo, and good luck," it read. Hardly overflowing with warmth, but something.

About a year later, I tried to look him up in the phone book. His name wasn't in any of the directories for the Washington metropolitan area. I hope that didn't mean anything.

Chapter Six

The night before I left the hospital, I had a dream. I was trying to get back to my apartment from Georgetown, but there was construction everywhere. The Taft Bridge was all but demolished. Finally, the cab I was in had to stop, and I had to walk the rest of the way home, picking my way through man-sized boulders of upended concrete, roaring bulldozers, ruined buildings.

Reality was not too different. In my apartment, the relics were still there: a mostly empty wine bottle, a stack of awards and plaques, with a scrawled note on top: "To be sent to Mother." Some of the letters I had written that night had been mailed, but nobody had replied; I had apparently veiled my intentions well. The others still lay on my desk. My cats regarded me as if I had just arrived from Mars, and followed me from room to room. My friend Robin had been collecting my mail, which now lay in a stack on the bookcase. In the pile of bills and junk was my brand-new American Express Gold Card. *What do you know*, I thought, amused. *Somebody thinks I'm a good risk.*

I was not. I was still very sick. The night before, I had made the last entry in my hospital journal.

> FEBRUARY 21: I wish I felt steadier. I wish I knew how to change things about my life …I think what I fear the most is that I'll get out and things will quickly become just as fucked up as they were before.

I wasted no time getting back to work. As I had been in college, I was afraid that the minute I stopped using my mind I would lose it. There were only a few polite inquiries at the *Post* about where I'd been. The relative dearth of curiosity was a sign that everybody who was interested already knew; after all, newspeople gossip for a living. When someone occasionally pressed me for details, I said I'd been hospitalized for depression. That was embarrassing, but I didn't have the energy to carry off a believable alibi. Some people awkwardly changed the subject. Others tried to cover their discomfort with bluster. "Well, snap out of it!" one person said cheerfully—implying, I guess, that feeling better was just a matter of trying harder. It was infuriating, especially when I thought about how many times I'd told myself the same thing.

But there were people who displayed some sophisticated awareness of what was going on. The first one I encountered was, of all things, a federal judge.

"Where have you been?" he asked me one day, stopping in the corridor of the courthouse. "We haven't seen you around here for a couple of weeks." He had turned around to face me; his body language suggested that this was no casual "Howya doin'?" kind of query.

"I've been in the hospital," I said, inwardly cringing, taken unaware and anticipating another excruciating social encounter. "I had a bad episode of depression."

"I'm sorry to hear that." His next question surprised me. "Are you taking anything for it?"

"Imipramine and lithium," I said.

"You know, my sister is a manic-depressive, and she takes lithium," he said. "She says it's changed her life." We chatted about lithium for a moment; than he had to get back to his chambers. As he turned away, he said warmly, "Hope you start feeling better."

This was amazing. Here was someone—a public official, no less—who had freely talked about mental illness in his own family. He was matter-of-fact, he treated the subject seriously, and he hadn't pried. I felt, briefly, relieved.

At work, I sensed my editors were watching me more closely than usual. Most of the time, reporters on beats set their own news agendas, and lived or died by the results. But this time my editors handed me my next assignment: a trial in federal court involving the head of a city agency accused of contract fraud. It was a DBW story—"dull but worthy"—promising to trap me for weeks in a mostly empty courtroom, listening to scratchy wiretap recordings and tedious legal maneuvering. The only way I'd get out of the back pages of the metro section would be if there was a shooting in the spectator section. But I couldn't argue. It was news. In my spare time, I decided to tackle a more ambitious topic, a story on trends in search-and-seizure law created by the war on drugs.

As I expected, the trial was about as exciting as a turtle race. But perhaps without realizing it, my editors had hit on the perfect assignment for an employee suffering from severe depression. Here was something I had to show up for, every day. It required some mental concentration, though not sustained or intense. If I found myself preoccupied with my own troubles, as I often did, the turtles never wandered too far down the road; I could catch up without much trouble. Every day, I had to make sense of a certain amount of information—not much, just pieces of a jigsaw puzzle, but enough to give me a challenge. And producing stories again, even if they were buried on the obituary page, gave me a sense of accomplishment.

The wisdom of taking on a daily assignment was made even clearer by the hard time I was having with the search-and-seizure story. It required reading a lot of federal appeals court decisions, each of which connected with others in different ways. My ability to concentrate was much improved, but it was still a slow process to make sense of the pattern of legal reasoning. In cognitive terms, depression had done the most severe damage to my short-term memory and my ability to grasp abstract concepts. In practical terms, it felt as if I'd lost about 15 IQ points. Every day, I had to review what I'd done the day or two before. I wrote long memos to remind myself of what I was doing, sometimes only to find a similar memo I'd written several days before. In all, the story took me two months to put together, including many weekends at the office—half again as long as it might have taken me under better circumstances. But this time, instead of flagellating myself for being stupid, I tried to remember that I was simply working with a handicap, one which I hoped would prove temporary. Just getting the story done was a relief. When the piece eventually ran in early May, on the front page, I thought, for perhaps the hundredth time, *Now things are going to get easier.*

I yearned to get better; I told myself I *was* getting better. In fact, the depression was still there, like a powerful undertow. Sometimes it grabbed me, yanked me under; other times, I swam free. It was hard to tell which things were signs of improvement, and which were evidence of the Beast's continued power. It was later clear that the imipramine I was still taking was doing only some good—the "discontinuation refractoriness" phenomenon again. The lithium boosted the effects of the imipramine, and seemed to slow down my mood swings. But what improvement I felt was bought at the price of uncomfortable side effects. I suffered from constant thirst; I was rapidly gaining weight; in the mornings my hands shook so much it was hard not to spill my coffee.

As winter gave way to spring, I alternated between days of deep fatigue and days of high anxiety. The fatigue may have been the side effects of the drugs, or evidence of my continued depression. For whatever reason, I craved sleep. Most nights I was in bed long before dark. The anxiety, I told myself, was a sign of improvement; at least it wasn't despair. But in some ways it was worse. It was like being locked in an airtight box, about to run out of oxygen. Impossible at those moments to sit still, impossible to complete a task, impossible to do anything but get outside and walk, for miles, trying to outrace it. It was like a crazy itch, way down under my skin, and I never knew when it would attack. I felt like a bumbling Inspector Clouseau being stalked by his homicidal houseboy, Cato. The anxiety, like Cato, was a permanent resident who now and then went on a rampage. Meanwhile, I blundered about in my mental attic, peering into closets and behind doors, my vigilance no match for the wiles of my adversary.

My anxiety centered on Thomas. "At some point," he said

while I was still in the hospital, "you're going to have to give me my life back." But even as he kept reminding me that our romantic relationship was finished, he kept in frequent touch by telephone. I carried a beeper, ostensibly so the city desk could reach me while I was in the courtroom. But the city desk rarely used it. Thomas used it a lot, sometimes three times a day. As the weeks went by, we began to see each other again—except, he kept saying, we were just friends now.

Which was true, as far as it went. There were many times when he was a valuable sounding board; when I felt discouraged, he could point out specific, incremental changes which told me I was, in fact, making progress.

"You're riding out crises much better than you used to," he would say—which was true. Or, "The buzziness is gone," which was something I would never have realized on my own.

And there were the kids. Sometimes, on weekends, I'd go along on family outings. Peter and Melissa were friendly, and took my appearances in stride. They were valuable therapy: I needed not to be self-absorbed, and self-absorption is difficult to practice around children. Before, I had felt I was in anxious competition with them. Now, their thirst for adult attention felt like a tonic, a welcome escape from the prison of my thoughts.

But we were not merely friends. Thomas was still the object of my obsession, the litmus test of whether I could be healthy. I could imagine no other yardstick than his approval. And he was obsessed with me. My daybook from that year carries cryptic notes—a "T" or a star, to mark the times our late-night telephone calls ended with his invitation to come over. I knew that there was something unseemly about the way I was at his beck and call; I understood that the power I was giving him must have been a temptation nearly impossible for him to refuse. It made no difference.

In his way, he struggled against it; he frequently told me I should see other people. I tried. My daybook from that period also shows reminders of my efforts to cultivate new friendships, even to find dates. But my weirdly tangled motives must have been painfully apparent. And Thomas was deeply ambivalent.

If I so much as went out for a drink after work with a male colleague, he was jealous. Once, when I told him I had done that, he reacted with stricken disbelief, as if I'd said I had started selling my favors by the hour. "You ... are ... *kidding*," he said. Then he apologized, and then he hung up, abruptly. I felt sick with self-reproach. We didn't talk for several days. But when we spoke next, he was friendly, playful, suggestive—as if our earlier conversation had never happened. And so the obsessive game started once more.

Yet sometimes, if a few days elapsed without my hearing from him, I would begin to feel anger—a quietly building fury, rage at him and at our entanglement, which was costing me so dearly despite what I derived from it. I knew he was seeing other women; he seemed to actually enjoy dropping hints about that. Needy as I was, some spark of self-respect would make me think, *Why am I doing this?*

Mostly, I had to admit, it was my idolization of intellect. Men who appeared older, more powerful, and smarter were obvious targets for my fascination and devotion—and Thomas fit that profile. In one or two superficial ways, he also resembled the father I had adored. And he met my longing to be rescued with his own intense need for control. As for the other things—his criticism, his rages, his intolerance of people he considered less intelligent—I just assumed they were part of the package. My own father, with his emotional remoteness and alternating black and buoyant moods, had left me unprepared for the idea that intellect could coexist with gentleness, patience, or sweetness of spirit.

But subtly, in ways visible only in retrospect, I was beginning to test my old assumptions and Thomas's version of reality. It was a process that began with my new psychiatrist.

Ironically, this was a doctor Thomas had put me in touch with. My former psychiatrist had declined to visit me at Georgetown, explaining that she was not on staff there or at any other hospital and tried to limit her practice to nonhospitalized patients. She was willing to see me once I left the hospital, she said, but while I was at Georgetown her policy was not to interfere with the hospital's treatment program. It had not occurred to me that it might make a difference whether my psychiatrist was part of some hospital staff; I had never expected to be hospitalized. In truth, I didn't much care. I had been so circumspect in what I told Phyllis that it couldn't be said there was much of a bond between us. But Thomas had been incensed when he heard about Phyllis's policy; he thought she was abandoning me. At his urging, I wrote her a letter saying I was firing her.

That had left me in the lurch, with no doctor to see once I got out. Thomas had called around and gotten the names of some psychiatrists on staff at the National Institute of Mental Health who saw patients in private practice. He started there, he told me, because the odds were better that they would have people who were aware of the latest developments in psychopharmacology. He came up with three names—two men and one woman.

Her name was Eleanor McAllister.

She was tall, angular, red-haired, plainspoken, and, unlike Amanda, not in the least maternal. At first, our sessions resembled traditional doctor's office visits, in which we talked only about medications—the side effects and limitations of various antidepressants. Unlike my sessions with Amanda, my visits with Eleanor did not seem to evoke in me any childlike yearnings for approval or comfort. She was friendly but businesslike. As before, I tried to limit my conversation to physical symptoms and how the drugs seemed to be working. Meanwhile, Eleanor was keeping tabs on the same thing: I had frequent blood tests to make sure my dosage of imipramine and lithium remained in a clinically accepted therapeutic range.

After the first few sessions, we agreed to meet twice a week in a tiny upstairs office in Takoma Park. It was in a building which also rented space to a wide variety of sisterhood-empowerment, New Age, holistic-healing, crystal-therapy, massage and primal scream therapy groups. In the tiny waiting area outside Eleanor's room there was a bulletin board advertising things like seminars on Women Who Run with the Wolves. This did not appeal to me; running *from* the wolves seemed much more sensible. Obviously, this was Flake City, and everybody knew it—an impression borne out by the furtiveness with which other patients seemed to greet each other, and me, in our comings and goings.

"Hi," Eleanor would say, in her peculiarly uninflected voice, as I sat down, and the session would begin. Usually I started by telling her about my physical state and any drug side effects, and then went on to assess my mental state for the past couple of days. But it was difficult to talk. For one thing, the topics were sensitive and I was trying to be honest in my reportage. But another problem was the god-awful wailing and thumping next door. I think it was a primal scream therapy group, or possibly a primal scream marriage encounter group; at times, there seemed to be people wailing in duets. I had the impression that at least some of them were on their hands and knees, pounding the floor. I tried not to pay attention, but how could I not?

"I feel convinced I will always be alone—" (AAAAAAAAR-RRRRGH! *Thump.*) "—but I don't really know where that feeling comes from, I mean, I can remember feeling this way when I was fourteen or so—" (Muffled sounds of sobbing from the next room.)

"So why do you think that? Is that part of feeling worthless?"

"Yeah. I mean, that has to be the reason Thomas would reject me, and it—" (NO! *Thump.* NO! *Thump.* NO! *Thump.* AAAAAR-RRRRGH!)

"Eleanor," I said, "could we just meet someplace like Dunkin' Donuts or something?"

She just grinned and said no; she liked this place because the rent was cheap. It was a nice moment; I had figured out a way to make her laugh. Slowly, I began to open up to her.

Eleanor's first impression of me, she said later, was the strength of my conviction that I was inherently "defective." But every time she tried to get me to talk about that, I veered off onto the subject of Thomas—reporting some observation he had made about me, or recounting some event with him or the kids that (I thought) illustrated how defective I was. The ultimate proof of my defectiveness lay in his rejection of me as a wife, after a courtship that had begun so ardently. When he really got to know me, he had been repelled. Didn't that speak for itself?

At first, as my doctors in the hospital had done, Eleanor strove for reticence. But after three or four sessions devoted to this theme, she burst out: "This guy has a *problem*."

This was not what I wanted to hear. As painful as Thomas's criticisms of me were, I was heavily invested in them. I *wanted* him to be right. If he was right, there was some chance that I could change my behavior and be a different person. Thomas was the first person to confirm what I had always known— that there was *something wrong with me*. That recognition was fundamental, but somehow people kept missing it. Instead, they tried to reassure me by telling me that I was a wonderful, lovable person who deserved the best. My reaction was either self-pity or silent rage at their platitudes. *You don't know what the fuck you are talking about*, I would think. But Thomas looked at me and saw what I saw: the lurking shadow of the Beast.

"You *are* defective," he told me once, "but not in the way you imagine. You are not defective in inherent worth, or attractiveness,or as marriage material. You have defective brain chemistry." It was the clearest and simplest summary of the problem I had yet heard. But at the time, the clarity of his summation was immediately destroyed by his rage, fueled by the disappointment of watching his vision of a reestablished, happily married life fade away. To find hope after his grief and then to have his hope snatched away must have made him feel like the butt of a nasty cosmic joke. He was a lapsed Catholic—a Jesuitical atheist, I used to say—and his universe was vacant of God. The only target for his anger was me. "You are a *selfish, fucked-up person*," he would say at such moments—and, as with everything else he said, I took that as fact. The subtle distinction he had made earlier, which I had begun to grasp for myself in the hospital, and which Eleanor was trying to make now, kept eluding me.

Eleanor's challenge to Thomas's judgment only confirmed what I already knew, but did not admit. I had not told Eleanor about the episode when he grabbed me by the collar, or the times he had casually humiliated me in public. ("You're going to have to lose weight," he said once in a movie line, loud enough for others to hear. "I don't want to wake up one day and have a whale for a wife.")

And so Eleanor and I reached an early impasse.

"I know you think you are defective," Eleanor would say, "but it would help if you could see yourself in a different way."

Yet trusting my own perceptions created another maddening problem: every time I spoke the one thing I knew to be true, people heard something slightly different. I would say, "I'm defective," meaning "I am broken"; people would hear that as "I lack self-esteem." It was like that simpleminded passage in Stanley Jackson's book: "As to how a clinical depression came about, Jacobson thought that a diminished self-esteem was the essential feature." This was like saying that arguing with imaginary companions in public was an essential feature of schizophrenia; it either equated a symptom with its cause or, at best, treated the cause as irrelevant. *Yes*, I wanted to protest, *but people do that because something is wrong with their heads.* And so it was with depression. Yes, my self-esteem was abysmal. But saying that was not synonymous with saying I was defective; my self-esteem was abysmal *because* I was defective.

"You try living this way," I would have said to Eleanor, if I could only have found the words. "You try going through life never knowing when your perceptions are getting distorted, and not knowing, when that happens, which ones are distorted and which ones are real. You try living at the mercy of moods that sweep you away, that you can explain only by relying on the worst of your distorted perceptions. Try going to work every day when you can't even remember how to do your job, and you start wondering why they even hired you. Try doing all this while trying to live an ordinary life, and see if *your* self-esteem doesn't suffer."

But I could not say that. All I could say was, "I am defective." Eleanor was left with the task of teasing apart the meaning.

In fact, we had stumbled up against the old "mind-body

problem." How were we to understand the "I" in the sentence "I am defective"? To Eleanor, the use of that word was a depressed patient's vicious attack on himself, a symptom of disease. To me, the statement was another way of saying, "My brain is sick"—a formulation that somehow distinguished between the "I" in that sentence and the brain it owned. But if so, who was "I"? It was as if the homunculus were speaking, that "little man" that medieval physicians believed was contained in every spermatozoon and that philosophers pictured as the being who "operated" whatever lay inside the human skull. In a way, I was using the same medieval imagery. The homunculus in my head was saying, "This machinery is defective." But to anyone outside my head, including Eleanor, the "I" had only one meaning: me, the whole person. The patient.

So: I could say, "My brain is sick," and think of myself in the way that had revolted me earlier—as the mere product of a chemical abnormality in the lumpy gray organ between my ears. Or I could say that what was speaking was not my brain but some mysterious property called "consciousness," which possessed a superior knowledge my brain alone could not comprehend.

Or maybe it worked another way. Maybe my brain wasn't an organ but an *organism*—one which had parts that worked even when other parts didn't. Maybe it was that healthy part of my brain which kept trying to say, "There is something wrong here"—but kept getting misunderstood and tangled in its own message. This somehow felt closer to being right than any other way of thinking about it. But it sounded nutty—as if I thought some kind of Captain Jean-Luc Picard was up there, getting reports from the helmsman: "Collateral damage in the main warp engine, sir."

"Okay," Eleanor finally said. "If you mean you have problems with depression, that's true. But it makes things harder when you put it in such a harsh, judgmental way." And so we left it. I had more immediate and pressing concerns.

Mindful of my promise to myself in the hospital, I began to develop a safety net of friends—people who understood that I was having anxiety attacks, who would stay with me until the crisis passed. The futon in my living room played host to a steady stream of guests. Robin and Linda, old friends from Atlanta who both happened to live on my street, got used to my panicky midnight phone calls. They would throw a coat over their pajamas and walk over, then stagger out at six-thirty a.m. in time to go home to get dressed for work. I felt ashamed of my neediness. But sometimes, as I lay awake in those dark nights, the only thing that helped was to sense the steady breathing of another human being, even if it was in the next room.

Meanwhile, I read. The chemistry of depression, I was discovering, was a very interesting and mysterious subject.

Psychiatry divides the universe of mental disorders into two major categories: thought disorders and mood disorders (also known as affective disorders). Schizophrenia is the classic example of the first; depression was the classic example of the latter, although the two categories can, and often do, overlap. The analogy that came to my mind was music. Someone with a thought disorder is like a tone-deaf person trying to play a piano: he may think he is producing a melody, but to bystanders it's just noise. People with mood disorders, on the other hand, have a sense of pitch, but they are playing on a piano which is woefully out of tune. The first group are convinced it is their listeners, not themselves, who can't recognize the melody. The second group are painfully aware that the dissonance emanates from them—but they have no idea of how to tune the piano.

The problem in either case lies with neurotransmitters in the brain.

A nerve cell looks a bit like a mashed spider, with a body and splayed branches going out in all directions. In between nerve cells are gaps, called synapses. The gaps are bridged by neurotransmitters, which convert electrical impulses from one nerve cell into a chemical form, then ferry them across the synapse to a specific site on the receptor neuron. It happens every second, waking and sleeping, billions of times per day, like shimmers of sheet lightning in the brain. Scientists have not cataloged all the neurotransmitters in the brain, or their location. But three have been identified as particularly important in the study of mental illness: serotonin, norepinephrine, and dopamine.

One of the problems with schizophrenics, for example, is that they have too much dopamine floating around, bombarding receptor cells with inappropriate messages. Their brains are speeded up, disordered, chaotic; these are people who, for example, hear voices or are convinced that government spies are speaking to them through their electric typewriters. I had run into such people several times over the years. A striking number of them wandered into newspaper offices because they were frantic for relief and had developed the notion that publicity would force their tormentors to stop. One man kept his head wrapped in aluminum foil; another wrote a long letter describing how he had mutilated his scalp, trying to dig under his hair to get the electrodes out. To sane people, such actions seem horrifying and bizarre. But I was beginning to see it differently, as the reaction of a brain keenly aware of an inner malfunction, and even vaguely aware of what it was—yet blindly trying to cure it by removing an external "cause." If you thought of schizophrenia that way, wrapping your head in aluminum foil made a kind of sad, intuitive sense.

People who are depressed suffer from low levels of at least two neurotransmitters, norepinephrine and serotonin. Arguments have gone on for years among researchers about which is more important, but the recent research I was studying seemed to confirm that low serotonin levels were a major factor. Again, here was a physical description of a problem which made intuitive sense. The expression "My mind was going in circles" might be not simply a metaphor but an actual physical description: if you didn't have enough neurotransmitters in your brain, the electrical impulses they were supposed to ferry could simply wander around in circles for lack of anywhere else to go, or they could get lost. So the depressed person would obsess about things, or forget them.

Learning more about my illness gave me some sense of mastery and control, two things the Beast had always robbed me of. It also helped me grasp a counterintuitive idea: that there were occasions when my emotions might actually be caused by something happening *inside* my head, not by anything outside. Always before, I had struggled to make sense of my black periods by finding a "reason" for them in people or events. At eight, the reason had been President Kennedy's assassination. At thirty, it had been my unmarried state. Both of those external perceptions had been real; both had caused me sadness. But neither was responsible for *all* of my feelings, or for their intensity, or for their stubborn refusal to be shaken. My feelings had been so strong that I had freighted outside events with significance they did not have, in order to justify them. Here, finally, was the reason for the nagging feeling I'd had over the years that these external explanations didn't really make sense: it was because they hadn't.

Now, walking from the subway back to my apartment at night, feeling the familiar sense of brooding hopelessness, I could try out an alternate explanation. *It's the sickness*, I would say silently to myself. *Just wait it out. It's the sickness.*

It was now almost summer, and for all the drugs and the medical attention I was getting, my improvement seemed very slow. And yet, though each day seemed an ordeal, I was beginning to think with a new kind of clarity. I began to come to a realization that, in retrospect, looks almost comically obvious. But at the time, it occurred to me with a kind of slow, cold terror: This illness could kill me.

This was no isolated battle I was fighting, no mere quest for personal improvement. It was a guerrilla war I had been fighting for many years, and recent events made it clear the tide of battle was not going in my favor. For the first time, I began to see a pattern over the past three decades in things I had previously ignored, or had made sense of only by attributing them to personal defects. Hiding behind the toilet in fourth grade. Taking the bottle of aspirin in high school. The nights of heart-pounding insomnia in college. The dogged search for rescue in relationships, the wrenching sobs on my bedroom floor and months of despair when those failed. The relief I had gotten so many times over the years when alcohol temporarily released me from my prison of self; the nights spent warding off the jitters with glass after glass of white wine (so yuppie, so chic—surely not harmful). "My hill-and-dale girl," my mother had called me, when I was five. Neither of us had any idea how right she had been.

The pattern was hard to track—my memories were so subjective, so jumbled—but I began to try. I took sheets of paper and drew graphs, trying to chart a lifetime spent falling through trapdoors. I couldn't re-create every dip and hill, but I could see the rough outline of a clear up-and-down pattern. It applied to everything in my life, in ways benign and sinister, not just to periods of depression. My working habits, for instance, had always been very uneven. I could put in extended spells of hard and productive work, followed by periods of relative slacking off that lasted weeks or even months; it had never gotten me in trouble because I was by nature pretty efficient and managed to stay afloat even during my down times. The overall pattern even applied to the up-and-down fluctuations of my weight since adolescence. Over the years, I had appeared in some snapshots as thin, almost haggard; at other times I had been decidedly plump. No amount of attention to diet had ever fundamentally altered this pattern.

At many points, I had recognized that various aspects of my life seemed to constitute a kind of sine curve, like the kind we drew in high school calculus; in those moments, I glimpsed my mental topography from the crest of a hill. Once, after a bad period on my first job, I'd bought a coffee mug to keep in the office which had a wavy green border around the bottom—a visible reminder which, I had thought, would recall past mistakes and help me negotiate around the next dip in the path. It didn't. I achieved great insights many times over the years, and lost them just as frequently.

Now, for the first time, I had begun to recognize the nature and form of my illness, and to force it into a grudging retreat. But I also now knew it would be back—if not next week, then next month, or next year. And if I could not find better weapons to fight it with, the next time I might be too tired to fight. If that happened, if I ever had to face going back to the hospital or living through another few months like the period I was living through now, I was going to choose death.

I saw this for the first time with clear eyes, a vision stripped of sentiment. This was not some problem susceptible to one-stop solutions; no pill, no hospital, no magazine article, no particular school of therapy, was alone capable of saving me. I was that person I had dreamed of years ago, headed out to a dark and chartless sea on my tiny raft toward that lighted pleasure ship on the horizon. On that lighted ship, I imagined the warmth of human flesh, people to be with, a life to be lived. On my raft, there was only me and my raggedy baggage. And now, like a weight pressing down between my shoulder blades, I felt the icy hand of necessity.

Ruthlessly, I began to ditch everything not essential to survival.

For several weeks in May and June, I threw away things—old college textbooks, mementos from trips, clothes I no longer wore but which had sentimental associations, books I had once loved, hair dryers, outdated prescriptions, letters from friends, old birthday cards, childhood jewelry. I quit wearing makeup. I took the family pictures on display in my living room and removed them from frames and stored them in a closet. I didn't know whether I was preparing for death, or preparing to ride out a storm. I only knew I could not afford excess baggage.

I was equally ruthless with people. Despite everything, I had always made friends easily. Now, I discovered, it was actually possible to have too many—too many well-meaning people who thought that all I needed was some ego stroking, that my difficulties would be alleviated "if you just take some time for *yourself*." I could not explain to them that taking time for myself was precisely what I was trying to *stop* doing, that breaking out of this glass box I was in required *not* being content with who I was. There were other people, too, who were like me, struggling with their own demons. I couldn't afford to keep them around, either. We were like veterans in the same combat unit—except that I had decided to desert this army; I had to leave them behind. Still others were simply comfortable with the Tracy they had always known. Either they didn't much care if that person was comfortable with herself, or they found it more convenient not to think about the question.

To all of them, I applied the same inflexible rule: If they could not offer immediate, concrete help, I cut them off. I had no time for them, their lives or their problems; I had no energy to explain. Years before, when Patti and I first became housemates and she was going through a divorce, she had rejected my idea of buying some house plants with the remark, "I don't want to be responsible for a single other living thing except myself." Now I knew how she had felt. As I had done once before, because of Thomas, I did not answer letters or phone calls. If people took offense, I steeled myself to live as I had not lived before, without their approval.

There were casualties. One of the first was my friend Linda, who lived across the street. We had been neighbors in the same apartment house in Atlanta before a career move took her to Washington several years before I arrived. Linda was a beautiful woman, an authentic Southern belle from Birmingham who bore more than a passing resemblance to a young Katharine Hepburn. She was also an unreconstructed prefeminist. She structured her life largely around men and made no apologies for it. Her code and mine were fairly similar; it was just that Linda was more overt about her preoccupation. Now, seeing me not even bothering to put on mascara before I left the house, Linda was baffled and alarmed. One day she came over, sat me down beside a window where the light was good, and actually started putting makeup on my face herself. I was irritated, but I tried not to show it. Then, over dinner a few days later, we got into a major argument. She told me that these changes I was making were a misguided attempt to forget my Southern roots, to deny my true self and become some kind of inside-the-Beltway creature of my new job—in short, to become a snob. I was furious. The part about forsaking my roots was silly. But I found myself unable to explain what I was doing. On one level, for instance, the makeup issue was also silly: when the most pressing issue seemed to be on what terms I would live my life from here on, makeup did not seem a priority. But on another level, it was significant: it was a shedding of the mask I had first put on in adolescence. I wanted not to be phony, not even in the most trivial of ways.

We were eating in a run-down Afghanistan restaurant around the corner from the street we both lived on. I tried to say these things to her, but as dinner progressed it became clear that we were talking past each other. Afterwards, we walked out to the street, increasingly frosty with each other.

"I'm sorry you feel this way," I said coldly, attempting to cut the conversation off. We were standing on the corner, just outside her apartment building.

"No, I don't think you are sorry," she retorted. I turned away from her and walked home. I cut her off—my exasperating but well-meaning friend, who had stayed with me on many dark nights. From that moment, we lived across the street from each other as strangers.

Later, I heard versions of the same accusation from other old friends in Atlanta, who had concluded that working for the *Washington Post* had turned me into a media social climber, that I had shaken them off like dust from my shoes. "You were out of here," one of them said, with bitterness. "You dropped off the radar screen." *Let them think that*, I thought grimly, and crossed names out of my address book. Thomas said, "I see you are finally making some serious choices here"—thinking, no doubt, that I was finally taking to heart his advice about ditching these provincial people from my past. My reaction to his remark was another shock: *I'm not doing this for you, buddy.*

It was painful, this shredding of the social network I had built up so carefully over the years, and I was extreme in doing it. I cut myself off not only from people who would have hindered me, but from some who would have helped. I wounded innocent people, and those relationships would later take time to heal. And yet, even now, I am not sorry. This discipline, harsh as

I made it, was a kind of mental toughness I badly needed. It was, at least, active. I was used to passivity, being overwhelmed by misery; I excelled in self-pity. Now I began to see self-pity as an unaffordable luxury, maybe a fatal one. There was a novelty button sold at the cash register of the American City Diner on Connecticut Avenue, probably intended for parents of small children, which I appropriated for myself. It had the word "WHINE" on it, overlaid by a red circle and diagonal slash. Underneath it said, "No whining allowed." That became my new liturgy. I repeated it a lot; I had to.

One book in my small but growing library on depression was a volume entitled *Cognitive Therapy of Depression*, by Aaron T. Beck, A. John Rush, Brian F. Shaw, and Gary Emery. I had put it aside earlier because the 1979 copyright made me think it might be out of date. The phrase "cognitive therapy" was not new. I vaguely associated it with an old vaudeville gag: Patient: "Doctor, it hurts when I do this." Doctor: "Well, then don't do that,"—that is, as a technique that taught people to deal with unpleasantness by avoiding it. Now I picked up the book and started to read; I was either going to use it or throw it away. It was slow going, especially in the early chapters—a sea of turgid prose, featuring a lot of words ending with "ize" and "ism." But as I skipped ahead, I began to realize it had something other psychiatric textbooks lacked: a step-by-step dissection of the mental habits bred by depression, and practical suggestions for changing them.

For example, the chapter entitled "Depressogenic Assumptions" contained an example of the distorted premises depressed patients depend on, without realizing it. "Major premise: 'If I don't have love, I am worthless.' Special case: 'Raymond doesn't love me.' Conclusion: 'I am worthless.'" *That* line of reasoning certainly sounded familiar; all I had to do was substitute "Thomas" for "Raymond." Seeing it in print made me realize the way some of my rigid, absolute "rules" had led, inexorably, to catastrophic conclusions. It was useful to get a better intellectual grasp of the flaws in that thinking. Yet, contrary to all the assumptions I'd ever made about therapy, understanding what I was doing did not help me stop. If I still *felt* worthless, as I often did, that was the explanation my brain produced. It was a matter of intense emotion, in the face of which logic was a puny ally.

I kept on reading the Beck book a little every night, as if it were a computer manual, skimming the parts I didn't need to know and focusing on what looked useful. In this manner I came to Chapter 7, "Application of Behavioral Techniques." Some of the suggestions seemed gimmicky; using a wrist counter to record my "dysfunctional" thoughts did not appeal to me. But the chapter also mentioned written homework assignments, such as scheduling specified daily "activities" and keeping a chart of my progress. I seized upon this. The idea of writing things down and keeping some kind of chart was a congenial concept for any former nerd. I talked about it with Eleanor, and decided to assign some homework to myself. The page is still in my notes, dated April 3, 1990: "My six goals for the next six months."

I remember that as a particularly bleak day—sticky and warm outside, the city a mass of blooming azaleas and forsythia, brightness outside and darkness in my mind. Marion Barry's drug possession trial was set to start in federal court in early June. It was attracting international attention, and I was one of four *Post* reporters assigned to it. My colleague Michael York and I would be writing the daily trial story. There was no chance I would be "cured" by then, whatever that meant. My goal was to avoid failure.

So I wrote my six goals.

Goal one was the most important: to reach out and cultivate friends—not just people I happened to strike up conversations with, but people I knew were living reasonably healthy and balanced lives.

Some of the most fascinating people I had ever known were alcoholics or people with problems like my own. Their lives tended to be dramatic and interesting, their love affairs tragic or passionate or both. Healthy people—the happily single, people with spouses and kids, people who had found that much discounted thing called ordinary love—I had dismissed as boring, even as I secretly envied the lives they led. Now I began to take a closer look at them, noting how they coped with their own problems, what their daily lives were like. They all seemed to have one basic similarity: they were all, in some way or another, outer-directed people. "Outer-directed" did not mean "altruistic." These were not necessarily people who spent their time in soup kitchens. In some ways, the focus of their energies was quite self-interested, aimed at their own families or close friends. But within those confines, I now saw, were individuals who didn't want or need a great deal of time to dissect their own psyches or analyze old pain. They were too busy *living*—putting in a full day's work, making a casserole, singing a child to sleep.

Years of therapy had instilled in me an unquestioning belief in the Platonic maxim "The life which is unexamined is not worth living." But what if the corollary was also true? What if the unlived life was not worth examining? Was self-examination an endless project, or was it the means to a larger end?

I started to take social risks. I began to experiment with straightforwardness. If one of these people asked me, with genuine interest, how I'd been, I would no longer try to parry that query with a shrug or a lie, or with the kind of combative "Wanna make something of it?" self-exposure I'd practiced at first. "To be honest, I've been struggling with depression the last couple of months," I would say. The tone mattered; it was important to say it simply, without defensiveness. From now on, I promised myself, I would maintain this kind of honesty in all my dealings with others; it would be honesty as unadorned as I could make it.

And, then as I am apt to do, I took my new rule to extremes.

Once I called up a male acquaintance to explain that one of the reasons I'd called him for lunch was to let him know I was available for a date. (He wasn't. He's probably still trying to work out what prompted that disclosure.) Sometimes I went back to friends to clarify some remark I'd made they didn't even remember. And there were a few times when I subjected people to the kind of unwanted self-disclosure usually offered by sloshed strangers on a nearby barstool. But there were other times when

I began to sense that, contrary to all my expectations, disclosing this deformity of mine actually made people like me better. Far from shutting down conversations, honesty seems to start them. Bizarre, but true. One night I went to dinner with a co-worker I was just getting to know, and though I don't remember exactly what we talked about, I recall that she impulsively threw her arms around me as I was on my way out. I was embarrassed and gratified; I had no idea what that was all about. Later, she told me, "You just seemed so fragile that night."

It was not clear to me at the time what this meant, but in retrospect I saw it as the beginning of a new realization—that friends could be more than security blankets for lonely times, that real friendship was the merger of the creative energies of two different people, a whole greater than the sum of its parts. It wasn't that I had never had that before, but where it had existed I had not valued it. Now, I began to recognize it in unexpected places—in an old friend whose worth I had overlooked, in a new friend whose value I was just beginning to see.

By whatever means, the unwritten assumption behind Goal one was to become less self-absorbed and more aware of others. Learning to do that was like learning how to ski. I had to watch how other people did it, risk doing it myself, and fall down a lot.

Often, I found the simplest mental tricks to be the most useful. I was not, for instance, accustomed to waiting to get on or off elevators. The minute the doors opened, I would step forward. *Outta my way*, I was thinking, except that my stated rationale tended to be more self-serving—something like, *These people will have more room if they just let me go first*. Now I started to train myself to give someone else first shot at the door. I called it "the elevator rule." It didn't change my life, but I found that if I paid attention to it, I somehow became more aware of other people—where their bodies were, whether they were holding packages, the expressions on their faces. And that was another small break from relentless self-absorption. I began to take note of people in this way in other places—on the bus, on the street corner. They revealed themselves in many ways; to the observant, we were all much closer to being naked than we thought.

The other goals tended to be more down to earth. Goal two, for instance: "Keep up with diet and exercise program." I often found that even when I felt exhausted, going to the gym and working out seemed to restore energy, not deplete it. Or goal three: "Pay a lot of attention to work. It's my solace, it's my career. It *matters*." I felt guilty about the way I had been performing at my job for so many months. But this wasn't just about assuaging guilt; it was practical. There were no trust funds in my future. Paying attention to my job at the *Post* was the best way of preserving my financial stability, not to mention a health insurance policy that had taken care of last winter's whopping $10,000 hospital bill from Georgetown. Then there was goal four: "Keep up with therapy and medication."

Goal five was: "Make serious efforts to meet men. Don't be passive about this; it turns you into a victim." This, to be blunt, didn't work. The fact that I even wrote it down was a measure of how much I was lying to myself about my continuing obsession with Thomas. But having this goal at least forced me to be active about meeting new people. If I had not had this fiction on which to base my efforts, it would have been much harder to break out of my social exile. Calling up people I barely knew and asking them to lunch felt like a form of emotional panhandling. It was especially tricky in a city like Washington, where it is assumed that no one goes to lunch unless they have an agenda they want to discuss. My agenda was: *I am lonely, I need friends.* Could you say that without clearing out the restaurant? I didn't think so. But oddly enough, trolling for dates was an acceptable lunch pastime; people regarded it as either a form of networking or a straightforward desire to get laid.

Goal six was an inspiration, though I wasn't to know that until much later: "Do volunteer work, preferably with children." At the time, I wrote it down because it sounded good, and because I had discovered through Thomas's kids how much relief children could be from relentless navel gazing. Of all the goals, this would prove to have the most far-reaching importance. But that would come later.

I remembered hearing from a friend in Weight Watchers

that weekly evaluations were better than daily ones, because day-to-day assessments were subject to momentary ups and downs. So Saturday mornings became my weekly assessment day. But on a daily basis, my job was to do *one thing* that would advance one of those six goals. I didn't have to succeed; all I had to do was seriously try. It could be something like making a lunch date. It could be calling a volunteer group to ask them for a brochure on signing up; it could be going to the gym. The only thing I did not allow myself was time off. There were no "mental health days" in my plan at this stage. I was so afraid of lapsing back into the abyss that I didn't dare take chances.

One thing per day. It doesn't sound like much, but sometimes it was almost more than I could do. A law clerk friend invited me to a party one Saturday night, and I went. The noise and bright social talk were almost physically painful. Standing in that crowded room holding a beer, I felt like some poor creature that had been boiled and peeled. But that night as I got into bed, I knew I had done my one thing for the day. Each day I succeeded at my one thing was one more small win against the Beast.

Other experiences were better. I signed up for "Christmas in April," a one-day volunteer project sponsored by the *Post*, in which employees picked out one house, usually belonging to an elderly person, and spent the day painting, repairing, cleaning, polishing, and spackling. The appointed Saturday arrived, and I woke up cursing myself for this foolhardy venture, this bleeding heart do-goodism which was going to wreck an entire weekend. I cursed myself as I dressed, and I cursed the traffic as I drove to a run-down neighborhood in an unfamiliar part of the city. This was a stupid, stupid idea, I said to myself, and then somebody gave me a paintbrush. At the end of the day I realized I had painted an entire bathroom and learned how to replace panes of glass in a French door. And I had a really unfamiliar feeling of *usefulness*.

On my weekly evaluations, I arbitrarily assigned a number to each goal, according to how well I thought I'd done at it. Each item was scored 0 through 10, so 60 was the maximum possible score. I tried to make the scoring generous but honest. Week after week, I found that adding up my numbers gave me a total that reflected more achievements than I was giving myself credit for. Here was experimental proof of what Eleanor kept telling me—that my perceptions were distorted, that I was doing much better than I realized. And since it was my own reality check, it was impossible to argue with it.

Another technique I picked up from the Beck book involved friends. If I felt overwhelmed with tears and anxiety, I called Eleanoror Thomas, or sometimes my friends Tim and Priscilla in New York. Their job was to list, specifically, things I had done lately I hadn't given myself credit for, to point out ways in which I was making progress. This had overtones of that sign I'd seen at Suburban Hospital the night I fled the mental ward there: "Cut out and make valentines." But even such simpleminded tasks had value. Priscilla might remind me: "You know, you did clean your apartment last weekend, you didn't just stay in bed." Or Eleanor would say, "Yes, I know you're feeling anxious right now, but anxiety never killed anybody; just wait and it will subside." Thomas would point out: "But your search-and-seizure story made the front page; I heard somebody in my department talking about how good it was." The only rule was that the comment had to be an unassailable fact. General statements I could easily defeat with another: "But you're a good person." "No, I'm not; I'm defective."

But the single most valuable tool was the one that sounds the most mindless: rote repetition. It could be verbal or written, spoken aloud or just thought. When an anxiety attack came, my thoughts began to funnel down, tighter and tighter, into a tiny point of concentrated, furious energy. Always before, the onslaught had been unstoppable. Now, I found that rote repetition could arrest its progress, and sometimes even make the anxiety go away. When I felt the familiar hollowness in the pit of my stomach, the first prickling of my skin, I would quickly try to come up with a phrase to repeat. It had to be a concrete, positive message, not a nonsense mantra but something that would help me through a bad moment. Sometimes I would write it down, as if I were a student kept after school; other times, I just repeated it to myself.

"Every day, I'm a little bit better."

"I *will* have a family someday."

Over time, I found the most effective way of doing this was to combine the message with some physical action—so that, for instance, walking down the street to work, I could time the words to the sound of my heels on the pavement. Then the words acquired a kind of poetic meter. The "family" one, for example, was in triplets, one foot per line, with the stress on the first beat in each foot and the "I" functioning as a kind of downbeat:

"I/WILL/have a/family some-/day."

It was the Parris Island method, the way Marine recruits got themselves through twenty-mile hikes carrying fifty pounds of gear. Sea chanteys were another example; so was the call-and-response singing African slaves had used in the cotton fields of the South. The words reinforced the action; the action reinforced the words. Taken together, it was as if a bulldozer were crashing through the underbrush of neurons in my brain, creating a new road, obliterating the paths that had been there before. Those old paths had been the automatic negative thoughts—"I am defective" or "I am not worth loving." Relentless and inexhaustible, they had existed on a level below conscious thought, which had been helpless to repel them. Seeing my distorted thinking patterns dissected on the page in the Beck book had clarified my intellectual understanding but had not touched the root problem.

Insight, self-analysis—all the techniques I had acquired so laboriously in years of traditional talk therapy—offered no help; applying logic to anxiety was like trying to reason with a swarm of bees. The tools of psychotherapy were useful in analyzing how I dealt with other people. But depression was a problem that began in my brain; whatever difficulties I had in getting along with people—and that had never been my worst problem—was a symptom, not the cause. Rote repetition went straight to the source of the malfunction. It was mental jujitsu, a way to take the very strength of my foe and use it for defense.

It was a crude method—anti-intellectual, in the sense that it did not rely on analysis—but it worked.

Later, I was struck by the similarities between the *ad hoc* program I created for myself that summer and the twelve-step recovery methods of Alcoholics Anonymous and Narcotics Anonymous. Their goals tracked closely with mine: honesty in all things, especially with myself; clear understanding of my strengths and weaknesses; the laying aside of defensiveness and pride to accept help from others; the sometimes painful moving away from people who could not support my efforts.

The reason for the similarity, I think, is that depression and substance abuse are rooted in the same behavior: psychological denial. Depression is an underlying condition behind a lot of substance abuse, including alcoholism—though the extent of that overlap, and the frequency with which one leads to the other, is a subject of debate. The emotional numbness of depression, the gradual sifting away of emotional response that occurs like color draining from a photograph, is a lot like the psychological denial of the drug addict. There are differences: an addict has to buy something to induce this numbness, while depression steals up on the brain; it is an altered state that develops more slowly, without the aid of external chemicals. But the effect of both kinds of denial is the same: the sufferer develops a delayed recognition of what his own feelings are, and at the same time loses the ability to see the effect of his emotional state on the people around him.

At some point, honesty—excruciating, self-lacerating, merciless honesty—becomes the only antidote, the only agent strong enough to tear through the mental labyrinth created by all those walls of denial. The difference, again, is that for substance abusers, it seems necessary for that honesty to work from the outside in—through the painful confrontations of AA group meetings, or in family "interventions" when the addict gets literally cornered by people who refuse to let him off the hook.

With depression, the honesty has to start on the inside. The classic substance abuser is the person who blames himself for nothing; the classic depressive is the person who blames himself—though perhaps in secret—for everything. The effect of bluntly confronting a depressed person with the evidence of the damage he has caused to himself and others can be devastating if it comes at the wrong time, or comes couched in harsh and judgmental terms. The honesty that I painfully acquired on my own, during that summer, was a version of the honesty Thomas had urged on me months earlier, in the worst of my despair, and a continuation of the journey I began while I was in the hospital. But at the time, Thomas's confrontations had felt like acid poured on my burns; I had been barely sturdy enough to withstand it.

And yet, through that process, I had learned another lesson which proved to be a crucial part of my healing: the difference between feeling shame and taking responsibility. Lacerated by Thomas's reproaches, I had felt nothing but shame—an essentially self-referential state in which my thoughts focused entirely on how awful *I* felt about the terrible things *I* had caused to happen. It was passive; it was a way to wallow in my feelings without doing anything about them. It was precisely that aspect which had so enraged Thomas, and had escalated our confrontations to vicious levels. Later, I was able to look back and see what I had done: I *had* been indifferent to the children; I *had* been self-absorbed; I had been emotionally shut down when Thomas had asked for my love. His reactions had been as destructive as my illness, but that did not change the fact that he was reacting to something real.

Looking back at that, I learned to say: *Yes, that is what happened. I did do those things*—and learned that the shame I felt at doing so would not kill me. The very act of looking back, in fact, was a way of taking responsibility for what had happened. I had been sick. Because of that, destructive things had happened, both to me and to people around me. Feeling shame about that was only the first step; the more important job was to try to understand my illness and its effects, and to take all the precautions I could to ensure those things did not happen again.

That subtle but crucial distinction—between feeling shame and taking responsibility—was illustrated for me in something that happened about a month after I got out of the hospital. Ironically, it was another sentencing hearing in a murder case. Like the Linda Johnson case, it happened in D.C. Superior Court; as in her case, the victim was a child.

Or, more precisely, two children. Padrica Hill had strangled her three-year-old son and her eight-year-old daughter on a morning in April 1988 while she had been in a cocaine-induced paranoid state. In the untidy pile of papers that constituted the public court file on her case, I found the results of an examination by a psychiatrist hired by the defense: "Major depression, recurrent, severe (underlying condition); cocaine dependence; cocaine delirium."

In the story I wrote for the *Post*, I quoted what Hill said to Judge Ricardo Urbina that day in court.

"I don't feel joy real often," she told Urbina. "I usually feel real sad all the time. But my kids cut across that sadness." She did not understand why she had turned to crack, why she had committed the murders, she continued. "'Sorry' doesn't fit … you do what you gotta do, Your Honor." Then she sat down at the defense table, put her head on her arms, and sobbed.

This time, I heard no self-defensive pleading in her tone. This was despairing acceptance of a horrific truth. Unlike Linda Johnson, Padrica Hill didn't have much to say; her statement took only about thirty seconds. And she pleaded for nothing. With Johnson, I had felt anger at her effrontery: how dare she kill a baby and then beg for our pity? Padrica Hill understood that her own feelings were irrelevant, in the face of the enormity of her deed: "'Sorry' doesn't fit." She asked for nothing; she awaited the consequences.

Urbina sentenced her to twenty-five years. "If there ever was a case that was a graphic and dramatic and tragic example of how drugs can kill, this is it," he said. I saw what he meant, but in this case I thought his formulation was only half right. For Padrica Hill, drugs had not been an isolated choice, but a response to depression. To say that only one of those factors had killed her children was like saying a gun could fire without a bullet.

Not all of this was clear to me at the time. In fact, there were only glimmers of understanding; the day I covered Padrica Hill's sentencing, I was still far from fully grasping the distinction I was seeing.

But, as I had done so many times before, I filed it away in my head.

By these means—imperfectly realized insights, mental tricks, self-assigned homework, antidepressants, and the help of a good psychiatrist—I made it through the summer of Marion Barry's cocaine possession trial.

Later, I counted up the clips: thirty-five days that summer when my name was on a front-page story, not counting smaller stories that ran inside. Every morning, I got up and spent most of the day at the courthouse, monitoring testimony, tracking leads, nabbing people in the hall to interview, responding to countless inquiries from the city desk. By midafternoon, I was usually back in the *Post* newsroom, writing the lead for the next day's story while Mike stayed behind to follow the courtroom proceedings to their conclusion for the day. When he was done, at about five-thirty or so, I incorporated his material into what I had already written for the first edition. Once that was done, we'd usually go back to do a more leisurely rewrite for the later editions, or try to fill stubborn holes in the story that had developed during the day. At some point, all the reporters assigned to the story would talk to each other or with editors, or both, to figure out who was doing what the next day. Most nights, none of us got home until nine, and I don't think I had a weekend off for two months.

But hard work was no act of heroism. It was self-preservation. Thomas was withdrawing from my life. Without work to distract me, I would have drowned. I drove myself so hard that my editors got worried—fearful, I thought, that they had foolishly assigned a major story to someone with a mental defect. I was prickly and defensive, determined to prove them wrong. In fact, my editors were being models of understanding. I was working hard, and so they took a risk. But they had no idea of what they were getting into.

Just before Christmas, I had had my first experience with a baffling health problem: an episode of severe, cramping stomach pain, centered just above my navel. It had kept me up all night, vomiting and writhing in intermittent agony, then mysteriously abated the next morning. Since then, the attacks of stomach pain had become gradually more frequent, several times sending me to a hospital emergency room in the middle of the night just for pain relief. That spring, my internist referred me to a gastroenterologist, who ordered a sonogram and discovered I had gallstones. I was not thrilled at the prospect of surgery—it seemed that lately I was spending as much time in hospitals as I had immediately after the car accident—but at least it promised to cure my mysterious ailment. There was one complication: because of abdominal surgery performed at the time of the car accident, twenty-two years earlier, I had scar tissue. That meant no quickie "Band-Aid" surgery of the type now most often used for gallbladder removal, but a full abdominal incision.

"I need to be back at work by the time jury selection is finished," I told the surgeon.

"Piece of cake," he said. "We'll have you out of here in no time."

Once again, my mother wanted to come up; once again, I refused. Consumed by the urgency I felt about my job, I just wanted to get this over and done with. No doting mothers, no languid convalescence for me. Before dawn one Thursday morning in early June, I caught a cab to Georgetown Hospital, checked myself in, and awoke several hours later minus a gallbladder. Two days later, I went home. The postoperative pain was much worse than I had imagined, but by that weekend I was out of the house, carefully taking my first walk up the street.

The hospital instructions had said to allow three weeks for recuperation. This was advice I might have paid attention to, except for one thing: the lack of physical activity was exacerbating my depression-related anxiety. Being still was a mental torture far worse than the pain in my gut. The following Thursday, exactly one week after my surgery, I was back in the newsroom, working at my desk. I wore a bulky cotton sweater to hide the thick surgical bandages wrapped around my middle.

In late afternoon, I looked down at myself and froze: spreading across my middle was a dark, reddish stain. I had been moving around too much, and my incision had begun to drain. I shoved my chair up against my desk, hiding my sweater, while I tried to think of what to do. I could imagine the sensation it would create if I rose from my desk, ghoul-like, and croaked, "Help!" But casually strolling out the door didn't seem the thing either; I looked like a recent gunshot victim. Finally I picked up the phone and called my immediate editor, John Mintz, who was sitting about thirty feet away.

"You have to come back here," I said, and hung up. John was on deadline, and normally he would have said, irritably, "What is it?" but something in my voice must have told him this was unusual. He appeared a few seconds later. When he saw me his face went white.

"Stay right there," he said. "Don't move." I did as he said, feeling really stupid. The appearance of bodily fluids in the workplace is not covered in etiquette books, and so I had no idea what to say or do. It felt as if I'd developed some weird female problem nobody had ever encountered before. In just a moment, John was back with our boss, Mary Jo Meisner.

"Come with me," she said. I picked up my purse and a manila file folder to hold across my stomach, and meekly followed her out the door. We drove to Georgetown Hospital's emergency room, which was starting to look really familiar. Mary Jo sat in the examining room, like a stern den mother, while an intern took a look and assured us that it was just the incision draining, nothing to worry about. He patched me up with a new bandage, and we drove back to the newsroom. Mary Jo went back to the city desk and I went to my desk and finished the story I'd been working on. But as soon as the first deadline was past, Mary Jo came back and took me into an empty office nearby. We needed, she said, to have a talk.

Milton Coleman, who ran the *Post's* metro section, was worried about me, she said. *She* was worried about me. Even before this incident today, it had been clear that I was under a strain. But this—coming to the office straight from surgery—this was more than worrisome. This was *strange*.

"You just don't look well," she said. Her face was grave. "We want you to go home." *Right*, I thought, *just long enough for somebody else to get their hands on my story*.

"It's okay," I said. "I'm sorry about what happened here, but—" Mary Jo wasn't having any of it. Reluctantly, I followed her orders and went home. I lasted there for three days, holed up inside my stuffy apartment with nowhere to go and nobody to go with. The enforced idleness raised my anxiety level to a white-hot temperature; I couldn't read or even sleep. The following Monday, I was back at the office. This time, perhaps wisely, Mary Jo and Milton backed off.

Jury selection in the mayor's cocaine possession trial was finished, and the first day of testimony was about to start. So much was at stake—for me, for the paper, for the city.

The proceedings lasted throughout one of Washington's infamous summers, in an atmosphere of tension between the mostly white news media and Barry's mostly black supporters. The same tensions were running through the *Post* newsroom; there were frequent and heated disagreements among reporters and editors about how to cast a story, the nuances of particular words, whether a particular fact deserved prominent mention or not. There was also a growing rift between Milton and Mary Jo, who sometimes conducted their arguments on opposite sides of my computer terminal while I was trying to write. The intensity of feeling was evident when the FBI videotape of Barry smoking crack cocaine was played in the courtroom. Sitting in the press section, I heard a collective intake of breath among everyone watching, as if we had all simultaneously been punched in the stomach.

I saw the mayor through my own peculiar lens: as a person who so feared his own weakness that he could not—simply *could not*—see himself as he really was. Where others saw defiance against a justice system racially oppressive to blacks, I saw cowardice. Whenever I saw him jauntily waving to his supporters as if the trial were a campaign rally, I felt anger, but it was mixed with shame. To the mayor, I was just another representative of the white media establishment, there to chronicle his humiliation. He had no idea how much we had in common.

At the time, I noted all this—my own feelings, the tension around me—the way a sleepwalker might note the temperature. One afternoon, on deadline, I sat at my computer terminal in the newsroom writing a lead paragraph over and over; Milton wanted a "big-picture" angle; Mary Jo wanted gritty specifics from that day's testimony. After three or four rounds, I got up to get some coffee and let them argue it out. "How many *Post* reporters does it take to write a Barry story?" I joked later to my colleagues. "Only one. But it takes at least three editors to move his fingers on the computer keys." In some ways, detached was the best way to be.

The verdict came late on a Thursday afternoon in early August. Foolishly, I had left the courthouse to wait at home for the cable-television installation man, who arrived five minutes before the city desk called. I left him in my apartment, doors unlocked, a signed blank check on the kitchen table (fortunately, he was an honest person), and made it to the courtroom, via the subway, in exactly sixteen minutes. The rest of that day is blur, as is most of the week that followed. The four of us who had been covering the trial—Mike, Elsa, Bart, and I—were assigned to interview jurors, which wasn't easy because they had all gone into hiding. I spent the week casing neighborhoods like a burglar, knocking at doors nobody would answer, getting hostile stares when I identified myself as a *Post* reporter. At the end of the week, I had struck out; not a single person had agreed to talk to me.

And then it was over—the daily deadline, the adrenaline jolts, the whole social construct that had sustained me. It silently imploded around me, and there was only Washington in August, weeks of accrued comp time, and daily life. Thomas was off, somewhere else, keeping company with someone else; I didn't know what he was doing and didn't want to. I wanted to get away, but I had no one to get away with. Even Eleanor was out of town for a few days. Earlier in the summer, she had recommended that I stop taking the lithium, and lately I had been pressuring her to let me stop taking the imipramine, too. I was tired of its side effects and wanted to change medications, and she had reluctantly agreed. We had been slowly reducing the dosage in preparation for this, and now I was down to almost no medication at all.

And then my friends Tim and Priscilla said, We are going to Cape Cod for a month with the baby; come with us. Gratefully, I fled.

This time, I never saw the Beast coming. I knew he was there, but I imagined him caged or in retreat; the ferocity of his approach was all the more stunning because I thought I was having a good time. We were staying at Tim's mother's place, a complex of whitewashed New England frame houses facing a green lawn, a few feet from the pond where Tim had learned to sail as a boy. There were theater people from New York there, and friends of Tim's and Priscilla's, their new baby—then barely two months old—and his new nanny, Philomene. Tim's family were all good cooks, and each night there was a feast: mussels dug up that morning, chicken pies, sweet corn, fresh-fruit tarts—and wine. Lots of alcohol. When the sun was past the yardarm, we broke out the gin-and-tonics, sitting on the lawn; then we had wine at dinner; then after dinner more gin-and-tonics, or maybe some brandy if the night was crisp. I paid no attention to how much I was drinking because I never actually got drunk. But I was drinking a lot—far too much for somebody struggling to recover from depression. I was drinking to relieve a building sense of tension.

And then, on August 26—the day before my thirty-fifth birthday—I left. I was conscious of feeling uneasy, as if I'd been sponging on my friends—or, more precisely, living a prolonged and humiliating adolescence, sleeping in my narrow bed while Tim and Priscilla juggled family and friends and baby and in-laws, all the accoutrements of adult life. When was *I* going to get to be a grown-up? I wondered. And then the thought came to me that I should be more self-sufficient; I should be traveling on my own, enjoying my own company and being an independent woman of the world. I was almost thirty-five years old, goddamnit; time to leave off the slumber parties. I said an abrupt goodbye to Tim and Priscilla, rented a car at Hyannis Port, drove to Woods Hole, and checked into a motel.

I had some vague thought of looking at the marine institute, but in retrospect I realized that some evil, self-destructive urge had drawn me to that place. Thomas had told me about a vacation he and his wife and the kids had taken there not long before her death. I drove through the town, imagining where they had walked, seeing them everywhere—the children so small then, emblems of the sweet unity of marriage and family which I, it seemed, was destined never to have or even to deserve. At the end of my first day there, as the light faded, I felt desolate. So much work, so many hopes, so much pain, and for nothing. I was thirty-five years old, and I was alone.

It was a crash—not the onset of a full-fledged major depressive episode, but an acute period of mental pain, an intense, seventy-two-hour version of the deadly despair of the previous winter. I had set myself up for it—distracting myself with amusements, fleeing from the surge of emotions that came with the end of a demanding assignment. Now it dawned on me that I was alone in a strange place, that I was still not well, that there was not a thing in Washington I looked forward to returning to. And then, for the past week, I had capped this off with strong, daily doses of alcohol. The gin-and-tonics were a much deserved break, I told myself. It was my vacation; I was entitled to relax. In fact, I wasn't relaxing at all, I was drugging myself. The alcohol was an insult to a body chemistry already severely out of balance.

This was not obvious to me at the time; for much of that week, I had even been comfortable. Now, sitting in my pine-paneled motel room, I felt myself hurtling once more into the abyss. The mental pain was physical, as if the marrow of my bones were being ground into dust. And that fierce loneliness was just the loneliness of the moment; the loneliness of the years to come was a horror I could not begin to describe. For me, it would always be this way, cut off from the sweetness of human love. I would have given everything I had for a chance at that love; I *had* given everything to Thomas and the kids, and I had lost them. I had probably lost many other chances, without even realizing the precise opportunity or when it had gone. It was my life story, this failure to connect.

At that moment I would have settled for any human comfort, any at all. A man, a woman, a child—it didn't matter; this wasn't about sex. Just a stranger's arm curled around my waist, naked flesh against my own. Anything, for just one night.

I had already had one gin-and-tonic at the motel restaurant. Staring at the bottle of imipramine I had with me (the leftover pills from the prescription I was no longer taking), I thought about walking down the street to the liquor store and buying enough of something to finish the job. This was it, I thought, the counterattack the Beast had been planning; this was the point at which I was going to negotiate a full surrender. No more of this; no more fighting unwinnable battles. I had given it my best, and I had lost. Tomorrow I would be thirty-five. I had done a few things in my life, enough to feel it hadn't been a waste. But if this was the pain I was going to have to live with, it was time to exercise the choice I had already thought about so clearly. It was time to quit.

The next thing that happened was a practical thought. I remembered my safety plan. I was supposed to call people when this happened.

At first I called Thomas, at home. It was late then, about ten, and after a few seconds it suddenly became clear to me from the tone of his voice that he was not alone. I hung up. *How dare he? By God, I'll make him pay for this.* I called back. "I just wanted to tell you that you'll never hear from me again—" I started, and he said, in cold fury, "I want you to hang up now and quit calling me." *Click.*

I was past pain. I called Eleanor, and left a message on her answering machine. I called my friend Arthur and we talked for a while. I couldn't bring myself to tell him what I was really doing. I just said I was feeling blue again. He tried to cheer me up, and after a while I pretended to be cheered and hung up. I called Robin; no answer. Then I sat and stared at the phone. After a while—thirty minutes? an hour?—it rang. It was Thomas. There were only two or three hotels in Woods Hole, and he had evidently been going down the list.

"Get back to Washington," he said. This time I sensed he was alone, but I did not dare ask. His voice sounded tight and strained, still angry. I said I would, maybe in a day or so. I hung up. Then, after another while, the phone rang again. It was Eleanor.

"Come home," she said, when I told her about the gin-and-tonics and the bottle of imipramine I had on hand. "Right now. Immediately."

I took the first flight out in the morning. By midafternoon, I was back in Washington, at the counter of my neighborhood pharmacy, where Eleanor had phoned in a new prescription. I took the bottle home with me, and at about four-thirty in the afternoon I swallowed the first of the little green-and-white pills inside. It was Prozac.

How do you describe the gradual lessening of pain? How do you describe the absence of something? The brain has no endorphins; technically, it doesn't feel. And yet memory is a form of pain; even recollections of happiness contain particles of grief, which we call nostalgia. It is all the same thing—billions of neurons firing in a billionth of a second—and when it stops, pain vanishes, and memory with it.

A broken leg can be remembered and located: "It hurt right below my knee, it throbbed, I felt sick at my stomach." But mental pain is remembered the way dreams are remembered—in fragments, unbidden realizations, like looking into a well and seeing the dim reflection of your face in that instant before the water shatters.

The Prozac did what the imipramine and lithium had done

imperfectly: it altered, or restored, the fundamental functioning in my brain. It didn't make me well. It made it possible for me to get well—something that was now even likely, given the work I had done and the medical therapy I was getting.

The first sign of this was not something that happened, but the absence of something happening.

It was midafternoon, about three days after I started taking the Prozac. I was sitting in my living room, reading a book, and this thing happened in my brain: a moment of silence. The buzz in my brain was there, and then it was not. I was a body floating to the surface of the water, and then my face felt the air and I breathed, for the first time in a long time, a long cool draft of oxygen. I did not hesitate or think. I got up from the sofa, walked to the telephone, and called Thomas.

"I'm not sure, and I may be imagining this," I said, "but I think I am feeling better."

He chuckled. "That's the way these newer drugs work," he said. "They can be very dramatic."

"Well, I thought you'd like to know," I said, and then I hung up.

And that was it, for a long time. The buzz came back later that day; the old hollow feeling returned. But then, a few days later, there was another deep breath of cool air. Then another.

There was no lightning bolt, nothing in any way dramatic. I took two more weeks off from work. I knew enough by now to be thoroughly frightened by what had happened in Woods Hole, thoroughly chastened and careful about myself. I treated myself as an invalid. I stayed home and drank Earl Grey tea and read books, and while I wasn't noticing, the buzz in my brain was getting gradually quieter.

After two weeks I returned to work, and things were okay. I went back to covering federal court—ordinary stories mostly, some leftover events from the Barry trial. The usual. September came and went.

And then, one day in early October, I walked out of the courthouse at the end of the day, my mind occupied with something I had to take back to the office and whether I should take the subway or catch a cab. Then I thought: *Neither. I'll just walk back. I want to walk in the sun.*

I felt a slight prickling of my skin; it felt nice. It was late afternoon, the sun still well above the horizon. The leaves had begun to turn. The air was warm, but there was a bustling breeze, and a hint of the cool night to come, a balm after months of sticky heat. I was standing on Indiana Avenue, facing west. Before me, the street sloped down to meet Pennsylvania Avenue, a marble boulevard where the edges of the buildings looked sharp, newly defined against the clear autumn sky. The light was coppery. All these things I noticed like a person just coming to consciousness after a long sleep. It felt familiar; it reminded me of something that had happened quite a while ago. (*The light through the window—My mother's warm arms around me—I was laughing—.*) Then I realized: this was pleasure, this feeling. Ordinary pleasure.

Hello, old friend, my brain seemed to say. *Hello back*, I said. And then I looked up into the busy air above me—bright, turbulent, a light-filled space reaching to infinity.

Chapter Seven

Life did not get easier. But living did.

As a child, I had been connected to the earth, following my grandfather and his mule across the newly plowed field, dozing in the afternoon sun in the grass outside the barn, imagining I felt the earth turn a degree on its axis. It was a connection I lost later, with living in cities and breathing artificial air. But while it lasted, it gave me the peculiar ability of knowing when it started to rain, even if I was deep in the bowels of some windowless building. I could feel it, some difference in the static charge of the air, like a ghost touching my cheek. "It's raining," I would say, and people would look up, surprised, and go to a window: Why, so it is.

So it was with the changes in my brain that marked my first steady steps toward health, starting in the fall of 1990. The changes began in a space no bigger than a molecule.

Every morning, I held between one and three green-and-white capsules in my hand. Every morning, I swallowed that dose, and a few billion molecules of fluoxetine—an intricate array of interlocking carbon, hydrogen, sodium, oxygen, fluorine, and chlorine atoms—made their way into my brain. Once there, they found their way to sites on the ends of particular neurons whose function was to absorb a neurotransmitter called serotonin. There, like a key fitting into a lock, the fluoxetine molecules slid into a spot on the neuron normally reserved for serotonin. That blocked serotonin molecules from being reabsorbed, increasing the number available in the synapse. As Satchel Paige might have put it, this was a pill that jangled my brain juices.

The effect was not magical. I was the product of the same environment, with the same values, the same IQ, the same capacity for emotion. The difference was that I felt *sturdy*. Resilient. Not happy, not blissed out, not numb, not hyper. Just: myself.

It took a while. At first, I felt like a wanderer on a storm-damaged landscape, seeing things that looked familiar but oddly askew. I kept trying to retrace my steps, and finding old paths blocked, or twisting off in new directions.

I still hoped for another chance with Thomas—and, for a brief period, that seemed possible. We saw each other frequently for the following year, and by the fall of 1991, the subject of living together had been broached again. Thomas suggested that I move in after spending Christmas with him and the kids at his parents' in Montreal. Some things about our relationship seemed very different. There was less tension between us, which I welcomed, not realizing that tension had been a measure of our connection. The responsibilities of two children, which had overwhelmed me when I first knew Thomas, now seemed taxing but manageable. Partly that was because I was healthier and more self-confident; partly it was because the children were growing up.

Peter, now eight, was continuing his lordly odyssey through childhood. Anything was fun to him, even lying on our backs on the front lawn at dusk and counting "butt bugs," which was his name for fireflies. Melissa, now eleven, hovered on the cusp of adolescence, a bud about to burst, a child of incipient beauty and strong passions. One night when everyone else was out—Thomas away on business, Peter sleeping over at a friend's house—she and I sat out on the deck long after dark talking about school, and then I heard her voice in the darkness saying, "I am happy now, just being here with you."

"Me, too," I said. And it was true: somehow, we had become friends.

And more: I felt, for the first time, like a parent, or at least the way I imagined a parent might feel. Melissa and Peter had become partly "mine" somehow—though I kept reminding myself this was not true, that not only did I have no legal connection to their father, but no one could replace their true mother. I knew this, and yet I was connected to those children in some way that made it okay to feel delighted when Melissa got her first phone call from a boy or when Peter's reading scores improved. Thomas's children had dragged me, kicking and screaming, out of my self-absorption; at times, I had bitterly resented them. Now it felt quite different. And they needed me: one night, Melissa mentioned a detail about their mother's death that Peter had probably heard before but, being so young, had never really absorbed. Peter got very quiet. Then he began to sob. Melissa, uncharacteristically, did not speak to him; I realized she was struggling with her own emotions. I went over to Peter and sat down on the kitchen floor beside where he was standing, leaning against the refrigerator. Without saying anything, he crawled into my lap and curled himself into a ball and continued to sob. I put my arms around him. We sat that way for a long time.

Later that night, as he was climbing into his bunk bed, he said something stunning: "I have said goodbye to a lot of people to be only eight years old." It was one of those mind-blowing assessments that children can come up with. I wanted to say, "Well, you won't have to say goodbye to me," but I didn't. I suspected that might not be true.

Things between me and Thomas were not right. It was ironic, considering how hard I had worked to get healthy, but it seemed to me at times that the Tracy he had fallen in love with was the one I had been before—the needy, sick one, minus a few of her more unattractive personality traits. The solution to the problem was simple and unavoidable—but there was this tangled history we had, the emotional intensity of the events we had been through together. There was also my growing attachment to Peter and Melissa. The simplest solution was the hardest.

The way it happened, then, was slow and, in the end, bitterly comic. It started with a fight over my bad driving on New Year's Day 1992, on our way home from Montreal. Over the next six months, he grew surly and distant. There were late-night phone calls he did not explain, mysterious "nights off" I feared to question. *You just have to trust him*, I told myself, though my instincts were going off like fire alarms. I avoided thought with nonstop activity, which was easy to do: Thomas had gradually relinquished many day-to-day decisions to me. I planned menus for the kids, took them shopping, went to parent-teacher conferences when he was out of town; I even made plans for the family vacation, a trip to South America Thomas and the kids had talked about for a year. Every day, Thomas became more of a stranger. Yet only once did I venture to broach the subject of our disintegrating relationship.

"So you are leaving me, then," he said flatly.

"No," I said, frustrated. "I'm saying that we have to talk." And then each of us waited for the other to say what was waiting to be said, and neither of us had the courage.

In June 1992, Thomas told me he had realized he was interested in someone else and wanted to "take a break." The trip to South America had been planned for the following month. I'd made the hotel reservations, planned for time off from work, arranged the complicated airline itinerary. Who was going to use my ticket? I asked Thomas. "No one is using your fucking ticket," he said tightly. But the day before he and the kids were to leave, I went by the downtown travel agency where I'd made the reservations. The woman behind the counter was a familiar face by now. I asked her to double-check the itinerary. And there it was: another woman's name on the plane ticket I'd reserved for myself.

The travel agent had been in the office when Thomas came by to make the switch, but she hadn't realized the significance of what had happened. Now she looked like she was about to cry. She kept saying, "But he seemed so *nice*." Then I remembered that the tickets had been bought on my American Express card. Thomas had paid me for all of them; I was short of cash, and he had agreed to let me owe him for my ticket for the time being. Now, as far as American Express was concerned, these tickets were still mine. Could I cancel the fourth ticket? I asked. Regretfully, the agent said no; I couldn't cancel one ticket without voiding the whole transaction.

"Fine," I said. I was angrier than I had ever been in my life. "Cancel the whole thing. Can you do that?" She nodded. I turned around to leave. And then I thought of Peter and Melissa, and I couldn't do it.

"Never mind," I said to the agent, who looked relieved. "Just leave a message at Mr. McCrary's office saying that his companion's ticket has been canceled, by me. Just tell him that." She nodded; she understood.

It was then a few minutes past six, the agency's closing time, and the plane was to leave around ten the next morning. By the time I got home an hour later, there were four or five messages from Thomas on my answering machine, each one more apoplectic than the one before. It would take him at least twelve hours, I thought, to reach someone at the agency and figure things out. In the meantime, I hoped he would pop a blood vessel. I hoped someone would find him in the morning with telephone in hand, eyes bulging with rage, dead as roadkill. As I stood there, imagining him dead, the phone rang again. I yanked the plug out of the wall, went to bed, and cried myself to sleep.

After that, there was little to say. He apologized; he said he wanted to remain friends. I hung up on him. I was so angry I did not even go back to his house to get my belongings, much less say goodbye to the kids. For a while, I wanted to kill him. It seemed odd, this desire to kill someone I had loved, but I seriously considered it. I thought I could get away with pleading temporary insanity. With my psychiatric history and the statement from American Express (which had by then thoughtfully sent me a receipt for the other woman's ticket, just for my records), what jury would convict me? Whatever was not fury was grief. I missed the kids. I dreamed about them, fragments in which I held Peter in my arms, or I heard Melissa, laughing delightedly at some joke. Eventually, I wrote them letters of goodbye.

"If I ever have a little boy, I would like him to be like you," I wrote to Peter. To Melissa, I said I wanted to be honest: I remembered our fights, and I was sure she did, too—but I wanted her to know that that night we had spent talking on the deck, just the two of us, had made me happy, that I had valued my connection with her all the more because I had thought we would never achieve it. And then I mailed the letters; it was the best I could do.

At times, some old depressive thought would emerge: *There must be something wrong with me, or he couldn't have treated me like this.* But increasingly, I found those thoughts muscled aside by a more realistic view. He had treated me badly—but I had allowed it to happen. For the first time, the end of a relationship did not bring on an orgy of self-blame—just a clean, healthy hate for this person who had hurt me. And even my grief seemed to have a floor under it. There was no bottomless abyss. Even at dark moments, I held on to a sense of perspective that had always eluded me before. *This is not going to last forever,* I could tell myself. That was the basic distinction between depression and grief.

Even so, the line got blurred. There were still times of anxiety, weeks when my thoughts were despairing and traveled in slow, plodding circles. At such times, Eleanor sometimes advised me to increase my dosage of Prozac for a few weeks, up to perhaps forty or even sixty milligrams a day from the usual twenty. But as time passed, she advised me to simply wait it out.

One day, walking past an art supply store near my apartment, I impulsively went in and bought a notebook of sketching paper, a handful of soft lead pencils, a sharpener and an eraser. It was a feeling I hadn't had since childhood, needing to put lines on paper. I started to get up early in the morning so that I could draw before work. I experimented with shapes and color; I tried to capture the line of my cat's body with just two or three pencil strokes. Words crept into those pages, but words were now only of passing importance. In the past, I would have endlessly explained and justified things to myself. Now I just drew. Loneliness was a cat asleep in an empty bed, my own face in a mirror, the dim bulk of an armoire in a shadowy room at four a.m. The images bypassed everything else. Drawing helped me feel.

Depression, as I well knew, did not consist merely in feeling sad; it was often heralded by the absence of feeling. My sketchbooks became a kind of diary, a daily self-monitoring device which helped me guard against sliding into that numbness. It was also a guard against self-absorption. Drawing required *seeing*, which required focusing on the outside world—even if it was on some trivial object, even if it was only for a few minutes at a time. It offered a middle ground between Plato's ancient admonition—"The life which is unexamined is not worth living"—and its corollary: "The unlived life is not worth examining."

And slowly—very slowly—I began to see things with some objectivity. I even found a certain kind of black humor in the way things had ended with Thomas. It had been a spectacular way to get dumped. Thomas believed that anything worth doing was worth doing well, and I had to admit that in the end he had lived up to his credo. As time passed, I began to think the story through, to imagine telling it—enhancing certain details to make it better, the way Southerners have always told stories, with a certain poetic license. "I had a lover once who left me for another woman," I would say, "and he took her to South America on my American Express Gold Card." It wasn't even that far from being true.

But Thomas would always defy all my attempts to neatly summarize our affair. It had been a complex, brutal thing; through him I had learned an important lesson, which is that intelligence, violence, and compassion can coexist easily in the same person. He had saved my life by recognizing the severity of my depression and taking me to the hospital when he did; he had helped me reclaim my life by leading me to books that helped me to understand the enemy I was facing. He had helped me face some agonizing truths about myself, had helped me stand when doing that seemed impossible. He had also savaged my self-esteem, over and over, with a kind of verbal cruelty I'd never encountered before. He had betrayed me. And he had taught me a great deal about my capacity to tolerate hurt, abuse, and betrayal. I would never again be shocked at some woman's complicity in an unhealthy relationship; I would never again be shocked to find vicious behavior in some pillar of the community. Thomas taught me some of the best and the worst that men and women can do to each other.

But the main thing I took away from that was simple. *Next time*, I told myself, *I'm going to find a man who will be good to me.*

At work, I had moved from covering federal court to a spot on the metro staff's Projects team. All during that tumultuous summer and the breakup with Thomas, I was doing research on teenage gunshot victims. For several weeks, I rode with D.C. ambulance crews, roaming the city until all hours, seeing a procession of drunks and sick people and, of course, young men lying in pools of blood on the sidewalk. It always seemed to be three a.m. at those shooting scenes, and there always seemed to be the same crowd there—the same blank-eyed teenagers, the same plainclothes detectives, the same small children dancing in and out of the adults. Some of the ambulance crews wore bulletproof vests; there had been instances, they told me, where the shooter was lurking in those crowds, making sure his victim was dead, and the marksmanship of these guys was notoriously bad. The nightly scenes of chaos and tragedy took me, if only briefly, out of my own head and away from my own troubles, and they matched the disordered life I was leading. I slept at odd hours, watching rented videos until dawn, eating cold pizza for breakfast at noon. It was a brutal assignment, but it led me to a story about a young teenager's shooting and its aftermath, which soon absorbed me; later, my editors would nominate it for a Pulitzer Prize.

One particularly horrific night, we picked up a woman who had stumbled onto the Anacostia Freeway into the path of a car. As the paramedics struggled to load her into the ambulance and avoid four lanes of onrushing traffic, she managed to tell fragments of her story: she had been in the woods next to the freeway, and a man had attacked her. It was not clear what she had been doing in the woods or if she'd been raped, but as she was running away from the man, she had tried to dart across the freeway on foot. The driver had not bothered to stop. It was pure chance that brought a D.C. ambulance going off duty along the same stretch of road a few minutes later to find her lying there, cars swerving wildly all around her. She had a fractured pelvis and what looked like internal injuries—the same injuries I'd had many years before, when I'd been hit by a car.

It was two a.m. before the Washington Hospital Center helicopter came and took her away, long past the *Post's* last news deadline. I went home and immediately poured myself a stiff Scotch. Then I sat in the dark living room while the liquor crept into my veins, and I had another drink, and after a while my hands stopped shaking and the mental image of what I had seen faded a bit from my brain. When I went to bed, the sky was growing light.

I woke up in midafternoon with my whole body feeling sore. It wasn't the flu, I knew; it was stress—and a wicked hangover.

It wasn't the first. I'd had lots of hangovers that summer. Usually I didn't even keep Scotch in the house, but that had changed too, a few weeks before: a swift jolt of Scotch after a night with the ambulance crews was much more relaxing, and a lot more efficient, than sipping a glass of white wine. But this time, shocked by my experience of the night before, I realized that, once again, I had started misusing alcohol to cope with stress.

This is really nuts, I thought. *I can't do this anymore.*

The slow drift I was on—from occasional use of alcohol to occasional misuse, toward dependency—was a story being played out allaround me that summer. Alcohol is the single best over-the-counter remedy for tension and anxiety, and for police officers and paramedics alcohol was often a blessed solace. I had already had the experience of finding myself in an emergency-medical-services car driven by someone who—I realized too late—had been dropping off in the men's room to drink all evening. Racing through red lights in an ambulance driven by a drunk person was an experience I would never forget. The paramedics I'd talked to about this were candid. It was a chronic problem, they said; everybody in their line of work either had a drinking problem or knew someone who did, and lots of people fit both descriptions.

Unlike the paramedics, I could quit this assignment if it began to affect my health, and I thought I should; fortunately, I had almost finished my research. But in another sense, my position was not that different from theirs. My decades-long pattern of recurring episodes of depression meant that I, too, frequently suffered from anxiety. It didn't matter if the source was a job or an illness; being constantly exposed to low-level psychic distress created a huge temptation to "self-medicate"—find a short-term cure for the symptoms and just keep going. I had known all this for years, in an academic sort of way. I had even gone so far as to admit that I had misused alcohol on some notable occasions. But me, in danger of becoming an alcoholic?

With a sense of acute shame, I finally brought the subject up with Eleanor. Her advice was simple: Stop drinking. Any short-term anxiety relief I got from alcohol was more than paid for in its long-term depressant effects, she said.

I agonized over definitions; I tried to backpedal and rationalize, to figure out a reason to get rid of the Scotch but keep the bottle of Chardonnay in my refrigerator. But those fake distinctions could not withstand even a sidelong scrutiny. "I am not an alcoholic," I said finally, "but I guess I'm at risk of becoming one." And Eleanor nodded vigorously in agreement.

Even so, I knew that without some other means of coping with anxiety, the temptation to use alcohol would still be strong. I had a feeling that if my choices were stark—use alcohol to control my anxiety, or give it up and suffer—then alcohol would become a consuming topic. That, in its own way, seemed another form of dependency; either way, it made alcohol the focus of my thoughts. Eleanor's solution for that was something that at first seemed hardly any better: antianxiety drugs.

Great, I thought. *I can either become a sot or a pillhead.* But as Eleanor and I talked, her rationale began to make more sense. Her recommendation was a drug called Klonopin, one of a class of drugs called benzodiazepines. That genre included other drugs I had heard about, such as Valium and Xanax—the latter a drug I had taken briefly in the fall of 1989. I knew that such drugs could be addictive. The difference, Eleanor explained, was that Klonopin took longer to get into the bloodstream than most benzodiazepines. This was important, because an important part of the mechanism of becoming addicted to a drug was the "quick kick" phenomenon, the instant gratification provided by fast-acting chemical compounds. Those compounds also tended to be the ones that induced a kind of mini-withdrawal when their effects wore off, which in turn tended to create the psychological craving for more. In some situations the quicker-acting drugs, such as Xanax, were useful, Eleanor said. But to treat chronic and intermittent anxiety for longer periods, they carried a much higher risk of dependency.

The fact that Klonopin took twenty to thirty minutes to get into the bloodstream made it useful for serious episodes of anxiety but gave me little incentive to pop a pill every time I felt a rush of nervousness. I already knew that a useful cognitive therapy technique for anxiety was to chart it—to mark the time it had started and when it subsided, as a means of reminding myself that most anxiety attacks were short-lived. I should use Klonopin only for those times when the anxiety didn't subside after fifteen minutes or so, Eleanor said. And, she warned, even that was a temporary measure; the prescription was not automatically refillable. If I found myself taking more than one milligram a day, I was to let her know.

It was an approach that appealed to my pragmatic nature. Like many people, I had started out with an ingrained distrust of prescription drugs; I equated them with illicit purposes or hopeless causes. Early experiences had done little to dispel my reservations. But over the years I had learned that psychoactive drugs, used responsibly, often did exactly what they promised: they could heal and relieve pain. Sometimes, as I knew, they could even perform something that looked like a miracle.

To some it might seem that I was well launched on the road to chemical slavery; having found one crutch, Prozac, I had now supplemented it with another. But to me, taking these drugs seemed no different from taking insulin if I had been diabetic or antiseizure medication if I had suffered from epilepsy. To be sure, this view assumed that depression and its related mental symptoms were distinct and observable physical ailments—which wasn't quite true. But it was getting closer to becoming true every day, thanks to advances like PET scans and other brain-imaging techniques.

But though I was starting to read more extensively in the scientific literature about research into the brain, my newfound confidence in drugs was not really based on anything rational. It was a kind of body knowledge gleaned from my experiences before and after Prozac. Those little green-and-white capsules didn't make me feel "different." They made me feel *less* "different," better able to surmount my black moods and be the person I really was. This knowledge was not proved by evidence; it was proved by its absence—my own subjective sense that the invisible weight I had hauled around my neck for years was now gone. How this had happened, I couldn't say; how to prove it, I hadn't the slightest idea. But I knew down deep in my bones that, at least for now, I was more "myself" on Prozac than off it.

And so, for a time, a little bottle of orange pills went next to the green-and-white ones in my medicine cabinet, replacing the liquor in the living room. As the months passed, I went through all the usual stages of grief: anger, denial, sadness, bargaining, and finally, acceptance. Indeed, my reaction to the loss of my relationship with Thomas and his children was absolutely normal: the reaction of an emotionally steady person who had suffered a significant blow—no more, and no less. So the orange pills were used regularly for a time, then retired. At some point since that moment on Indiana Avenue when I had turned my face up to the sun, I had stopped being a victim of depression, and become a survivor.

It was a strange interregnum, that period between the fall of 1990 and the summer of 1992. It began at the point at which I started my first steady progress toward health, and ended when I parted from the person who had accompanied me on much of that journey. And yet, throughout that whole period, I comforted myself with this thought: *Whatever happens, it will be all right.* For the first time, apart from some wordless moments of childhood security before I became acquainted with my particular doom, I believed it. With or without Thomas, I would survive; my happiness did not depend on him. I no longer faced annihilation by abandonment.

The unbearable weight lifted in tiny increments, day by day. Amazing, to realize how heavy it had been; amazing, to understand how much effort it had taken to carry it. For the first time, I developed a small, shaky faith in the future.

Something else began to happen: time seemed to expand. I was no longer constantly dealing with mood swings, anxiety, and the assorted life crises caused by being in those mental states. I was no longer devoting great chunks of time to introspection and analyses of why I was unhappy. There seemed to be more hours in the day, and during those hours I seemed to have more energy than I remembered having before. Having a natural abundance of energy had enabled me to pursue a career despite the handicap of chronic and sometimes incapacitating depression. Now, as that weight lifted, I had energy to spare.

And I wanted to be needed.

Until I knew Peter and Melissa, my idea of being needed had fallen into two categories. One was the martyr mode—to find a man and make myself indispensable to him. That was one way of getting love and security. The other was the avoidance mode—protecting myself by staying away from those who might use their own helplessness to demand love and security from me. But with Thomas's children, I had learned that being needed was neither an emotional quid pro quo nor an encounter with a bloodsucker. It was a deep pleasure. One day Peter hurt himself on the playground and came running toward me, his face contorted with tears. Without thought, I dropped to my knees and opened my arms, and when he fell into my arms something inside me resonated like a bell tolling deep underwater.

I wanted that feeling again.

The old ways of filling up time didn't work anymore. Just spending extra hours in the office wasn't the answer—nor was shopping, or going to the gym, or reading books. "You know what you should try?" said Robin, whose own weekend work schedule made me look unemployed by comparison. "Go to Elizabeth Arden and get a facial. It's such a treat." But I wasn't in need of pampering. I signed up for scuba-diving lessons. That was not the answer either. It was connection I craved. I wanted the thing I had been offered by Hugo in the hospital, by Peter on the playground. I wanted to get out of my own head.

I had tried. But in those group therapy sessions years ago in Atlanta, bridging the gap between myself and another person had been excruciating. Every venture outside my own consciousness seemed to be accompanied by the sound of shattering glass; it took a mighty effort to leave my soundproofed box. I could see the same story in the eyes of the others, too. Like me, they harbored the inner certainty that something was wrong; like me, they defended themselves with exaggerated shame at being imperfect, or with furious, defensive hostility. To expose ourselves was like submitting to a caress on burned flesh. And yet, escaping the prison of self was what it was all about.

It wasn't just about some transcendental moment of connection; it was about immortality. One of the lessons I had learned by being around Thomas's children was that they reflected my most trivial ideas and ways of being in the world. Once I'd told Peter a joke. "Why did the chicken cross the road? To show the possum that it *could* be done." After I'd explained to him that dead possums were a common sight on back roads in the South, he thought the joke hilarious and told it often. I suspected that Thomas, an urban sophisticate with no taste for cornpone humor, was going to be hearing that possum joke for a long, long time. I had left my mark on Peter, and he had never been my child.

The course of action that presented itself to me, after I thought about it for a while, seemed self-evident: I volunteered to mentor a high school student.

Her name was Lisa, and she was not what I expected. She was a straight-A student who was already being courted by several colleges. She was also so drop-dead beautiful that once, when we were eating dinner together, I saw a strange man cross the restaurant floor to leave his business card by her plate, hoping vainly that this poised seventeen-year-old would give him the time of day. Lisa was blasé; it had happened before, she said. I had expected to meet some teenager who was a victim of poverty or parental neglect or both. Lisa came from a loving, stable, middle-class family. I couldn't think of a single thing she needed from me. I also wondered what her mother would say if she knew her daughter was being "mentored" by a former psychiatric patient.

But after several weeks, it came to me that perhaps I did have something to offer her: my own experience with the perils of over-achievement. Lisa was black, and I knew our lives would always be different in fundamental ways. But in a few ways, she and I came from similar backgrounds. We were both from middle-class families with roots in the South; with her and her mother, I had the sense that the word "home" meant the same Southern landscape, the same food, even the same hymns I had known as a child. We were both products of a culture steeped in fundamentalist Christianity, which placed prime value on education and the kind of respectability that comes with a healthy bank account. We were both teachers' pets, star students who had learned to cultivate that kind of attention and to thrive on it.

I saw a piece of myself in the part of Lisa that so highly prized a certain type of accomplishment—achieving perfect grade point averages, winning essay contests, getting scholarships, setting out on the path that would lead someday to a comfortable income. Over that school year, I talked to her about the perspective on life I had acquired, at some cost, after my own youth as a superachiever. I told her how I'd imagined my own tombstone in my diary, when I was fifteen—"Here lies Tracy Thompson, she made straight A's"—and how empty and sad that had made me feel, even when I had thought straight A's the only thing about me that people could value. Perfect grades and scholarships were wonderful, I said, but don't make the mistake I made, and conclude that they are what makes you a worthwhile person. Don't fall into the trap of always needing the good opinion of other people; don't do harm to yourself in trying to please them.

I don't know if she found my advice useful. She was not as desperate to please as I had been at her age, and so perhaps my mistakes were wasted on her. But she seemed to weigh what I said, and file it away for future reference. As the year went by, she would sometimes diffidently mention things that had happened at school, and I realized that she wanted me to know about her achievements, that my opinion had come to matter to her. We became girlfriends, going to the movies, meeting for dinner, talking about men. After a while, I stopped worrying about whether I was "mentoring" properly.

At the end of the year, Lisa left Washington to accept a full scholarship to the University of Virginia, one of the schools that had courted her so assiduously. I decided to reenlist as a mentor.

I had been looking for something I needed; in the process, I had discovered that I already possessed true luxury, which existed in feeling able to give. Before, I had been like those people who haunt flea markets, who collect pieces of other people's lives—a bit of jewelry, a mirror—and hoard them, whose pleasure consists in having. I had collected proofs of love and esteem; I had been a bottomless well of human need. Now I felt as if I were cleaning out my garage, finding treasures—or at least usable items. *Take this*, I felt like saying. *Does anybody need an end table? Can anybody use this perfectly good lamp?*

When I thought about this in the context of my struggle with depression, I stumbled on a radical notion. Perhaps this was one of the costs of depression I'd never considered. Depression had not simply robbed me of pleasure in life; those around me had suffered an ongoing loss too.

There were risks in saying that. For one thing, doing volunteer work gave me a considerable sense of self-worth. It made me feel important—but that, in itself, proved nothing about the actual value of what I was doing. There was also the risk of assuming that I was the helper and not the one being helped. And there was the risk of arrogance. The religion of my childhood had been vigilant about squelching pride; we were helpless creatures, our Bible taught, we were nothing without God. "Just as I am, poor, wretched, blind ..." we sang. It was a religion suited for a culture of poverty and defeat; the afterlife it promised had been, for my mother, a rock of stability and hope. But for me, it had only bred a kind of reflexive self-deprecation.

I had always considered self-deprecation a bad habit that harmed nobody but me. Now I reexamined that idea, and found a kind of self-indulgence lurking in it. Confusing hubris with self-confidence fostered a kind of willful blindness, a deliberate dishonesty. A person who did not own up to his abilities, like a person who was blind to his own faults, would always be limited by his lack of self-knowledge. A person who refused to acknowledge his own abilities was engaged in a form of emotional miserliness.

Worse, this habit could also become a kind of emotional armor. As long as I presented myself as weaker than I was, people could not demand as much of me. If I was skillful, I could even use that technique to turn the tables and demand things for myself. The tyranny of the weak: my grandmother had done that. I had thought that her refusal to be anything but a victim had been a conscious decision to manipulate others. But it was just as likely—maybe more likely—that she had begun simply by indulging herself in a lie, by refusing to acknowledge the strengths she possessed. The effect was deadly. It was the emotional equivalent of putting a healthy arm in a cast and whacking people over the head with it.

How could I avoid that trap?

The answer had been percolating in the back of my mind for some time. It was summed up in that button I had found a year or so earlier at the American City Diner—the one that said "No Whining Allowed." That phrase combined two concepts which were very popular, but which rarely got mentioned in the same sentence. One was the search for self-esteem. The other was the concept of "tough love."

The latter, the idea of expressing love by imposing discipline, seemed to appeal most strongly to people who wanted to be the ones *applying* the discipline; I didn't notice anyone queuing up to receive any. In fact, American culture bombarded us with the opposite message: Whatever happens, whatever you've done, don't think ill of yourself. The *Post* sometimes ran stories about someone who had committed a crime, but was described by family and friends as "a good person," someone "trying to get his life together," someone forced by circumstances to do something highly out of character—a conclusion that often went unchallenged. When they got caught, perpetrators never said, "I'm sorry." They said, "I regret what happened," as if they had just been standing there while the gun in their hand had magically emptied itself of bullets, or the child had choked to death, or the pension fund had gotten looted. A genuine apology had become synonymous with groveling.

But where did the truth—the awkward, inconvenient truth—fit in?

Years ago, a co-worker had told me about a self-improvement seminar he had attended at a local junior college. "It was great," he said earnestly; it was clear he'd bought the whole spiel. "This guy's theory is that your brain only processes the information you allow into it. Think of yourself as having this grid, or a filter, which allows some information in and keeps other information out. All you have to do to think positively about yourself is to rearrange your grid. If the only kind of input you allow is positive, then the only kind of thoughts you can have about yourself are going to be positive too."

"Okay," I said. "But what if you *think* that you're terrific, but you're really an asshole?"

My co-worker looked disgusted. "There's a person like you in every office," he said.

I had been teasing him, but I'd also been genuinely puzzled. At the time, I had been wrestling with my own inability to tell if *I* was really terrific, or just an asshole; my opinion varied daily. To arrive at a more realistic assessment of myself had taken many years, and my approach had been the opposite of my friend's: my self-esteem had been wholly dependent on how other people thought I was doing, not on what I thought about myself.

Now, at long last, I realized: it was both—both loving myself, and putting myself out there to be judged in the eyes of others. If I loved myself, I could learn to forgive my mistakes. And yet as long as my self-esteem relied in some part on what other people thought of me, I would be motivated to try for tangible accomplishments—a far sturdier foundation for my self-regard than empty ego puffery or "I feel good about myself" psychobabble.

The trick was unsparing, unsentimental honesty. There were bad things in view when I looked in the mirror; my job was to figure out what they were, to see them in proportion, and not to flinch. "No Whining Allowed." The button was stuck on the bulletin board above my desk at work as a silent reminder: tough self-love. Learning how to love myself had given me a reason to survive a debilitating and terrifying episode of depression; it was the rope I had hung on to in the pit of despair. But being tough on myself was the pulley. It was the thing that got me out.

Chapter Eight

It is barely daylight. As my mind floats up from the still pool of sleep, its first conscious act is to note the blue-gray light creeping under the bedroom curtains. Then, like a 1950s television screen coming on, objects in the bedroom gently come into view: bookshelf, television, dresser. The neighbors' dog is yipping outside, and I hear the wood-flute call of a mourning dove. Drowsily, I roll over and look at my husband.

He is deeply asleep, his hand thrown outside the covers, and as I move, he stirs slightly. Soon the clock radio will come on, and the day will begin.

Last night, I dreamed of anxiety, something about being trapped in a car in a traffic jam, in an agony of needing to be somewhere else. The car was full of people who knew about my pain but could do nothing about it. Their helpless sympathy made me unreasonably angry. The dream was vivid; I can feel the aftermath of the anxiety now, in the muscle tension in my stomach and back. The anxiety in the dream was the diffused, free-floating type I associate with depression. It seems odd, to dream about depression—though no different, I suppose, from having any other kind of dream-memory. Maybe a person lost in schizophrenia dreams of normal life, of taking out the garbage; I don't know. But the dreams always alarm me, because the feelings in them seem so real. I am superstitious, afraid that merely dreaming about them will release them, like an evil genie escaping from a bottle. Anyway, as far as my brain is concerned, which *is* more real—these dream feelings or the present, waking, moment?

Which is now, as David rolls over, half awake, and stretches out his arm to draw me close. The present comes into focus;

my mind starts to fill with what I have to do today—ordinary things like my writing schedule, some gardening I plan to do afterwards. These things seem lovely to me, my pleasure in them effortless. David's arm is around me; there is something nourishing in the touch of his skin on mine, the warmth of his chest against my back. We have been together for almost two years now, married for one. He is a physicist, I am a writer, our work has almost nothing in common. *Not the man I'm looking for*, I thought that night almost two years ago, when he first made an awkward pass at me. I told him so, and he listened, sitting there on my sofa wearing his wire-rimmed glasses—the kind, he told me, laughing, that all science geeks wore. He heard me out. "That's okay," he had said, when I was through. "You're worth waiting for. Besides, I'm a good guy. If you stick around long enough, you'll figure that out." That story is a joke on me now, part of our shared folklore, along with the tale of our first date, when I came to the door in a fashionable silk outfit and David thought I was still in my pajamas. He thought if it was silk, you wore it to bed. *For smart people, we aren't too bright*, I think, and grin to myself. We lie there, limbs tangled in drowsy disarray, until the radio clicks on. This is the way my life is now.

It has been four years since that sunlit moment on Indiana Avenue. The Prozac I started taking in 1990, and which I still take today, has spawned books, television shows, and innumerable news articles, as well as several "copycat" drugs. Until Prozac, antidepressants were the chemical offspring of drugs originally developed to treat other illnesses—tuberculosis, say, or hay fever; their effects on depression were discovered by accident. Prozac is the first "designer" antidepressant, developed to affect the specific neurotransmitter, serotonin, whose malfunction is at least one of the causes of depression. But now even Prozac is passé; by refining the methods of discovery that led to it, researchers are developing more powerful drugs with even more specific influences on brain biology, including previously intractable illnesses such as severe schizophrenia.

There are the wonder drugs of the 1990s, which scientists are calling the Decade of the Brain, and they inspire awe and fear. To me, awe seems fitting. Perhaps only someone who has experienced a mental illness like the black free-fall of depression—which is not even the worst mental illness there is—can really appreciate the magnitude of this achievement. I started taking Prozac after more than a year of a debilitating depression only partially relieved by traditional antidepressants. Within weeks, that mental hurricane had stopped dead in its tracks. I offer no proof; first X happened, and then Y. But it is hard not to attribute that miracle to the little green-and-white pills, difficult not to give them credit for the fact that since then, I've lived something like a normal life. It's been a gift.

Maybe even a miracle. Prozac seems to offer a shortcut on that old American journey, the pursuit of happiness. It promises social assertiveness, relief from pesky personality quirks, a cheerful disposition for the terminally cranky—but at what cost? On the filing cabinet in my study I have a *New Yorker* cartoon that explores what great thinkers of the nineteenth century might have been like on Prozac. My favorite is Edgar Allan Poe, greeting a raven with a sprightly "Hello, birdie!" It sums up our ambivalence.

I'm ambivalent sometimes too. Will I pay a price for this normal life sometime, somewhere—a cancerous tumor, a learning-disabled child? I don't know. Nobody knows. I have rolled the dice, I have made a gambler's bargain. To some, this seems a reckless venture into a Brave New World of personality enhancement. People tell me I'm foolish, that I've donated my brain to science before I'm even dead, that I've opted for an artificial life instead of the authentic one I could have had. At one point in Aldous Huxley's *Brave New World*, protagonist Bernard Marx declines an offer of *soma*, the pharmaceutical cure-all of Huxley's futuristic society. "I'd rather be myself," Marx explains. "Myself and nasty. Not somebody else, however jolly." *Just say no to drugs*, people say; we've been repeating this mantra for a decade now, and the repetition has become automatic. People are afraid of this drug I'm taking, in some way they can't quite define. Miracles just don't come free.

That doesn't stop a lot of people from taking this drug—

an estimated four million in the United States alone. Yet government estimates put the number of people who suffer from a serious depressive episode in any given year at roughly ten million. Of that number, fewer than half seek any medical treatment at all, preferring to suffer in silence than risk the stigma of being diagnosed with a mental illness. A respectable argument could be made that the problem isn't too many people taking drugs for this illness, but too few. Yet the debate over psychotropic drugs is based on a very different assumption: that doctors are prescribing drugs like Prozac, Paxil, and Zoloft with careless abandon to people who don't need it. We even have a name for this: "cosmetic psychopharmacology"—a term coined by psychiatrist Peter Kramer to describe basically healthy people who "are not so much cured of illness as transformed" by taking Prozac. Kramer has taken pains to point out that patients seeking cosmetic psychopharmacology are a minority in his practice, but few people have heard that part of what he is saying. It's not surprising; our speeded-up culture has trouble digesting complex information.

In fact, both sides may be right. Some people—adventurers, those who push the limits in search of whatever the next enlightenment may bring—are probably getting psychotropic drugs when they don't need them. But millions more who could benefit from those drugs are too frightened or ashamed to seek them out. If you are really sick, if you are frightened that you are losing your mind, few things are more terrifying than taking a pill that will further alter the way your brain is working. Most people have to be desperate to do it.

The result of our misconceptions is the proliferation of myth. People think these drugs are uppers, like amphetamines. In comic strips, they are the latest self-indulgence for touchy-feely emotional dilettantes. An op-ed piece in my own newspaper compares them to worthless nineteenth-century patent medicines. At a private girls' school in New Jersey, six teenagers get together, chop up some Prozac capsules, and inhale the contents, trying to get high. And the people who aren't looking for some illicit bliss in these drugs are suspicious that everybody else is doing so behind their backs.

"I don't know about this Prozac," a man says to me at a party. "Seems like everybody's taking it. Pretty soon I'll have to take it too, just to keep up." He is only half joking.

I smile politely and sip my drink. Here is a person who has never visited the featureless white room of mental illness, I think, who has never formed an intimate acquaintance with the Beast. He has no concept of what it means to go through an ordinary day hauling an invisible 150-pound lead weight—one you'd just as soon not discuss, since its very presence constitutes a social embarrassment.

Try being that *person*, I want to tell him, *if you want to understand what it means to live at a disadvantage. Try that for a while, and you'll have something to fear.*

In the fall of 1975, I awoke in my dorm room at Emory University in the grip of a dream. In it, I was in the basement of my old house, which had been converted into a restaurant. The light was glaring, the walls white and stark. I was eating something mushy and brown, a food designed not to give pleasure but only to sustain life. And then out of nowhere, I began to have a marvelous feeling that I had a stupendous secret: it was spring outside.

I excused myself and slipped out the door. Outside was my grandfather's old cornfield, the same field he had plowed so long ago with Becky the mule. It was covered with the stubble of last year's cornstalks; this year's planting had not yet begun. It was chilly, like the day I followed behind him in the furrows of his plow, but there was warmth in the sun. The earth was brown, the sky drab, but I could hear music from somewhere. It was faint, but growing stronger.

I took off my sweater and hat and shoes, feeling the earth slowly warming beneath my feet, letting my hair go loose. And then wolves appeared. They were my secret gods, my helpers; nobody but me knew about them, but I had actually dared to name them. They were dangerous, but I was not frightened. I felt supremely happy. I began to run across the cornfield, the wolves loping along beside me as if we were all part of the same pack, and the wild, strange music filled the sky.

It is tempting to romanticize, to look back to say that dream presaged my eventual triumph over the Beast. But there is no triumph here, only wiser ways of fighting. I suspect that after all these years, the Beast and I are life partners. But it's okay. I have an ordinary life—and though some might think this is dull, I tell you it is sweet. Ordinary life is a miraculous thing.

There are times when the old despair seems to return, only to disappear seventy-two hours later; there are weeks of being in a low-grade funk. I have had bad times since that fall day in 1990. The worst have been in August and in February, for reasons that remain inscrutable to me, and during those periods this life I've built at such pain and cost has seemed to me as flimsy as cardboard. I think: *This is it, I've been kidding myself. No drug works forever; sooner or later, this illness will kill me.*

And then it passes. "How are you feeling?" my friend Gus asks me, leaning over my desk at work in a quiet moment. He looks at me meaningfully. "Fine," I say blankly. "Why?" Then I remember: in our last conversation over lunch, a week ago, I had said, "It seems like I'll never really feel better." Now, a week later, I've already forgotten. At home, going through papers on my desk, I find some notes I jotted down a month earlier:

> This anxiety is I think the worst of anything. [It's] not attached to anything—though I want to focus it at David, to blame him somehow. He's having a bad month himself. I feel guilty that I'm not being more supportive to him. Fulfills my worst fears—that I am just not able to be a good wife ... Goddamnit, I thought I was through with this shit. I keep expecting happy endings. I should know better.

Reading this, I think: *Really?*

Or I stop by the desk of a friend in the Style section, to catch up. He and I are charter members of the Kemistry Klub, an ad hoc organization of Post employees who take psychotropic drugs. Membership is anonymous, and meetings are held at the water cooler. One day he tells me about walking down 15th Street and glimpsing from the corner of his eye a woman wearing a coat with an elaborate fur collar. In a billionth of a second, the outline of her fur collar against the winter sun made her into a gigantic, horned lizard. My friend said he had a flash of panic—*am I going nuts?*—and then the visual trick righted itself; it was just a woman in a fur collar.

"That hasn't happened in a long time," he says, patting his heart, as if to calm its beating. "But, boy, the lizard lady—she set me back."

We laugh together the way war veterans do. I know exactly what he means—the dislocating sense of never knowing when something really bad, really impossible to escape, may happen.

But it hasn't. And in the meantime, there is daily life, a fever of activity which occasionally resolves into a moment of clarity—the warmth of my husband's body, an early morning slant of light—that shows me life is no tangled mystery, but simplicity itself. I navigate cautiously; I will always need a map. I leave guideposts around, reminders of what to do when I lose my way.

"Don't attempt big tasks—divide them into smaller ones," I will write, and tape the note to my desk for times when I am distracted and anxious. Or, in the infrequent dead times, I keep lists of everything I've done on a particular day. *Look at this*, I say to myself at night, bending over the bathroom sink to wash my face. *You accomplished this today. Today was not so bad. Lighten up.*

I'm closing in on forty, the point at which youth stops being taken for granted and becomes a relative term. It's too early for grand summary statements—but even so, I find myself weighing conclusions about how much this illness has come to define me, and how much I have imprinted my personality on it. I'm casting about for some rule, some unifying principle, by which this puzzle of my life can be seen as a whole. And it seems to me that my illness has been the product of three forces: genetics, culture, and chance.

I was born with a predisposition to suffer from depression. I was also fated to grow up in a culture filled with anxiety—some the product of the times I lived in, some the product of the religious sensibilities imposed on me by my parents, who were themselves transmitting the culture they were born into. Part of it was the residual fearfulness I sensed from my mother, who could not escape her own past. And then there was a childhood accident which marred my face just as I was entering adolescence—a chance event, a unique stressor, which forever altered my trajectory.

Over time, all these things worked together—and, in doing so, they permanently altered the "wiring" in my brain, which was not perfectly "wired" to begin with. This is a way of thinking about depression which scientists are exploring, which is known informally as "kindling." It makes sense to me. It describes the way my brain works in other spheres—mastering an algebra problem in eighth grade, learning to serve a tennis ball: a bombardment of stimuli, a repeated reaction, the spark of comprehension, the eventual effortlessness of what had once seemed foreign and impossible. Emotions, I believe, are also partly learned. And can be relearned—with help.

For me, help began with psychoactive drugs. Drugs were not a miracle cure or a replacement for therapy; they were what enabled me to derive the maximum benefit from therapy, which was hard work. Drugs are tools, nothing more—but that is no small thing. To a person scaling a cliff, a grappling hook is the difference between life and death.

I make no summary statement, then; I only say that at one crucial point, I chose life. It was an arduous choice, and I tried my best to avoid it. When I could avoid it no longer, it came down to the realization that I owned a moral responsibility for my life. The question then became: how do I live now? And then, having faced that question, I realized something else: every day, the question is asked again.

Which may be the reason why at all times I carry a scrap of paper in my purse. It's something I wrote down one day, based on the six goals I made for myself in those first months after I got out of the hospital. It's not a magic formula, just something I scribbled on a day when I needed a basic reminder of what keeps me on course.

Honesty in all things, large and small (social and job exceptions as required).

When you are angry, express it, resolve it if possible, then forget it. No grudges.

Admit mistakes promptly and make amends if possible.

Help others. Be of service. Only in this way will you find your way out of the prison of self.

Work hard at your profession. It's your most valuable possession.

"The Rules," I have scrawled, in my bad handwriting, across the top of the page, which is a much folded piece of green steno paper, just like the paper I began my journal on many years ago. Once in a while, this piece of paper turns up in the welter of dry-cleaning receipts and coupons and business cards that accumulate in the bottom of my purse. Every time, I look at it, thinking I should toss it.

And then, after a minute, I fold it up and put it back.

Acknowledgments

There are many people who helped me with this project as if it were their own, to whom I am deeply grateful. My employers at The *Washington Post* generously gave me time off to write. Two editors at the *Post* provided particular help. Abigail Trafford encouraged me to write the feature story that was the origin of this book, and Gene Weingarten provided creative and insightful commentary on the manuscript, for which I am indebted. Others also proved invaluable—notably Robert Content, whose thoughtful and scholarly comments challenged me and helped me refine my conclusions. Dan Baum and Meg Knox provided a critical eye and early encouragement. Ray Fuller at Eli Lilly went out of his way to help me understand some of the newest discoveries in brain biology; Robert Post, at the National Institute of Mental Health, was generous in supplying me with relevant scientific literature. My psychiatrist helped me reconstruct and understand some of the personal events which are recounted here. I am particularly grateful to my agent, Beth Vesel, who devoted a year of nagging to convince me that this book was worth writing, and to my editor at Putnam, Laura Yorke, whose energy, enthusiasm, and intelligence made even the most mundane tasks a pleasure.

Over the years, the encouragement and love of many people have sustained me in dark times, and these are debts which can never be fully repaid. My pain has often been my family's pain, too; despite this, they have never failed to love and believe in me. My friends are too many to mention, though some will recognize themselves here. Finally, there is my husband, David, who has given me unfailing love, support, and encouragement. For him, mere gratitude is not enough.

Author's Note

The events and persons in this book are real. However, in order to protect the privacy of certain individuals, I have sometimes used pseudonyms, and on occasion I have gone so far as to alter personal descriptions.

CPSIA information can be obtained
at www.ICGtesting.com
Printed in the USA
BVHW081249210819
556415BV00007B/696/P

9 781626 815209